READING STORIES FOR COMPREHENSION SUCCESS:

Grades 4-6

BY

KATHERINE L. HALL

45 High-Interest Lessons with Reproducible Selections

The Center for Applied Research in Education
West Nyack, NY 10994

Library of Congress Cataloging-in-Publication Data

Hall, Katherine L. (Katherine Louise)

    Reading stories for comprehension success / Katherine L. Hall.

      p.   cm.

    Includes bibliographical references.

    ISBN 0-87628-889-1 (paper adhesive). — ISBN 0-87628-890-5 (paper
spiral)

    1. Reading (Elementary)—Problems, exercises, etc. 2. Reading
comprehension—Problems, exercises, etc. I. Title.

LB1573.7.A35   1996

372.4—dc20   96-41535

                                      CIP

© 1996 by The Center for Applied Research in Education

Printed in the United States of America

10 9 8 7 6 5 4 3 2 1

ISBN 0-87628-889-1 (pbk)
ISBN 0-87628-890-5 (spiral)

ATTENTION: CORPORATIONS AND SCHOOLS

The Center for Applied Research in Education books are available at quantity discounts with bulk purchase for educational, business, or sales promotional use. For information, please write to: Prentice Hall Career & Personal Development Special Sales, 113 Sylvan Avenue, Englewood Cliffs, NJ 07632. Please supply: title of book, ISBN number, quantity, how the book will be used, date needed.

**THE CENTER FOR APPLIED RESEARCH
IN EDUCATION**
West Nyack, NY 10994
A Simon & Schuster Company

On the World Wide Web at http://www.phdirect.com

Prentice-Hall International (UK) Limited, *London*
Prentice-Hall of Australia Pty. Limited, *Sydney*
Prentice-Hall Canada, Inc., *Toronto*
Prentice-Hall Hispanoamericana, S.A., *Mexico*
Prentice-Hall of India Private Limited, *New Delhi*
Prentice-Hall of Japan, Inc., *Tokyo*
Simon & Schuster Asia Pte. Ltd., *Singapore*
Editora Prentice-Hall do Brasil, Ltda., *Rio de Janeiro*

DEDICATION

To my Mother, Doris L. Hall
Thank you always for your love, support, patience, and confidence,
not only during the writing of this book, but through all the
ups, downs, pains, and joys of our lives.

ACKNOWLEDGMENTS

We wish to thank the following for allowing us to use their photographs and artwork:

READING LEVEL 4

Warning! Earthquake!: Official photograph courtesy of Los Angeles Police Department
The Mystery of Saint Elmo's Fire: D. Kasterine/Daily Telegraph Colour Library/ International Stock
The Source of Saint Elmo's Fire: Courtesy of Marc Anderson
The Newbery Medal: The Newbery Medal and the name Newbery Medal are property of the American Library Association and are used with permission.
It's Roadeo Time: Peter Krinninger/International Stock
Who Wrote the Tortoise and the Hare?: Scott Hanrahan/International Stock
The Many Faces of Catfish: Scott Thode/International Stock
The Runestone: Katherine Hall
Bone Hunter: George Ancona/International Stock
Who is Uncle Sam?: Bill Tucker/International Stock
They Stood on Top of the World: Bob Firth/International Stock
Stephen Hawking: Reuters/Martin Langfield/Archive Photos, photo no. 822 15012
Black Holes: National Aeronautics and Space Administration, no. S90-50866
To Clean or Not to Clean: John Zoiner/International Stock
Chief Seattle: J.G. Edmanson/International Stock

READING LEVEL 5

Robert J. Acosta: Teacher: Courtesy of D. Henrioud
Columbus' Mysterious Light: Roger Markham-Smith/International Stock
The Remarkable Life of Howard Hughes: National Archives, no. 255-PA-135A-4
The Battle of the Ironclads: National Archives, no. 111-B-40
How Fast the Trees Grow: Chad Ehlers/International Stock
Beethoven: Courtesy of Dover Publications, Music: A Pictorial Archive of Woodcuts & Engravings
The Flags of the American Colonies: John Michael/International Stock
The Flyer: Smithsonian Institution photograph by Charles Phillips, no. 87-3137-6
The Magic of Special Effects: The Museum of Modern Art, Film Stills Archives
Making Cartoons Move: The Museum of Modern Art, Film Stills Archives
Make Your Own Phenakistocope: Katherine Hall
Mount Pinatubo Erupts: Reuters/Tim Alipalo/Archive Photos, photo no. 91240057
A Folktale Comes to Life: Bob Firth/International Stock
Freedom: National Aeronautics and Space Administration, photo no. S95-14270
The Telephone of the Future: Courtesy of AT&T Company Photo Service

READING LEVEL 6

From the Imagination of Theodor Geisel: Ted Geisel estate
Bushnell's American Turtle: Naval Historical Foundation Photo Service, photo no. 3294
The Five-Dollar-A-Day Job: Chad Ehlers/International Stock
The Birth of McDonald's: Courtesy of McDonald's Corporation
Leonardo's Secret Notebook: Maria mit dem Kinde, 66 x 47.5 cm., Alte Pinakothek
Antipater's Travel Guide: John Zoiner/International Stock
The Seven Wonders of the Ancient World: J.G. Edmanson/International Stock
George Washington Carver: The National Portrait Gallery, photo no. NPG.65.77
The Smithsonian Institution: Smithsonian photograph by Charles Phillips, photo no. 88-13106
Franklin Delano Roosevelt's Secret: The National Portrait Gallery, photo no. NPG.64.14
The March of Dimes: Richard Pharaoh/International Stock
The Secrets of the Rosetta Stone: Miwako Ikeda/International Stock
Reading Hieroglyphics: Katherine Hall
The Great Explosion of 1908: National Aeronautics and Space Administration, photo no. S74-17688
The Good Master Kung: J.F. Genaro/International Stock

ABOUT THE AUTHOR

Katherine Hall attended the University of Texas at El Paso and earned her bachelor's degree in elementary education and special education in 1982. She has worked with students at the elementary school level for many years as a teacher for the first grade, English as a Second Language program, and resource room as well as a private tutor.

An interest in reading comprehension was first sparked by her experience in elementary school resource rooms. Disillusioned by her students' lack of progress, she found that the multiple-choice question format often became monotonous and did not excite students or offer opportunities for self-expression. The challenge of opening up the world of literature to her students, including the learning disabled, prompted the creation of a new format for teaching comprehension skills. Katherine developed *Reading Stories for Comprehension Success* to increase students' confidence, interest, and involvement in learning. She found that when she used high-interest, nonfiction stories, her students' curiosity about learning began to grow. From her own experience, she has found that *Reading Stories for Comprehension Success* also creates a rewarding teaching experience that can be implemented in schools, homes, and tutoring centers.

During the past ten years, Ms. Hall was an active member of the Texas State Council of the International Reading Association and of a Parent Teacher Association. Katherine taught and developed summer programs for the Learning Disabilities Association. She has presented inservices for teachers and was published in several magazines. In addition to reading and teaching, she also enjoys music and is an avid performer of the harp, flute, and piccolo. She resides in Hurst, Texas, where she continues to tutor students at the elementary to college level.

INTRODUCTION

USING READING STORIES FOR COMPREHENSION SUCCESS

Reading Stories for Comprehension Success includes an entire week or more of activities for each story lesson. Turn to the beginning of any of the three reading levels, and you'll see that they all follow this format:

Contents

The Contents page lists all the story titles, along with the reading grade level of each story and the story's page number. The reading grade level tells the teacher the story reading difficulty within the reading grade level.

About the Story

A brief description of the story introduces the teacher to the topic.

Preview Words

The Preview Words are *not* words that the teacher drills before the lesson. These words allow the teacher to expose the students to words they may not know or are unable to pronounce. Young students should prepare for unknown words before reading in public.

Choose all or only a few of the words, based on your students' needs. Write the Preview Words on chart paper or on overhead projector transparencies before the day of the story lesson.

Throughout the Week or Prior to the Lesson

Some of the stories include these topics. *Throughout the Week* presents such activities as reading from chapter books or decorating the classroom on a theme. *Prior to the Lesson* tells you about any important preparations you must make before the week begins.

Books to Read

A list of books that relate to the subject of each story lesson is provided. These books are at many levels, from picture books to chapter books to books found in the adult section of the library. Your librarian can provide you with additional sources.

Important—Always review any books, videos, and other materials before introducing them to your students, whether they are on the Books to Read *list or suggested by a librarian. What is considered appropriate for the students varies from state to state, or from school district to school district.*

Videos

This section lists videos on the story lesson subject. Many public libraries lend videos without charge.

Use caution, however, when showing videos to your class. Make sure your situation does not require special fees to show the film. Avoid violating copyright laws!

CDs, Records, and Cassettes

Here you'll find other materials that coordinate with the story lesson.

Introductory Activities

Introductory Activities introduce the student to the story lesson. In Reading Level 4, *The Many Faces of the Catfish,* the Introductory Activities begin with a visit to an aquarium. The students make a list of the types of catfish they see. These experiences encourage more logical, well thought out answers to interpretive questions.

Story Lesson

The stories—each with an accompanying photograph—are the foundation of *Reading Stories for Comprehension Success.* Prior to the lesson, make a copy of the black-line master for each student. If you choose question 11, "Write a title for the story" (Identification of Main Idea), make one copy of the story. Erase the title of the story with correction fluid, then make the number of copies needed for your class.

The design of the story meets the needs of the learning disabled and students with lower reading skills. The story is only one page long, about 150 words. The margins are wide to reduce the clutter on the story page, and there are no pictures, questions, or illustrations on it. This helps students with perceptual problems, attention deficits, short attention spans, or other disabilities to see the text more clearly.

If a student has an extremely short attention span, cut the stories apart between paragraphs. Present only one paragraph at a time. When the student masters reading one paragraph without losing attention, increase the page length to two paragraphs. Continue in this way until the student reads an entire story at one sitting.

Following the lesson plan, choose the questions the students will answer. Make one copy of the black-line master of the Questions Sheet and cut out only the questions you wish to present in the lesson. Mount the questions on plain white paper. Erase the numbers with correction fluid, then renumber the questions and make your copies.

For students with short attention spans, run one question per page to reduce distractions. Place one question in front of the student at a time.

Follow the *Presenting the Story Lesson* instructions (p. xv) for each story. Every story follows the same presentation procedure. The consistent format is important for learning disabled students.

The nonfiction, multicultural stories of *Reading Stories for Comprehension Success* are high-interest, and encourage the students to learn more. The biographies tell about such people as Stephen Hawking and Beethoven, who reached beyond themselves and their circumstances to achieve their dreams.

Extension Activities

Each story includes a list of *Extension Activities,* which allow the students to experience the subject beyond the story. Art projects, plays, and special activities for the whole school are offered.

Questions

The question format of *Reading Stories for Comprehension Success* requires students to answer in complete, well thought out sentences. There is no answer key because students create their own answers. Count any answer within reason as correct.

When presenting the Questions Sheet, encourage the students to debate possible answers to the interpretive questions. For example, the Drawing Conclusion question in the story about Chief Seattle reads, "What one word best describes Chief Seattle?" Many words describe Chief Seattle; the word I believe is best may not be the word you choose. Discuss the choices made by the students. Each student's opinion is valuable, and they must know this every time they choose an answer to an interpretive question.

One exercise the students enjoy is a discussion group. The students play-act a television discussion group. The teacher acts as moderator and the students discuss ideas presented in the story. Ask individual students interpretive questions about the story; encourage them to state their own opinions, and to back up their opinions with evidence.

This exercise helps students to realize that not all questions have the same answer. After using *Reading Stories for Comprehension Success,* students can better evaluate the choices presented in a multiple-choice test.

Unlike many other reading comprehension programs, *Reading Stories for Comprehension Success* bases all of the comprehension questions on the text of the story. You choose the number and difficulty of the questions, based on the needs of your students.

Comprehension exercises include literal and interpretive questions, using the following format:

I. *Literal questions:* The students find and retrieve answers directly from the text.

   A. *Description* (questions 1-4 on the Questions sheet): literal questions in which the student takes exact answers from the text.

   B. *Sequence* (questions 5-6): ask the students to demonstrate an understanding of the sequence of events in the story.

II. *Interpretive questions:* The students are asked to draw logical conclusions, based on the information presented in the text. Answers to these questions might vary from student to student.

   A. *Conclusion* (question 7): These questions ask students to look at the facts of the text, then draw a conclusion based on these facts.

   B. *Inference* (question 8): Here, students must look beyond the stated text to what is inferred by the author.

   C. *Prediction* (question 9): To answer questions dealing with prediction, the students must imagine a future influenced by the events described in the text.

   D. *Identification of Cause* (question 10): The students speculate on the cause of an event or someone's actions.

   E. *Identification of Main Idea* (question 11): This seems to be a difficult concept for many children with or without learning disabilities. One of the best ways to teach this concept is to ask students to write a title for the story. The title must state the topic or main idea of the story in only a few words.

      1. Throughout *Reading Stories for Comprehension Success* the question for main idea is basically the same, "Write a title for the story. Use as few words as possible."

      2. First, remove the title from the story page with correction fluid, then make the number of copies needed for your class.

   F. *Comparison* (question 12): Students must compare subjects, concepts, and events found within the story.

   G. *Summarize* (question 13): These questions ask the students to summarize an event in their own words.

   H. *Effect* (question 14): The questions ask students to consider the effects of the events presented in the story.

   I. *Fact and Opinion* (question 15): Students determine if a statement from the story is a fact or an opinion. The question also asks the students if they can prove their answers. For example, can they find sources in reference books to back up their answers?

III. *Teacher-Created Question* (question 16): In this section, you can create your own question. Add your question to a copy of the Questions sheet. Inject the students' own experiences into the questions. The questions must relate to the text.

Student Data Sheet

■ Students track their progress on the Student Data Sheet.

■ All students record their time on task. Those with attention deficits see concrete evidence of their improvement.

Reading Ability Guidelines

■ *Reading Stories for Comprehension Success* provides a chart enabling teachers to follow a lesson procedure that matches a student's reading ability.

■ Routines for Poor Readers, Average Readers, and Upper Level Readers further allow you to tailor the lesson to the student's abilities. As the student improves, move to the next level of the Guidelines.

WHO CAN USE *READING STORIES FOR COMPREHENSION SUCCESS?*

TO TEACHERS

While working in the public schools as a Resource teacher, I saw more of the educational responsibility for students with learning disabilities fall on the shoulders of the regular classroom teacher. Some of these teachers had important and valid concerns:

■ "Tommy's attention span is so short. What can I do when I have twenty other students in the classroom?"

■ "Julia reads two years below grade level. How can I modify my lessons to include her in a subject dependent on reading?"

I could give the teachers only the same list of modifications: Reduce distractions. Seat Tommy close to your desk. Underline the important information in Julia's books. These modifications, however, only emphasize the special students' disabilities in front of their peers.

Reading Stories for Comprehension Success has all the modifications built into the program. The entire class works on the same lesson without singling out the learning disabled student. This book works well for students in a variety of settings, including the following:

1. Public schools
2. Private schools (both regular and special education)
3. Classes for the learning disabled
4. Behavior disorders classes
5. Bilingual education classes
6. Tutoring centers
7. Home schools
8. Adult education classes

According to the U.S. Department of Education, the population of students with attention deficit disorder (ADD), dyslexia, and other learning disabilities is rising faster than any other educational group. *The Fifteenth Annual Report to Congress on the Implementation of Individuals With Disabilities Education Act (1993)* states:

> ... Since 1976–77 ... the number of students with specific learning disabilities has increased by more than 1.4 million (183 percent).

As the number of students with specific learning disabilities has increased, so has the percentage of learning disabled students served in the regular classroom. Over the past several years, *The U.S. Department of Education's Annual Report to Congress on the Implementation of The Individuals With Disabilities Education Act* showed a steady increase in the percentage of learning disabled students served within the regular classroom setting.

Percentage of Children Age 6-21 with
Specific Learning Disabilities Served
in Regular Classes Throughout the U.S.

1989–90	*1990–91*	*1992–93*
20.70%	33.75%	34.83%

Percentage of Students with Specific Learning
Disabilities Exiting the Educational
System Across the United States[1]

During the 1990–91 School Year

Age Group	Graduated With Diploma	Graduated With Certificate	Reached Maximum Age	Dropped Out	Other
14–21+	51.67%	10.80%	0.69%	22.16%	14.67%

Note that while this population grows, nearly 50% of learning disabled students fail to graduate with a diploma.

TO TUTORS

Students in tutoring centers can benefit from the use of *Reading Stories for Comprehension Success*. As a tutor, you can tailor the lessons to the individual student's needs.

The week before the story lesson, give the student a list of books, videos, and activities to which the parent should expose the student. At the end of the list, add activity suggestions from the *Introductory Activities* and the *Extension Activities*, which the parents can do with the child.

TO PARENTS

Parents can use *Reading Stories for Comprehension Success* to supplement a child's education. When using this program with your child, follow the instructions for the teacher. Ask your child's teacher to administer an Individual Reading Inventory and inform you of your child's independent reading level. Many teachers already have this information in your child's file.

---

[1]Current (1995) figures are not available.

Remember to be consistent. Use complete sentences whenever you talk to your child. For example, your child might ask, "Where are we going?" Answer in the complete sentence, "We are going to the store." Do not answer with the sentence fragment, "to the store." Reduce visual distractions and clutter around the home and use natural light whenever possible.

Read one story a week with your child. Before reading the story, complete the *Introductory Activities,* and take your child to the library to check out books on the story subject.

Follow the *Presenting the Story Lesson* instructions on the day you read the story. If your child has a very short attention span, begin with only one paragraph of the story, and only one question from the Questions sheet. Note the length of time the child stays on task on the Lesson Plan (Objective 3 on p. xviii), and monitor progress on the Student Data Sheet. Over time, slowly increase the length of the story read, and the number of questions on the Questions sheet.

After reading the story, complete the *Extension Activities.* All the activities are great family projects, and a parent has more freedom than a classroom teacher to expose students to a variety of learning experiences.

CLASSROOM ENVIRONMENT

When creating a classroom environment, keep the distractions to a minimum. The classroom decorations don't have to be plain and dull — just not too busy. Some suggestions are:

1. Hang the same color of bulletin board paper throughout the room. White paper does not fade, so the same paper will last all year.
2. Use bulletin board borders that are not busy. Even plain borders can be attractive.
3. Play soft instrumental music as the students enter the room or while they are doing seat work. The music masks such random noises as dropped pencils and squeaky chairs.
4. Use natural light whenever possible; students seem more at ease without fluorescent lights.
5. If you store your materials in open bookcases, put them in boxes. Cover the boxes with shelf paper without a busy design. Use the same design on every box.
6. Keep a few plants in the room. They add beauty and act as living air filters.

"IF YOU DO IT FOR ONE, DO IT FOR ALL"

The most important rule a teacher can follow is: "If you do it for one, you do it for all." Too often, teachers make modifications for special education students that are visible to the entire class. These modifications, which are put in place to help the student educationally, can destroy the student's morale. You *must* use modifications for learning disabled students; however, modifications should be subtly implemented. Publicly announcing a student's special needs in front of her or his peers embarrasses and demoralizes a child already struggling for acceptance. These students will withdraw in shame or act out to find approval from their peers.

Watch your special education student throughout the day; note how many times you make special allowances or modifications of which the entire class is aware. For example:

■ Seating the student in an isolated area, even when there is no disruptive behavior involved.

■ Stating the modifications when giving an assignment. Avoid statements like these:

"Read Chapter One and answer questions one through ten. Frank, you need to do only questions one through five," or "Everyone read Chapter Six. Susan, I'll underline the parts you need to read after everyone begins working."

Later, look over your notes. Are there modifications that the entire class can participate in? If you do it for one, can you do it for all? For example, students with learning disabilities have difficulty keeping their work organized. If one modification is to set up a notebook with individual folders for each subject area and homework, all the students should have such a notebook.

Sometimes you cannot use modifications with the entire class. It is best to meet with the student privately to discuss these modifications. When you meet with the student, write down all the modifications she or he can expect and how you will implement them. Remember to make the implementation as private and subtle as possible. After the student understands and agrees to these modifications, sign a contract. File it in the student's file; it will be invaluable as proof of modifications if school district or other officials ask for it.

ATTENTION DEFICIT DISORDER

Aside from the recent surge in drug therapy, few programs offer innovative teaching aids for learning disabled students, including those with ADD. Focus on strategies that go beyond medication, and remember to use these strategies with the entire class whenever possible. For example, the rate at which the teacher reads a story affects the student's comprehension level during auditory presentation. According to one study, hyperactive students were less active and stayed on task when the teacher read the story fast "without added nonrelevant detail." Comprehension improved, however, when the teacher read the story slowly without added detail.[2]

According to Fiore, Becker, and Nero, the following techniques are most likely to be effective in academic areas:

Positive Reinforcement

1. Social praise
2. Group reward contingencies
3. Parent rewards
4. Token economies

Punishment ("a contingency that reduces the frequency of behavior")

1. Hyperactive students remained on task longer using negative feedback. However, errors increased significantly.
2. Short, strong, and consistent reprimands reduced disruptive behaviors.

In her book *When Children Don't Learn,* Diane McGuinness states that educators must meet the following three needs before hyperactive students can change their behaviors and begin to improve their academic performance.[3] We should apply these needs to all students, with or without learning disabilities.

1. *ACHIEVABLE GOALS: Reading Stories for Comprehension Success* allows the teacher to determine "achievable goals" for each student on an individual basis. The teacher chooses the type and number of questions used. As the students achieve success, the teacher gradually increases the number of questions.

---

[2]Thoms A. Fiore, Elizabeth A. Becker, and Rebecca C. Nero, "Educational Interventions for Students With Attention Deficit Disorder," *Exceptional Children,* v 60 (Oct.–Nov. 1993), 163 (II).

[3]Diane McGuinness, *When Children Don't Learn: Understanding the Biology and Psychology of Learning Disabilities* (New York: Basic Books, 1985).

2. *GOALS BASED ON ACADEMIC SUBJECT AREAS: Reading Stories for Comprehension Success* incorporates the needs of learning disabled students in an academic subject (reading comprehension) in a format that benefits every student in the class. Students can develop reading comprehension skills at any reading level.

   The teacher chooses a reading level based on the learning disabled reading skills, and uses this level for the entire class. The high-interest, factual stories mask the true reading level. Everyone in the class, learning disabled or not, learns comprehension skills with modifications built into the program, without being aware of special provisions for learning disabled students.

3. *FREQUENT PRAISE:* As the students progress through *Reading Stories for Comprehension Success,* they complete their assignments without undue stress. They participate in making the Data Sheets, proving to themselves that they can succeed. The factual, fascinating content of the stories inspires students to learn more, and possibly to set goals based on newly found interests.

TEACHING STRATEGIES

Teachers can use several teaching strategies with the entire class to improve the reading comprehension skills of students with or without learning disabilities. *Reading Stories for Comprehension Success* begins with one to two days of introductory activities before the story lesson. From these experiences, the students develop a better understanding of the story. The Extension Activities build on the students' comprehension; with them, you create a "total sensory experience."

Students with learning disabilities have difficulty remembering what they learned even minutes after reading the story. Use this activity presented by Jerome Rosner in his book *Helping Children Overcome Learning Difficulties: A Step-by-Step Guide for Parents and Teachers* with the entire class. (Note: This skill also prepares all students for achievement tests, which require strong short-term memory.)

Give each student a paragraph written at the child's independent reading level. The students copy as much of the paragraph as they can in two minutes. Set a timer for two minutes and say, "Go." The students stop when the timer rings.

At the bottom of the page, the students write "number of words copied = _____" and "number of spelling errors and omissions = _____." On a separate page, the students copy the following chart:

Day	Number of Words Copied in Two Minutes	Number of Errors and Omissions
1		
2		
3		
4		
5		

The chart can be kept for the number of days needed. The goal is to increase the number in column 1 while decreasing the number in column 2. Tell the students to try to keep larger sections of the story in their memory while they write; it will increase the number of words they copy. It is also helpful to say the words to themselves as they write. According to Rosner, repeating the information to themselves will improve short-term memory. Keeping larger pieces of the paragraph in their heads will improve reading speed.

Language Development

The Preview Words of *Reading Stories for Comprehension Success* introduce the students to new vocabulary words without drill. The students not only hear the words in the story, but continue to use them in speech and writing during the Introductory and Extension Activities. Encourage the students to find new words based on the concepts presented in the story. Remember to model the use of these words in your own speech.

Team Learning

Throughout *Reading Stories for Comprehension Success,* students work in groups or teams. This allows the learning disabled students to participate in an activity without depending solely on their own abilities. Break the class into groups of two to three students. Subtly assigning a higher level reader to each group helps the others in the group with difficult words or passages, and learning disabled students don't feel singled out when other students in the group also ask for help.

Set up a permanent book center in the classroom. Encourage the students to read books that interest them.

Read to the Class

Chapter books supplement several stories in *Reading Stories for Comprehension Success.* Look for these titles in the *Throughout the Week* section. Read chapters from these books each day. Soon students will ask the librarian for books on the same topic or by the same author. An active interest in reading quickly improves a student's reading comprehension skills.

Reading Stories for Comprehension Success aims to improve reading comprehension by introducing and reinforcing basic concepts of the subject matter through multisensory Introductory and Extension Activities. With the high-interest, factual stories, students expand their vocabulary, reinforcing the Preview Words.

READING ABILITY GUIDELINES[4]

The guidelines suggest teaching procedures, based on the students' reading comprehension skills. As poor readers improve, move to the next level.

A student's answers to interpretive questions may not be logically sound. Conduct a short, open discussion about other possibilities. Consider the answer correct, however, if the student arrived at the conclusion based on his or her best effort. Remember that the purpose of *Reading Stories for Comprehension Success* is to create joy in learning and expressing oneself.

Note: Do not include interpretive questions in your question list until the student demonstrates mastery of literal questions. Then introduce only one interpretive question until the student shows confidence.

---

[4]Based on information from: Dolores Durkin, *Teaching Them to Read,* 3d ed., p. 442 (Boston: Allyn and Bacon, 1979).

Poor Readers

1. Read the literal questions orally.

2. Read the story silently.

3. Discuss the answers to the literal questions. (Encourage students to speak in complete, understandable sentences.)

4. Read the interpretive questions orally.

5. Read the story silently (second reading).

6. Discuss the answers to the interpretive questions.

7. The students complete the Questions sheet independently, writing all the answers in complete sentences.

Average Readers

1. Read the literal and interpretive questions orally.

2. Read the story silently.

3. Discuss the answers to the interpretive questions.

4. The students complete the Questions sheet independently, writing all the answers in complete sentences.

Upper Level Readers

1. Read the interpretive questions orally.

2. Read the story silently.

3. Conduct a discussion based on the questions. (Guide the students in the use of complete, well thought out sentences.)

4. The students complete the Questions sheet independently, writing all the answers in complete sentences.

PRESENTING THE STORY LESSON

Important: Remove all extra stimulation from the students' view or reach. The work area must be clear of distractions.

1. Review the Introductory Activities. Discuss what the students did and learned.

2. Display and discuss the Preview Words, then remove the words from the children's sight.

3. Display the story picture. Engage the students in a discussion about the illustration. Focus on the topic of the story and guide the students in such a way as to focus their attention on the subject.

4. Read the quote found in the Story Lesson section of each story. This question prepares them for the content of the story. For example, "The title of the story we're reading today is *Mount Pinatubo Erupts*. What do you think the story is about? What do you already know about volcanoes?"

5. Hand out the story pages.

6. Choose the lesson format in the guidelines that suits your students' reading ability. Remember to remove the story from the students' view when they work on their question sheets to avoid distractions. They can refer to the story if needed; however, remove the story from the students' view as soon as possible.

7. Grade the questions in front of the students when they complete their work. Because you monitor the work closely, there should be few errors.

8. Students record their scores on the Student Data Sheet.

SENTENCE WRITING LESSONS

MATERIALS

■ photographs or drawings with simple subjects

Do not use complicated, busy photographs. Calendars provide a good source for photographs and drawings because they usually focus on a single subject (e.g., a dog in a simple pose).

PROCEDURE

Week One

1. Display a calendar picture in front of the class.

2. Teacher:

> Every picture has a subject. A subject is the most important figure in the picture. Look at this picture. The subject of this picture is a dog. What is the subject of this picture? (Answer: The subject of the picture is a dog.)

3. Show five more pictures. Display the pictures one at a time. Ask the students the subject of the picture. Model a complete sentence for the answer whenever the students answer in sentence fragments.

4. Repeat the exercise with five photographs each day for a week, or until the students demonstrate mastery of the skill.

Week Two

1. Display the same dog picture used in Week One, step 1.

2. Teacher:

> Each subject in a picture is doing something. What is the subject in this picture? (Answer: The subject in the picture is a dog.) What is the dog doing? (Answer: The dog is sitting in a basket.)

> The part of a sentence that tells us the subject of the picture is the subject. The part of the sentence that tells us what the subject is doing is the predicate. What is the part of the sentence that tells us what the subject is doing? (Answer: The part of the sentence that tells us what the subject is doing is the predicate.)

> If we were to tell about this picture in a complete sentence, we would say, "The dog is sitting in a basket." (Write the sentence on the board.)

> What is the subject of this sentence? (Answer: The subject of this sentence is "The dog." Underline the words "The dog.")

What is the predicate of this sentence? (Answer: The predicate of this sentence is "is sitting in a basket." Draw two lines under the words "is sitting in a basket.")

The sentence "The dog is sitting in a basket" is a complete sentence. It has a subject and a predicate. What must a complete sentence have? (Answer: A complete sentence must have a subject and a predicate.)

3. Remove the dog picture and display another picture. Follow the procedure outlined in step 1.
4. Erase the sentence and remove the picture from the students' view.
5. Repeat the procedure for three more photographs.
6. Do this exercise with five photographs each day of the week, or until the students demonstrate mastery of the skill.

Week Three

Students who have difficulty writing can do these exercises orally. Remember, if one student does the exercise orally, everyone does the exercise orally.

1. Display one picture.
2. Ask the students to write or state a complete sentence about the picture. If the students answer orally, write the sentence on the board.
3. The students will underline the subject of the sentence. They will draw two lines under the predicate. If this is an oral exercise, ask students to come to the board. They will underline the subject and draw two lines under the predicate. If the students write their answers, call on individuals to read their sentences. Ask them to tell the subject and the predicate.
4. Erase the sentence on the board and remove the picture.
5. Repeat the exercise with four more pictures. Show only one picture at a time.
6. Practice this exercise with five pictures each day of the week, or until the students demonstrate mastery of the skill.

Supplemental Lessons

Repeat Week Three throughout the year to refresh the students' skill. Remember to model complete sentences at all times. Ask the students to speak in complete sentences all day in every subject.

PRETEST

Determine the reading grade level of each student in the class. Survey each student's reading grade level using your favorite Individual Reading Inventory (IRI). You are looking for the student's independent reading level, *not* the instructional level. *Reading Stories for Comprehension Success* aims to improve comprehension skills only. If you begin the program at the student's instructional level, the reading of individual words becomes the focus of his or her efforts. If you present the stories at the student's independent reading level, he or she comfortably reads the text and concentration is on the content.

Look over the IRI scores. Which score is the lowest? Begin *Reading Stories for Comprehension Success* one level below this score, unless the lowest score is grade 1. In this case, begin on Reading Level 1. For example, if your students are fifth-graders, look at the lowest IRI score. If the lowest independent reading level is grade level 3, begin *Reading Stories for Comprehension Success* at Reading Level 2.

This procedure ensures that the student with the lowest reading level will feel comfortable reading with the rest of the class. Never tell the students the reading level they are working on. Because of the factual, high-interesl nature of the stories, they will not realize that they are reading at a lower reading level. You can teach any reading comprehension skill at any reading grade level.

TEACHER LESSON PLAN

The Lesson Plan form in *Reading Stories for Comprehension Success* saves valuable teacher time. First, choose the type and number of questions you will ask the students. Begin with only literal questions on the first lesson, presenting one to no more than five questions in one lesson. The number of questions asked depends on the students' ability and attention span.

LESSON PLAN FORM

1. *Basic Information*

   ■ Fill in the class information at the top of the page.

2. *Objectives*

   ■ The lesson format of *Reading Stories for Comprehension Success* is consistent and predictable throughout the series. Therefore, each lesson teaches and reinforces the same basic objectives.

   Objective 1

   ■ Circle if the student is to read orally or silently.

   Objective 2

   ■ Circle if the student is to answer the questions orally or in writing.

   Objective 3

   ■ Fill in the number of minutes the student will stay on task. Use this objective to monitor students with short attention spans. By beginning with a short question list and increasing the number of questions over time, you can actually help the student to increase his or her time on task.

3. *Comprehension Skills Taught in This Lesson*

   ■ Check off the comprehension skills you will present in the lesson.

4. *Materials*

   ■ Every lesson uses all the materials listed.

LESSON PLAN

Date: _____   **Teacher Edition page ____**

Class Period: _____   **Student page ____**

Student: _____

Reading Group: _____

Story: _____

Objectives:

(circle one)
1. The student(s) will read the story orally/silently.

(circle one)
2. The student(s) will orally state/write the answers to the following comprehension skills in complete, understandable sentences.

3. The student(s) will complete the given assignment in _____ minutes.

Comprehension Skills Taught in This Lesson:
(Check the skill to be taught.)

I. Literal questions

  A. Description _____

  B. Sequence _____

II. Interpretive questions

  A. Conclusion _____

  B. Interference _____

  C. Prediction _____

  D. Identification of Cause _____

  E. Identification of Main Idea _____

  F. Comparisons _____

  G. Summarize _____

  H. Effect _____

  I. Fact and Opinion _____

III. Teacher-created question _____

Materials:
__ Story page   __ Questions Sheet   __ Data Sheet

STUDENT DATA SHEET

STUDENT DATA SHEET (Example)   Student: ___Frank___

Story	1
Date	4/6/97
Description	2
Sequence	1
Conclusion	1
Inference	0
Prediction	
Cause	
Main Idea	
Comparison	
Summarize	
Effect	
Fact/Opinion	
Score	4/5
Percentage	80%
Time on Task	6 min.

Consider a comprehension skill mastered when the student has five correct answers in a row. Move on to the next skill; however, intermittently include the mastered skills in the Questions Sheet as review.

STUDENT DATA SHEET

Student: _____

	Story	1	2	3	4	5	6	7	8	9	10	11	12	13	14	15	AVERAGE
L I T E R A L	Date																
	Description																
	Sequence																
I N T E R P R E T I V E	Conclusion																
	Inference																
	Prediction																
	Cause																
	Main Idea																
	Comparison																
	Summarize																
	Effect																
	Fact/Opinion																
	Score																
	Percentage																
	Time on Task																

Purpose of Student Data Sheet

The easy-to-use Student Data Sheet helps both teacher and students track their progress through *Reading Stories for Comprehension Success*. The Data Sheet serves several purposes:

1. The students track their own performance, which serves also as a motivational reward system.
2. The students track their time on task, and thus see tangible evidence of their efforts. This is also a powerful, yet often overlooked, reward system.
3. You can use the Data Sheet to monitor the student's mastery of comprehension skills.
4. School districts require teachers to keep a written record of any provisions made for students who qualify as learning disabled. The Data Sheet is a good record to keep in your files.

Using the Student Data Sheet

1. After the students complete their Questions sheets, grade the answers in front of each student. At the top of the page write:

$$\frac{The\ Number\ of\ Correct\ Answers}{The\ Total\ Number\ of\ Questions}$$

For example, if a student answered four out of five questions correctly, write the following at the top of the page:

$$\frac{4}{5}$$

2. Give the student her or his Student Data Sheet.
3. Write the date under the number of the story read.
4. Look at the list of reading comprehension question styles listed down the sheet. In front of the student, enter the number of correct responses to each question style. Because of the presentation of the material, there should be few errors.
5. The student enters the score from the Questions sheet into the space marked Score.
6. Using the score numbers, enter the percentage into the Percentage box. If the student has the skills to calculate the percentage, he or she will enter the number into the Data Sheet; otherwise, you must calculate and enter the percentage. (You can also use this number as the grade for the lesson.)
7. The student enters the time in minutes that he or she stayed on task in the Time on Task space.
8. At the end of the reading level, average the percentage scores and enter the total score under the Average box. For example, Frank's Questions sheet contained two description questions, one sequence question, one conclusion question, and one inference question on Story 1. He answered every question except the inference question correctly. The score on his paper would read: 4/5. His time on task was 6 minutes.

IN CONCLUSION

The aim of *Reading Stories for Comprehension Success* is to incorporate modifications for learning disabled students into one program. This program gives teachers maximum flexibility in lesson presentation. Unlike other reading comprehension programs, this book gives you the freedom to base a lesson on your students' needs. Always keep in mind the following:

1. Keep the room and work area as distraction free as possible.
2. If you do it for one, do it for all.
3. Always model complete sentences in your own speech.
4. Encourage the students to speak in complete, well thought out sentences.
5. Create an environment in which students feel free to develop and communicate their unique ideas. Allow them to debate the interpretive questions, and to learn from the variety of backgrounds each student brings to the class.

Katherine L. Hall

CONTENTS

INTRODUCTION

Using *Reading Stories for Comprehension Success* (vi) Who Can Use *Reading Stories for Comprehension Success?* (ix) Classroom Environment (xi) Teaching Strategies (xiii) Reading Ability Guidelines (xiv*) Presenting the Story Lesson (xv) Sentence Writing Lessons (xvi) Pretest (xvii) Teacher Lesson Plan (xviii) Student Data Sheet (xx) In Conclusion (xxii)

READING LEVEL 4

CONTENTS   1

WARNING! EARTHQUAKE!

About the Story (2) Preview Words (2) Prior to the Lesson (2) Books to Read (2) Introductory Activities (3) Extension Activities (4) Warning! Earthquake! Story (6) Questions (7)

THE MYSTERY OF SAINT ELMO'S FIRE

About the Story (9) Preview Words (9) Books to Read (9) Introductory Activities (9) Extension Activities (11) The Mystery of Saint Elmo's Fire Story (13) Questions (14)

THE SOURCE OF SAINT ELMO'S FIRE

About the Story (16) Preview Words (16) Books to Read (16) Introductory Activities (16) Extension Activities (17) The Source of Saint Elmo's Fire Story (20) Questions (21)

THE NEWBERY MEDAL

About the Story (23) Preview Words (23) Books to Read (23) Introductory Activities (24) Extension Activities (25) The Newbery Medal Story (27) Questions (28)

IT'S ROADEO TIME

About the Story (30) Preview Words (30) Prior to the Lesson (30) Books to Read (30) Introductory Activities (31) Extension Activities (32) It's Roadeo Time Story (34) Questions (35)

WHO WROTE "THE TORTOISE AND THE HARE"?

About the Story (37) Preview Words (37) Throughout the Week (37) Books to Read (37) Introductory Activities (38) Extension Activities (38) Who Wrote "The Tortoise and the "Hare" Story (41) Questions (42)

THE MANY FACES OF THE CATFISH

About the Story (44) Preview Words (44) Prior to the Lesson (44) Books to Read (44) Introductory Activities (45) Extension Activities (45) The Many Faces of the Catfish Story (48) Questions (49)

THE RUNESTONE

BONE HUNTER

WHO IS UNCLE SAM?

THEY STOOD ON TOP OF THE WORLD

STEPHEN HAWKING

BLACK HOLES

TO CLEAN OR NOT TO CLEAN

CHIEF SEATTLE

BIBLIOGRAPHY   113

READING LEVEL 5

CONTENTS   115

ROBERT J. ACOSTA: TEACHER

COLUMBUS'S MYSTERIOUS LIGHTS

THE REMARKABLE LIFE OF HOWARD HUGHES

THE BATTLE OF THE IRONCLADS

HOW FAST THE TREES GROW

BEETHOVEN

THE FLAGS OF THE AMERICAN COLONIES

THE FLYER

THE MAGIC OF SPECIAL EFFECTS

MAKING CARTOONS MOVE

MAKE YOUR OWN PHENAKISTOSCOPE

MOUNT PINATUBO ERUPTS

A FOLKTALE COMES TO LIFE

FREEDOM

THE TELEPHONE OF THE FUTURE

BIBLIOGRAPHY   226

READING LEVEL 6

CONTENTS   227

FROM THE IMAGINATION OF THEODOR GEISEL

BUSHNELL'S AMERICAN TURTLE

THE FIVE-DOLLAR-A-DAY JOB

THE BIRTH OF MCDONALD'S

LEONARDO'S SECRET NOTEBOOK

ANTIPATER'S TRAVEL GUIDE

THE SEVEN WONDERS OF THE ANCIENT WORLD

GEORGE WASHINGTON CARVER

THE SMITHSONIAN INSTITUTION

FRANKLIN DELANO ROOSEVELT'S SECRET

THE MARCH OF DIMES

THE SECRETS OF THE ROSETTA STONE

READING HIEROGLYPHICS

THE GREAT EXPLOSION OF 1908

THE GOOD MASTER KUNG

READING LEVEL 4

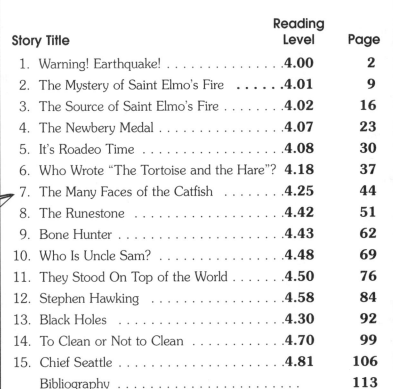

WARNING! EARTHQUAKE!

ABOUT THE STORY

This story tells about "earthquake lights." During earthquakes in Japan and California, bright white and red lights appeared in the sky above the center of the earthquakes. Scientists hope to find out how to use the lights to warn people before an earthquake strikes.

PREVIEW WORDS

earthquake	Japan	California
scientists	sparks	warning

PRIOR TO THE LESSON

Learn about warning systems in your community. Does the community use tornado sirens? How does the Emergency Broadcast System work in your area? What happens if hazardous materials are spilled? During the week, the students will investigate the effectiveness of these warning systems.

BOOKS TO READ

Pompeii, Ian Andrews (M.N. Lerner, 1980).

Magic Dogs of the Volcanoes, Manlio Argueta (Childrens Book Press, 1990) English and Spanish.

Volcanoes and Earthquakes, Martyn Bramwell (Franklin Watts, 1986).

Activities in the Earth Sciences, Helen J. Challand (Childrens Press, 1982).

The Magic School Bus: Inside the Earth, Joanna Cole (Scholastic, 1987).

Earthquakes, Disaster! Series, Dennis Brindell Fradin (Childrens Press, 1982).

Can Bears Predict Earthquakes?: Unsolved Mysteries of Animal Behavior, Russell Freedman (Prentice-Hall, 1982).

Disastrous Earthquakes, Henry Gilfond (Franklin Watts, 1981).

Paul's Volcano, Beatrice Gormley (Houghton Mifflin, 1987).

Earthquake, Christopher Lampton (Millbrook Press, 1991).

Earthquakes: New Scientific Ideas About How and Why the Earth Shakes, Patricia Lauber (Random House, 1972).

If You Lived at the Time of the Great San Francisco Earthquake, Ellen Levine (Scholastic, 1987).

The Changing Earth, Keith Lye (Rourke Enterprises, 1985).

The San Francisco Earthquake and Fire, Helen Markley Miller (Putnam's, 1970).

The Marshall Cavendish Science Project Book of the Earth, Steve Parker (Marshall Cavendish Corp., 1986).

Earthquakes, Seymour Simon (Morrow Junior Books, 1991).

I Can Be a Geologist, Paul P. Sipiera (Childrens Press, 1986).

Caught in the Moving Mountains, Gloria Skurzynski (Lothrop, Lee & Shepard Books, 1984).

Cornerstones of Freedom: The Story of the San Francisco Earthquake, R. Conrad Stein (Childrens Press, 1983).

The Amateur Geologist: Explorations and Investigations, Raymond Wiggers (Franklin Watts, 1993).

VIDEOS

Born of Fire, National Geographic (Vestron Video, 1983). Length: 60 minutes.

The Great San Francisco Earthquake, PBS Video, 1988. Series: The American Experience. Length: 58 minutes.

INTRODUCTORY ACTIVITIES

DAY ONE

Objective: A community official will visit the class and discuss warning systems. The students will learn about the emergency plans of their community.

Curriculum subject: Social Studies

Invite a community official to class to discuss warning systems used in your area. Contact City Hall and ask for the appropriate department. They can direct you to a speaker.

Before the speaker arrives, help the class develop a who, what, when, where, and why question list. For example:

◆ Who is involved in warning the community in emergencies?

◆ What types of emergencies might the community face (examples: tornadoes, earthquakes, hazardous material spill, etc.)?

◆ When are the warning systems activated?

◆ Where should you go if you hear a warning?

◆ Why is it important to maintain a warning system?

End the discussion with a question-and-answer session. Ask if the emergency system in your community can be improved. How can the students become involved in improving the system? How can the students inform the community about the system?

DAY TWO

Story Lesson

Follow the *Presenting the Story Lesson* instructions in the Introduction. Each story lesson follows the same procedure; however, say the following in step 4:

"The title of the story we're reading today is *Warning! Earthquake!* What do you think the story is about? What do you already know about emergency warning systems?"

EXTENSION ACTIVITIES

1. Read from the book *Can Bears Predict Earthquakes?: Unsolved Mysteries of Animal Behavior,* pages 3–10. Ask how bears and earthquake lights are alike. How are they different? Which would make the best warning system? Why?

◆ Read from the book *Why in the World?: Books for World Explorers,* page 81, by the National Geographic Society (Washington, D.C.: The National Geographic Society, 1985). Compare the man-made warning instruments to bears and the earthquake lights. Which is the best warning system? Why?

2. List improvements that need to be made in your community warning system. The students will write letters to community, state, and federal officials voicing their concerns. Obtain these names and addresses from your local library. The students must write about specific improvements and clearly explain why they are needed.

3. The students will make fliers and posters that inform the community about warning systems. List the types of warnings and what people must do when they hear the warnings. Make special posters that address the needs of the elderly, hearing impaired, and others with disabilities.

◆ Post the fliers and posters in centers for the hearing impaired, community centers, libraries, grocery stores, and senior citizen centers.

WARNING! EARTHQUAKE!

No one knows when an earthquake will shake the ground. Early warning of an earthquake would save lives. Everyone could move to a safe place until the quake was over.

Scientists think they have found nature's warning lights. During earthquakes in Japan and California, many people said they saw "earthquake lights." Bright white and red lights appeared in the sky above the center of the quake. Is nature turning on warning lights?

Many scientists say yes. They think the lights are like giant sparks. If you rub your bed sheets together quickly, you can make little sparks. You can see the sparks in a dark room. Scientists think that earthquakes rub big rocks together very quickly. The rocks are much bigger than your sheets, so the sparks are very big. The sparks are so big that they light up the sky.

"Earthquake lights" don't happen during every earthquake. After scientists study the lights, they hope to find out how to use the warning lights of nature.

QUESTIONS FOR WARNING! EARTHQUAKE!

1. Where have "earthquake lights" been seen?

   _____

   _____

2. What colors are "earthquake lights"?

   _____

   _____

3. What rubs together to make "earthquake lights"?

   _____

   _____

4. What do scientists hope to use "earthquake lights" for?

   _____

   _____

5. When did the lights shine in the sky: before, during, or after the earthquake?

   _____

   _____

6. What do scientists hope to find out after they study the lights?

   _____

   _____

7. Would "earthquake lights" be a good earthquake warning system? Why do you think so?

   _____

   _____

8. The story says, "'Earthquake lights' don't happen during every earthquake." Why do you think "earthquake lights" do not happen during every earthquake?

   _____

   _____

9. How might scientists use "earthquake lights" as warning lights?

_____

_____

10. A seismologist studies earthquakes. Are you interested in becoming a seismologist? Why do you think so?

_____

_____

11. Write a title for this story. Use as few words as possible.

_____

_____

12. Compare the sparks made by rubbing sheets together to the sparks made when rocks rub together. How are they alike? How are they different?

_____

_____

13. In your own words, tell what scientists believe make "earthquake lights."

_____

_____

14. Someday scientists might use "earthquake lights" to warn people about an earthquake. How might this affect people living where earthquakes are common?

_____

_____

15. The story said, "They (scientists) think the lights are giant sparks." Does this mean scientists know for a fact what makes these lights? Why do you think so?

_____

_____

16.

_____

_____

Name _____   Date _____

THE MYSTERY OF SAINT ELMO'S FIRE

ABOUT THE STORY

This story tells about a sailor who sees a ship glowing in the distance. The sailor becomes alarmed because he believes the ship is on fire. His captain reassures him that Saint Elmo is visiting the glowing ship. He explains, "Saint Elmo comes down from heaven in the form of fire to protect ships from violent weather."

*Do not tell the students the scientific reasons for these occurrences. They will explore these explanations in the next story.

PREVIEW WORDS

Saint Elmo's fire	blustery	hull
deck	masts	rigging
Columbus	Atlantic	London
crow's nest		

BOOKS TO READ

The Flying Dutchman: A Guide to Opera, Frank Granville Barker (Barrie & Jenkins, 1979).

"Rip Van Winkle," *The Rand McNally Book of Favorite Nursery Classics,* adapted from Washington Irving's legend by Dorothy Bell Briggs (Rand McNally, 1961).

Tales of Thunder and Lightning, Harry Devlin (Parents' Magazine Press, 1975).

Jason and the Argonauts, Bernard Evslin (William Morrow, 1986).

Rip Van Winkle, Washington Irving (William Morrow, 1987).

The Flying Dutchman: Legends and Folktales Series, told by Catherine Storr (Raintree Steck-Vaughn, 1985).

VIDEOS

Rip Van Winkle: American Heroes and Legends, Rabbit Ears Productions, 1992. Length: 30 minutes.

Rip Van Winkle, Claymation Classics, Will Vinton Productions, 1987. Length: 30 minutes.

INTRODUCTORY ACTIVITIES

A note about Saint Elmo's fire:

According to Peter Kemp, Saint Elmo's fire is "the brushlike electric discharge which, under certain atmospheric conditions, takes place at the masthead and yardarms of a ship." Greco-Roman mythology tells us that Poseidon made the heads of Castor and Pollux glow in a storm during the first voyage of the Argonauts.

Some sailors believed that Saint Elmo's fire was a sign of good luck. Others feared that if their face was lit by the glow of Saint Elmo's fire they would die within the day. Still other sailors would not look at Saint Elmo's fire, fearing they were looking at the ship of the Flying Dutchman. Some of the famous seamen to record sightings of Saint Elmo's fire include Columbus, Vasco da Gama, and Magellan.[1]

Because thunder and lightning are also caused by electrical charges of a storm, I begin the lessons with folktales about thunder and lightning. In this way, the students might better understand why sailors told stories about Saint Elmo's fire.

DAY ONE

Objective: The students will listen to folktales from around the world, told to explain the occurrence of thunder and lightning.

Curriculum subject: Language Arts

Teacher: Long ago, people didn't know what caused thunder and lightning. They watched the flash of bright lightning and heard the clap of thunder. Even today, children can be very afraid of thunder and lightning. Do you become afraid during a thunderstorm? Why are you afraid?

Imagine being a small child many years ago. Your parents might tell you a story to explain thunder and lightning to make you feel better.

Today I'll read some stories called folktales. These folktales come from around the world. They are stories parents told their children so they wouldn't become frightened during a thunderstorm.

Read the book *Tales of Thunder and Lightning*. Afterward, discuss the stories and how they might help calm a child's fears. Will the students remember these stories during the next thunderstorm? Will the stories make them feel better?

DAY TWO

Objective: The students will watch the video *Rip Van Winkle*. They will discuss why people told stories about things they did not understand.

Curriculum subject: Language Arts

Teacher: Yesterday we listened to stories from around the world about thunder and lightning. Why did people make up stories about things they did not understand?

Today we'll listen to an American folktale by Washington Irving. As you listen to the story, think about what thunder sounds like.

Show the video *Rip Van Winkle: American Heroes and Legends*. Afterward, ask the students if thunder sounds like little men bowling up in the mountains.

Teacher: We have listened to many stories about thunder and lightning. Why do you think people made up so many stories about thunder and lightning? (Answer: People wanted a story to explain something they did not understand.)

Tomorrow we'll read about some strange lights sailors see on their ships during storms. People made up stories to explain what made these strange, glowing lights, just as they did for thunder and lightning.

---

[1]Kemp, Peter, *The Oxford Companion to Ships and the Sea*, p. 744. New York: Oxford University Press, 1976.

DAY THREE

Before the story lesson, display a picture of a ship. Write the words *crow's nest, hull, deck, rigging,* and *masts* on the board. Point out each of these features on the picture of the ship.

Story Lesson

Follow the *Presenting the Story Lesson* instructions in the Introduction. Each story lesson follows the same procedure; however, say the following in step 4:

"The title of the story we're reading today is *The Mystery of Saint Elmo's Fire.* What do you think the story is about?"

EXTENSION ACTIVITIES

1. Read the story "The Flying Dutchman."

The Flying Dutchman

Long, long ago, a Dutch skipper sailed the sea. The captain was a fine seaman. One cold and stormy day, the captain was determined to sail from Batavia to Table Bay.

"No storm has beat me yet," he boasted. "All men aboard!"

Many a good sailor followed the captain that thundering day. They weren't afraid of anything with their captain to guide them home.

But that night, the wind began to blow harder. The waves began to rise higher. The ship creaked under the brave sailors' feet.

"Keep on to Table Bay!" cried the captain from the wheel. "No storm will hold us back!"

Hours passed and the wind grew stronger. The ship pushed into the wind. The mighty gales pushed back against the helpless ship. The captain and his crew made no progress against the storm.

Finally the captain turned his face up to the beating rain. His fist reached up toward heaven and he bellowed, "By *Donner* and *Blitzen* I'll beat God's winds, and sail into Table Bay!"

Suddenly, the ship began to shake. Down from heaven came a thundering voice. "Tempt me not, Flying Dutchman, for I condemn you to sail against my winds through all eternity!"

To this day the Flying Dutchman continues to sail against the winds. The captain's bony white fingers still grip the ancient wheel. So beware if you sail around the Cape of Good Hope. You might see a ghostly ship glowing in a storm. If you listen closely, within a roll of thunder you'll hear the good captain cry, "Keep on to Table Bay! No storm will hold us back!"

◆ Teacher:

Some people believe the legend of the Flying Dutchman is one way sailors explained ships that glowed during storms. How is this story like The Mystery of Saint Elmo's Fire? How is it different? How is the story of the Flying Dutchman like the legend of Rip Van Winkle?

2. The students will make up a legend of their own to explain why ships glow during storms. Break the class into groups. They will write the legend, and draw pictures to go with their story. Share the stories with the class.

THE MYSTERY OF SAINT ELMO'S FIRE

It was a cold, blustery night. Strong winds blew over the waters. From my perch in the crow's nest, I could clearly see another ship struggling against the storm.

Suddenly, a bright ball of ghostly fire burst out on the other ship's hull. The fire danced about the deck as if alive. The spirit then slipped up the rigging, leaving a blazing trail behind, until it reached the top of the masts. There it exploded into flames that leaped into the night sky. The ship and all hands would surely burn.

"Calm yourself, old man," my captain said when I told him my story. "That ship is safe. What you saw was a visit from Saint Elmo's fire. Saint Elmo comes down from heaven in the form of fire to protect ships from violent weather. The fire gives off a bright light, but does not burn. Saint Elmo visited Columbus's ship during a storm to protect her as she sailed across the Atlantic. So calm yourself. You'll find the ship safely docked in London tomorrow."

QUESTIONS FOR
THE MYSTERY OF SAINT ELMO'S FIRE

1. What was the weather like the day the story takes place?

   _____

   _____

2. Where was the sailor when he saw the other ship?

   _____

   _____

3. What happened on the hull of the other ship?

   _____

   _____

4. How did the captain explain the sailor's story?

   _____

   _____

5. What was the weather like before the sailor saw Saint Elmo's fire?

   _____

   _____

6. What did the sailor think happened to the other ship before he talked to the captain?

   _____

   _____

7. Do you believe these ghostly fires are the glow of Saint Elmo? Why do you think so?

   _____

   _____

8. What was the weather like when Saint Elmo visited the ship? How might weather help make Saint Elmo's fire?

   _____

   _____

9. If Saint Elmo's fire appears on ships, do you think it might show up in other places? Where do you think you might see Saint Elmo's fire?

_____

_____

10. What do you think causes the bright lights called Saint Elmo's fire?

_____

_____

11. Give the story a title. Use as few words as possible.

_____

_____

12. How did the sailor feel about Saint Elmo's fire? How did his captain feel? Why do you think they felt differently?

_____

_____

13. In your own words, tell what the sailor saw as he watched the other ship.

_____

_____

14. The captain said that the fire the sailor saw was Saint Elmo's fire. He said that it would not burn the ship. How will the sailor's feelings change the next time he sees Saint Elmo's fire?

_____

_____

15. Is the captain's story about Saint Elmo's fire a fact or his opinion? How do you know?

_____

_____

16.

_____

_____

Name _____   Date _____

THE SOURCE OF SAINT ELMO'S FIRE

ABOUT THE STORY

This story explains what causes Saint Elmo's fire. Static electricity builds up on the masts and riggings of a ship. When this electricity suddenly releases, the ship glows as if on fire.

PREVIEW WORDS

static electricity   corposant   corpo santo

BOOKS TO READ

Why Does It Thunder and Lightning?: A Just Ask Book, Chris Arvetis, and Carole Palmer (Rand McNally, 1985).

Thunderstorm, Thelma Harrington Bell, (Viking Press, 1960).

Science Fair Project Index: 1985–1989 for Grades K–8, edited by Cynthia Bishop, Katherine Ertle and Karen Zeleznik (Scarecrow Press, 1992).

Flash, Crash, Rumble and Roll, Franklyn M. Branley (Thomas Crowell, 1985).

How Things Work: It's Electric, Andrew Dunn (Thomson Learning, 1993).

Safe and Simple Electrical Experiments, Rudolf F. Graf (Dover Publications, 1973, c1964).

Lightning and Thunder, Martin L. Keen (Julian Messner, 1969).

Simple Science Experiments with Everyday Materials, Muriel Mandell (Sterling Publishing, 1989).

Science Mini-Mysteries: Easy-to-Do Experiments Designed to Keep You Guessing, Sandra Markle (Atheneum, 1988).

Experiments in Magnetism and Electricity, Harry Sootin (Franklin Watts, 1962).

Experiments with Static Electricity, Harry Sootin (Norton, 1969).

Exploring Electrostatics, Raymond A. Wohlrabe (World Publishing Company, 1965).

Physics for Kids: 49 Easy Experiments with Electricity and Magnetism, Robert W. Wood (TAB Books, 1990).

INTRODUCTORY ACTIVITIES

DAY ONE

Objective: The students will create static electricity in a variety of ways. They will make sparks in a dark room.

Curriculum subject: Science

*This lesson must be conducted on a dry day, or the students cannot make sparks.

Teacher: We read a story called "The Mystery of Saint Elmo's Fire." Can anyone tell me what the story was about? What might cause a ship to glow without catching it on fire? Today we're going to do some experiments. We're going to see if we can make bright light without fire.

Materials

◆ several blown-up balloons
◆ clean plastic combs
◆ pieces of wool
◆ a piece of carpet
◆ a doorknob

Procedure

◆ Set up three stations around the room. In station one, keep a box of balloons. In station two, keep clean plastic combs and pieces of wool. In station three, keep a piece of carpet in front of a doorknob.

◆ Divide the students among the three stations. Ask each station to do the following:

Station One: Rub your head with a balloon.

Station Two: Rub a clean plastic comb on a piece of wool and comb your hair.

Station Three: Rub your feet on the carpet then touch the doorknob.

◆ As the students are working, discuss what is happening.

◆ Warn the students that you will turn off the lights. They are to carefully continue what they are doing. Try to make the room as dark as possible.

◆ The students should see the sparks they are creating glowing in the dark.

◆ What is happening? What is causing the sparks to glow?

◆ Read *How Things Work: It's Electric* to the class. Emphasize the information on pages 8 and 9.

◆ Ask the students, "What do static electricity and lightning have in common? Could Saint Elmo's fire involve static electricity, too? Why do you think so?"

DAY TWO

Story Lesson

Follow the *Presenting the Story Lesson* instructions in the Introduction. Each story lesson follows the same procedure; however, say the following in step 4:

"The title of the story we're reading today is *The Source of Saint Elmo's Fire*. What do you think the story is about? What do you already know about Saint Elmo's fire?"

EXTENSION ACTIVITIES

1. Bring several rectangular magnets, with the positive and negative ends marked, to class. Break the students into groups. Give each group two magnets. Allow the students time to play with the magnets. What have they discovered?

   Read the book *Why Does It Thunder and Lightning?: A Just Ask Book* to the class. As you read, encourage the students to do the magnet experiments the animals are doing in the story.

2. Invite a scientist to your class to demonstrate experiments using static electricity. This person might be a high school teacher or a college professor. High school teachers might prepare their students to perform demonstrations for your class.

3. Conduct the experiment "Static Electricity Light" from *Physics for Kids: 49 Easy Experiments with Electricity and Magnetism* by Robert W. Wood, pages 11–12. Do not allow the children to do this experiment. It requires a fluorescent tube, which can be dangerous. Use caution while doing this experiment.

◆ Next, break the class into groups. Assign each group an experiment using static electricity. Share the experiments with the class. Some books with examples of static electricity experiments are:

Markle, Sandra. *Science Mini-Mysteries: Easy-to-Do Experiments Designed to Keep You Guessing,* "The Balloon Trick," pages 45–46.

Mandell, Muriel. *Simple Science Experiments with Everyday Materials,* "Flash!" page 33 and "Take a Bubble Dancing," page 126.

Sootin, Harry. *Experiments in Magnetism and Electricity,* "What You Should Know About Charging and Discharging an Electrophorus," pages 140–143 and many other experiments.

For more experiments refer to *Science Fair Project Index: 1985–1989 for Grades K–8.* Look under the heading "Electrostatics."

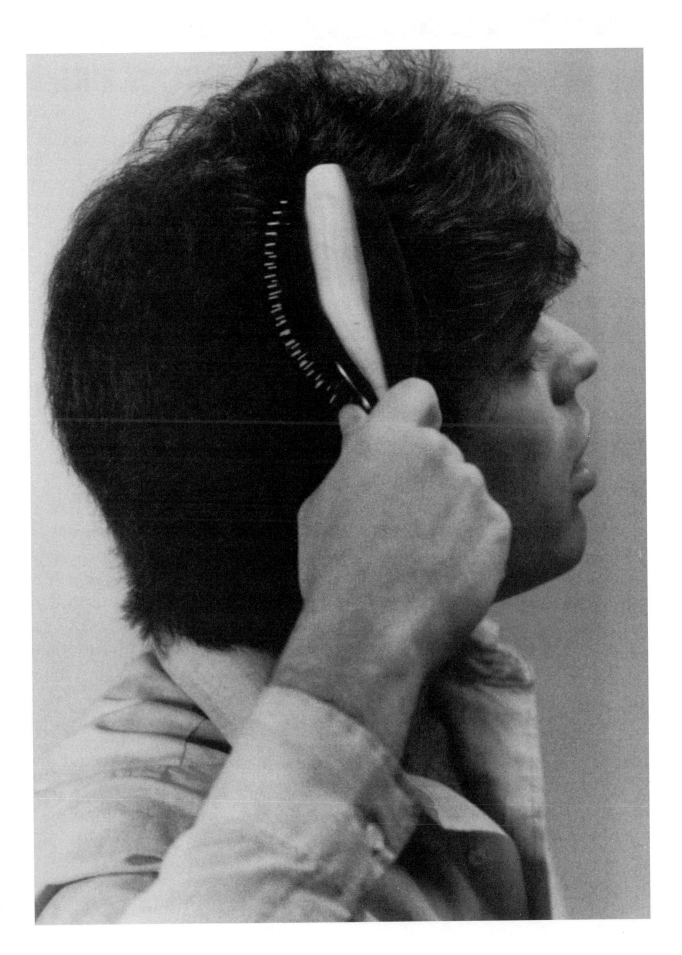

THE SOURCE OF SAINT ELMO'S FIRE

Have you ever seen sparks in the fur of a cat when you pet it? While combing your hair in the dark, you might see small sparks of light. Static electricity causes these sparks, and the glowing lights of Saint Elmo's fire.

Sparks of static electricity don't hurt your hair or your cat. They may look like flames, but, like Saint Elmo's fire, they do not burn.

During thunderstorms, static electricity builds up on the masts and riggings of ships. When this electricity suddenly releases, the ship glows as if on fire.

Airplane pilots report seeing Saint Elmo's fire on their planes' wings. When the static electricity quickly leaves the plane, it makes a loud, thunderlike noise.

Scientists call Saint Elmo's fire corposant. Corposant comes from the words corpo santo, meaning "holy body." As you can see, the legend of Saint Elmo's fire even touches the imaginations of scientists.

QUESTIONS FOR THE SOURCE OF SAINT ELMO'S FIRE

1. What causes the bright lights of Saint Elmo's fire?

    _____

    _____

2. What name did scientists give Saint Elmo's fire?

    _____

    _____

3. What does <u>corposant</u> mean?

    _____

    _____

4. Where do airplane pilots report seeing Saint Elmo's fire?

    _____

    _____

5. What must build up in the masts and riggings of ships before they can give off Saint Elmo's fire?

    _____

    _____

6. What happens after static electricity builds up on the masts and riggings of ships?

    _____

    _____

7. Why do you think scientists named Saint Elmo's fire "corposant"?

    _____

    _____

8. In what weather condition would you <u>not</u> see Saint Elmo's fire?

    _____

    _____

9. Imagine riding on a plane in a thunderstorm late at night. Looking out the window, you see Saint Elmo's fire on the wing and engines. If people didn't know about the cause of Saint Elmo's fire, what might their reaction be?

_____

_____

10. When you walk across a rug and touch a doorknob, you might feel the shock of static electricity. If it is a strong shock, you might also hear it snap. Saint Elmo's fire makes a thunderlike bang when the static electricity leaves an airplane. Why do you think static electricity makes a noise when it is suddenly released?

_____

_____

11. Give the story a title. Use as few words as possible.

_____

_____

12. How are Saint Elmo's fire and the static electricity found in a cat's fur alike? How are they different?

_____

_____

13. Briefly explain what causes Saint Elmo's fire. Include when it occurs and why.

_____

_____

14. What happens when static electricity builds up on the rigging and masts of ships?

_____

_____

15. Sailors once thought that Saint Elmo visited ships in storms in the form of a fire that didn't burn. They believed Saint Elmo protected the ship. Is this belief based on fact or opinion? How can you prove your answer?

_____

_____

16.

_____

_____

Name _____   Date _____

THE NEWBERY MEDAL

ABOUT THE STORY

This story tells about the history of the Newbery Medal. The medal is named after John Newbery (1713-1767). He was one of the first people to promote the writing and selling of children's books.

PREVIEW WORDS

Newbery Medal	library	librarian
St. Paul's Churchyard	London, England	John Newbery

THROUGHOUT THE WEEK—Read the latest Newbery Prize-winning book. Periodically discuss why this book received the award.

BOOKS TO READ

Newbery Prize Winners

(Consult your librarian for a complete list.)

The Giver, Lois Lowry (Houghton Mifflin, 1993).

Missing May, Cynthia Rylant (Orchard Books, 1992).

Shiloh, Phyllis Reynolds Naylor (Atheneum, 1991).

Maniac Magee, Jerry Spinelli (Little, Brown, 1990).

Number the Stars, Lois Lowry (Houghton Mifflin, 1989).

Joyful Noise: Poems for Two Voices, Paul Fleischman (Harper & Row, 1988).

Lincoln: A Photobiography, Russell Freedman (Clarion Books, 1987).

The Whipping Boy, Sid Fleischman (Greenwillow Books, 1986).

Sarah, Plain and Tall, Patricia MacLachlan (Harper & Row, 1985).

The Hero and the Crown, Robin McKinley (Greenwillow Books, 1984).

Dear Mr. Henshaw, Beverly Cleary (William Morrow, 1983).

Dicey's Song, Cynthia Voight (Atheneum, 1982).

A Visit to William Blake's Inn: Poems for Innocent and Experienced Travelers, Nancy Willard (Harcourt Brace Jovanovich, 1981).

Jacob Have I Loved, Katherine Paterson (Crowell, 1980).

A Gathering of Days, Joan Blos (Scribner, 1979).

The Westing Game, Ellen Raskin (Dutton, 1978).

VIDEOS

Jacob Have I Loved, based on the book by Katherine Paterson (Public Media Video, 1989). From the series Wonderworks Family Movie. Length: 57 minutes.

Roll of Thunder, Hear My Cry, based on the book by Mildred Taylor (McGraw-Hill Media, Random House Video, 1986). From the Newbery Video Collection. Length: 95 minutes.

Sounder, based on the book by William H. Armstrong (Paramount Home Video, 1984). Length: 107 minutes.

Bridge to Terabithia, based on the book by Katherine Paterson (Public Media Video, 1985). From the series Wonderworks Family Movie. Length: 58 minutes.

A Visit to William Blake's Inn: Poems for Innocent and Experienced Travelers, based on the book by Nancy Willard (Random House Video: Newbery Video Collection, Newbery Award Records, 1986). Length: 17:30 minutes.

CDS, RECORDS, AND CASSETTES

Sarah, Plain and Tall (cassette), based on the story by Patricia MacLachlan, performed by Glenn Close (Caedmon, 1986).

The Grey King (cassette), based on the book by Susan Cooper (Newbery Award Records, 1977).

Mrs. Frisby and the Rats of NIMH (cassette), based on the book by Robert C. O'Brien (Newbery Award Records, 1972).

INTRODUCTORY ACTIVITIES

DAY ONE

Objective: The students will watch a film based on a Newbery Medal book. They will discuss why they think this book received the award.

Curriculum subject: Language Arts

   ***Note:** There are several videos based on Newbery books. Look at the Videos list for names of films you might find at your local library.

Teacher: Many books are published for children. Every year a group of people choose the best children's book. They give the author of this book the Newbery Prize.
   Today we'll watch a video based on a Newbery book. After the movie is over, we'll discuss why you think this story won the Newbery Medal.

   Show the film. After the film is over, ask the students why they think this story won the Newbery Prize. What did they think was special about the story? Would they like to read the book?

DAY TWO

Story Lesson

Follow the *Presenting the Story Lesson* instructions in the Introduction. Each story lesson follows the same procedure; however, say the following in step 4:

   "The title of the story we're reading today is *The Newbery Medal.* What do you think the story is about? What do you already know about the Newbery Medal?"

EXTENSION ACTIVITIES

1. The students will create an award for best picture book. They will name the award and choose a winner.

◆ Teacher:

There are several awards for children's books. The Caldecott Award goes to the best illustrator or artist of a children's book. The Newbery award goes to the best author of a children's book. Today we'll create our own award for the best overall picture book. This means we'll look at the author's work on the story itself as well as the illustrations.

Procedure

◆ Encourage the students to brainstorm and work together to choose a name for their award. Like the Newbery Medal, it should reflect the purpose of the award.

◆ Break the class into groups of four to five students. Take them to the library. Their goal is to find a picture book with the best story and illustrations. Everyone in the group must agree on the selection. They will check out the book and return to class.

◆ Each group will write a nomination proposal for their book. They will tell why they chose this book. Why does this book deserve the award? What is special about the way the author told the story? What is special about the illustrations? They must try to convince the rest of the class that their book deserves the award. They can use every creative means possible to reach this goal (i.e., charts, graphs, etc.).

2. Each group will present their proposal to a visiting class. They must try to persuade the class that their book deserves this award.

◆ After the presentations, the visiting class will vote for the best picture book. If two books tie for the vote, conduct a run-off election.

◆ Make a blue ribbon with the name of the award written on it. Present the award to the librarian with the winning proposal.

3. The class will write to the author and illustrator telling them about the award, and why their book was chosen. The reference desk of your local library can help you find an address for the author and illustrator. Publishers might also forward the letter.

4. Break the class into groups of three to four students. The group will choose and read a Newbery book. (Learning disabled students may need to listen to the story on cassette. Some examples are listed in the *CDs, Records, and Cassettes* list.)

◆ Next, the students will make a poster promoting the Newbery book. The poster, like a movie poster, should encourage others to read the book. Give the completed posters to the librarian to display in the library.

THE NEWBERY MEDAL

Sometimes you don't know what book you'd like to read. All you know is that you want to find a good book. Then you walk into a library filled with hundreds of books. Where should you begin?

You might ask the librarian for a list of Newbery Prize books. This list tells you which books won the Newbery Medal. The Newbery Medal goes to the author of the best children's book.

The Newbery Prize began in 1921, but the name of the prize comes from a man born over two hundred years ago. John Newbery (1713–1767) lived in London, England. In 1745, Newbery began selling books in St. Paul's Churchyard.

Few people wrote books for children. John Newbery wanted children to have good stories to read. He asked authors to write more children's books. Newbery then made the children's books he sold.

QUESTIONS FOR THE NEWBERY MEDAL

1. What does the list of Newbery Prize books tell you?

   _____

   _____

2. When did the Newbery Prize begin?

   _____

   _____

3. What did John Newbery want children to have?

   _____

   _____

4. Who has a list of Newbery Prize books?

   _____

   _____

5. What happened first: the beginning of the Newbery Prize, or John Newbery selling books?

   _____

   _____

6. What did John Newbery do after the authors wrote children's books?

   _____

   _____

7. What one word best describes John Newbery?

   _____

   _____

8. Did John Newbery like children? Why do you think so?

   _____

   _____

9. Will you ask for the list of Newbery Prize-winning books the next time you go to the library? Why do you think so?

_____

_____

10. Why was a prize for good children's books named for John Newbery?

_____

_____

11. Write a title for the story. Use as few words as possible.

_____

_____

12. Good picture books win an award called the Caldecott Medal. The Caldecott Medal goes to the illustrator. How are Newbery Medal books and Caldecott Medal books alike? How are they different?

_____

_____

13. In your own words, tell about the life of John Newbery.

_____

_____

14. How will the list of Newbery books change the way you look for books at the library? Why do you think so?

_____

_____

15. The story says, "The name of the (Newbery) prize comes from a man born over two hundred years ago." Is this a fact or an opinion? How can you prove your answer?

_____

_____

16.

_____

_____

Name _____   Date _____

IT'S ROADEO TIME

ABOUT THE STORY
The story tells about the Roadeo, a safe-driving competition for truck drivers. The first Roadeo took place in 1937. This event rewards truck drivers who maintain a safe record.

PREVIEW WORDS

Roadeo	rodeo	truckers
track	prize	safest
truck drivers	ticket	cowboys
fences		

PRIOR TO THE LESSON
Organize teachers to conduct a school-wide bicycle Roadeo. The students will navigate their bikes through streets the teachers make on the blacktop. Make stop signs and collect child-size toy cars to put in your streets. Some local police departments have their own practice streets to teach bicycle safety.

BOOKS TO READ
I Can Be a Truck Driver, June Behrens (Childrens Press, 1985).

The Look Out! Book, Cindy Blakely and Suzanne Drinkwater (Scholastic, 1987).

A Day in the Life of a Cross-Country Trucker, Miriam Anne Bourne (Troll Associates, 1988).

Bicycles Are Fun to Ride, Dorothy Chlad (Childrens Press, 1984).

BMX's, Paul Estrem (Crestwood House, 1987).

Sincere's Bicycle Service Manual, William Ewers (Sincere Press, 1975).

Things to Know Before Buying a Bicycle, Joanne Fink (Silver Burdett, 1985).

Trucks, Ian Graham (Gloucester Press, 1990).

Truck and Tractor Pullers, Rosemary Grimm (Crestwood House, 1988).

What's Inside?: Trucks, edited by Hilary Hockman (Dorling Kindersley, 1992).

Bicycle, Cynthia Fitterer Klingel (Creative Education, 1986).

Safety First! - Outdoors, Cynthia Fitterer Klingel (Creative Education, 1986).

Bicycle Safety, Sally McNulty, illustrated by Mike Higgs (Rourke Corp., 1983).

Model Trucks, Ed Radlauer (Childrens Press, 1983).

Truck Tech Talk, Ed and Ruth Radlauer (Childrens Press, 1986).

The Big Book of Real Trucks, Walter Retan (Grosset & Dunlap, 1987).

Truck Driver, Judith Bauer Stamper (Troll Associates, 1989).

Cars and Trucks, Philip Steele (Crestwood House, 1991).

Here Come the Monster Trucks, George Sullivan (Cobblehill Books, Dutton, 1989).

Trucks and Trucking, Ruth and Mike Wolverton (Franklin Watts, 1982).

INTRODUCTORY ACTIVITIES

DAY ONE

Objective: The students will listen to a story about being a truck driver. They will discuss how truck drivers practice safe driving.

Curriculum subject: Social Studies

Read the story *A Day in the Life of a Cross-Country Trucker* to the class. Before the story, tell the students to look for precautions taken by the driver to ensure a safe trip. Examples are:

◆ The driver must pass road and medical tests.

◆ The truckers take refresher courses once a year.

◆ The rig is inspected before it begins a trip.

After the story, discuss the precautions truck drivers take to have a safe trip. List the precautions on chart paper.

DAY TWO

Objective: The students will talk to a truck driver about safety.

Curriculum subject: Social Studies

Before the truck driver comes to class, display and review the list the students made on Day One. Help the students to make a who, what, when, where, and why question list on another piece of chart paper. For example:

◆ Who oversees truck drivers to make sure the public is safe?

◆ When do truck drivers take safety tests?

◆ Where do these safety checks take place?

◆ Why is it important to make sure truckers drive safely?

End the discussion with a question and answer session. Ask the truck driver if the students can look at his or her cab.

DAY THREE

Story Lesson

Follow the *Presenting the Story Lesson* instructions in the Introduction. Each story lesson follows the same procedure; however, say the following in step 4:

"The title of the story we're reading today is *It's Roadeo Time*. What do you think the story is about?" If the students mention trucks, ask, "What do you already know about trucks?"

EXTENSION ACTIVITIES

1. Ask a police officer to speak to the class. Tell the officer that the students learned about truck driving safety. Ask him or her to tell the students about bicycle safety. How are truck safety and bicycle safety alike? How are they different? What should the students know to be safe bicycle drivers?

2. Hold a bicycle Roadeo. The students must ride a bike or tricycle that fits their size and a bicycle helmet.

◆ Create a ministreet on the blacktop. Make crosswalks and set up stop signs. Put child-size toy cars along the sides of the street. Adults act as pedestrians.

◆ The students ride through the ministreet from the set starting point to a set end. Each student receives points for following bicycle safety rules.

◆ The Roadeo can have a carnival atmosphere with booths. The P.T.A. can sell bicycle shaped cookies, reflecting tape, and so on. Ask a bicycle helmet vendor to sit at a booth to take orders. The school nurse might talk about how to care for wounds if an accident does occur. Try to involve the community as much as possible.

◆ Inform the news media about the event. This will allow the students to spread the word about bicycle safety.

IT'S ROADEO TIME

When you think of the rodeo, you think of cowboys and their horses. The rodeo is a place where cowboys can show how good they are at what they do. There is another kind of rodeo. Truck drivers ride their big trucks like the cowboys ride their horses. Truckers call it the Roadeo.

The first Roadeo was in 1937. The truckers wanted to show how safe the big trucks were. Everyone liked the Roadeo. Now the truckers meet for a Roadeo every year.

To ride in the Roadeo, the truck drivers must show they are good drivers. If the truck driver gets one ticket during the year, he or she can't be in the Roadeo.

At the Roadeo you will see trucks with 14 to 20 wheels. They ride along a special track. To make it harder, the driver must go around flags and fences.

The winner of the Roadeo gets a prize. The most important prize goes to everyone on the roads. We know that our truck drivers work hard to be the safest in the world.

QUESTIONS FOR IT'S ROADEO TIME

1. Who rides in a rodeo?

    _____

    _____

2. Who rides in the <u>Roadeo</u>?

    _____

    _____

3. In what year did the first Roadeo take place?

    _____

    _____

4. How many wheels are on the trucks in the Roadeo?

    _____

    _____

5. What must a driver do before he or she can be in the Roadeo?

    _____

    _____

6. What does a driver get after he or she wins the Roadeo?

    _____

    _____

7. What is the main purpose of the Roadeo?

    _____

    _____

8. Why do you think the truck drivers call their show the Roadeo?

    _____

    _____

9. The story tells us that the Roadeo makes truckers safer drivers. Do you think that truck drivers would be less careful about their driving without the Roadeo? Why do you think so?

_____

_____

10. Other than to promote safe driving, what other reasons might truck drivers have for driving in the Roadeo?

_____

_____

11. Write a title for the story. Use as few words as possible.

_____

_____

12. Compare a rodeo to the <u>Roadeo</u>. How are they alike? How are they different?

_____

_____

13. In your own words, tell what truck drivers do in the Roadeo.

_____

_____

14. What effect does the Roadeo have on the drivers of big trucks?

_____

_____

15. The story said, "We know that our truck drivers work hard to be the safest in the world." Is this a fact or someone's opinion? How can you prove your answer?

_____

_____

16.

_____

_____

Name _____   Date _____

WHO WROTE
"THE TORTOISE AND THE HARE"?

ABOUT THE STORY

This story tells about Aesop, who lived about 2,500 years ago. Some historians believe Aesop was a black slave from Athens, Greece.

PREVIEW WORDS

Aesop	believe	tortoise
Athens, Greece	hare	Croesus
fable	grasshopper	lesson
library	royal	

THROUGHOUT THE WEEK

Aesop's fables usually centered around such animals as lions, mice, crows, foxes, tortoises, and hares. Decorate the classroom with photographs and drawings of these animals.

Read fables from *Aesop and Company: With Scenes From His Legendary Life* prepared by Barbara Bader (Boston: Houghton Mifflin Company, 1991). As you read the fables, ask the students to look for their own personalities in the characters of the stories.

BOOKS TO READ

Anno's Aesop: A Book of Fables by Aesop and Mr. Fox, retold by Mitsumasa Anno (Orchard Books, 1989).

Aesop and Company: With Scenes From His Legendary Life, prepared by Barbara Bader (Houghton Mifflin, 1991).

The Best of Aesop's Fables, retold by Margaret Clark (Little, Brown, 1990).

Feathers and Tails: Animal Fables From Around the World, David Kherdian (Philomel Books, 1992).

Animal Fables From Aesop, adapted by Barbara McClintock (David R. Godine, 1991).

Aesop's Fables, retold in verse by Tom Paxton (Morrow Junior Books, 1988).

Androcles and the Lion and Other Aesop's Fables, retold in verse by Tom Paxton (Morrow Junior Books, 1991).

Belling the Cat and Other Aesop's Fables, retold in verse by Tom Paxton (Morrow Junior Books, 1990).

Henry and Theresa's Race, Ronne Peltzman (Golden Book, 1984).

The Fables of Aesop, illustrated by Frank Riccio (Contemporary Books, 1988).

The Tortoise and the Hare: An Aesop Fable, adapted by Janet Stevens (Holiday House, 1984).

The Town Mouse and the Country Mouse: An Aesop Fable, adapted by Janet Stevens (Holiday House, 1987).

The Ant and the Dove: An Aesop Tale Retold, Mary Lewis Wang (Childrens Press, 1989).

The Aesop for Children with pictures by Milo Winter (Rand McNally, 1984, c1919).

VIDEOS

Bill Cosby in Aesop's Fables: The Tortoise and the Hare (Karl-Lorimar Home Video, 1986). Length: 30 minutes.

INTRODUCTORY ACTIVITIES

DAY ONE

Objective: The students will watch a video about Aesop's fables. They will discuss what a fable is and why Aesop's fables are entertaining.

Curriculum subject: Reading or Language Arts

Teacher: This week we'll read and write about Aesop's fables. Can anyone name one of Aesop's fables? Watch the video *Aesop's Fables*. After the video is over, I want you to answer these questions. What is a fable? Why are Aesop's fables entertaining?

Show the video *Bill Cosby in Aesop's Fables*. After the video, discuss what makes a story a fable. Why did the children in the video enjoy listening to Aesop's fables?

DAY TWO

Before the story lesson, read the book *The Tortoise and the Hare: An Aesop Fable* adapted and illustrated by Janet Stevens. Discuss why this story is called a fable and why it is entertaining.

Story Lesson

Follow the *Presenting the Story Lesson* instructions in the Introduction. Each story lesson follows the same procedure; however, say the following in step 4:

"The title of the story we're reading today is *Who Wrote the Tortoise and the Hare?* What do you think the story is about? What do you already know about the fable 'The Tortoise and the Hare'?"

EXTENSION ACTIVITIES

1. The students will rewrite one of Aesop's fables placing themselves in the role of the main character.

◆ Teacher:

I've read several of Aesop's fables to you so far this week. Have you seen parts of your own personality in the characters? For example, have you ever been like the hare in "The Tortoise and the Hare"? Have you put off finishing something you had plenty of time to do until it was too late? Maybe you're more like the tortoise. Do you keep working on something until you finish it in the best way you can?

◆ Continue to discuss this idea. Read the story "The Shepherd Boy Who Cried 'Wolf'" in Barbara Bader's *Aesop and Company*. Has anyone in the class "cried wolf"? Ask the student to tell what happened.

◆ Teacher:

Today you'll rewrite one of Aesop's fables. Write the story so that you are the main character. Maybe someone you thought was too little to help you did something that helped you a lot.

That's what happened in "The Lion and The Mouse." (Read the fable "The Lion and the Mouse" in *Aesop and Company*.) Tell your story so that you're in the lion's role and your little friend is in the mouse's role. What did you need help with? How did your little friend help you? The moral or lesson of the story will be, "Little friends may prove to be great friends." Draw a picture to go with your story.

2. The students will prepare plays based on one of Aesop's fables.

◆ Break the class into groups. Assign one Aesop fable to each group. The groups should include as many students as there are characters in the fable. Try to pick fables with the fewest characters. The students will write the fable in play form and practice it. End the play by stating the moral of the fable.

◆ Supply props when they are needed. For example, the ant in "The Ant and the Grasshopper" needs plastic corn.

◆ The students will make masks of their characters to wear during the play. Make the masks from construction paper. Punch holes in the side of the mask. Tie one string to each hole. Tie the strings in a bow at the back of the student's head. Allow the students to use their imaginations and creativity to make the masks.

◆ Suggested fables:

The Grasshopper and the Ant
The Lion and the Mouse
The Fox and the Crow
The Tortoise and the Hare
The Belling of the Cat
The Young Crab and Her Mother

3. The children will perform their plays for your students without any other classes in the room. This gives them an opportunity to practice their plays. Later, invite other classes to come to your room to see the plays. Before the plays begin, tell about Aesop's life and fables.

WHO WROTE "THE TORTOISE AND THE HARE"?

Everyone knows the story "The Tortoise and the Hare." Your parents read this story when they were children. So did your grandparents, and their parents. This story, along with many other tales, is part of a group of fables written by Aesop.

Some people believe a man named Aesop never lived. They say the fables are stories many different people told.

Others say that Aesop lived about 550 B.C. in Athens, Greece. He was a slave, possibly a black man. King Croesus owned Aesop. Aesop's job was to tell stories to please the royal family.

Aesop told funny stories about animals who talked. Every fable ended with a lesson. Do you remember the lesson of "The Tortoise and the Hare"?

Look in your library for Aesop's Fables. Read "The Lion and the Mouse," or "The Grasshopper and the Ant." You will be reading stories 2,500 years old.

QUESTIONS FOR
WHO WROTE "THE TORTOISE AND THE HARE"?

1. Some people believe that there was never a man named Aesop. Who do they think told the fables?

   _____

   _____

2. Where did Aesop live?

   _____

   _____

3. When did Aesop live?

   _____

   _____

4. Name two of Aesop's fables.

   _____

   _____

5. Which fable by Aesop did the story talk about first?

   _____

   _____

6. What did Aesop end his story with?

   _____

   _____

7. The story tells us that Aesop was a slave. Slaves did not go to school. How do you believe Aesop learned to tell such good stories?

   _____

   _____

8. Each of Aesop's fables ended with a lesson. Why do you think he wrote stories that taught lessons?

   _____

   _____

9. The story tells us that "The Tortoise and the Hare" has been told to children for hundreds of years. Do you think this fable will continue to be enjoyed for many years to come? Why do you think so?

_____

_____

10. Why do you think Aesop's fables continue to be popular 2,500 years after they were first told?

_____

_____

11. Give the story a title. Use as few words as possible.

_____

_____

12. Listen to your teacher read the stories "The Ugly Duckling" by Hans Christian Andersen, and "The Tortoise and the Hare" from Aesop's Fables. How are the stories alike? How are they different?

_____

_____

13. In your own words, tell about the life of Aesop, who some people believe lived long ago.

_____

_____

14. Listen to your teacher read the story "The Lion and the Mouse" from Aesop's Fables. What did the story teach you? How can the lesson affect your life?

_____

_____

15. The story said, "Some people believe a man named Aesop never lived." Is this a fact or an opinion? How do you know?

_____

_____

16.

_____

_____

Name _____   Date _____

THE MANY FACES OF THE CATFISH

ABOUT THE STORY

This story tells about the large variety of catfish. Catfish range in size from one inch to ten feet. The catfish family includes the electric catfish, walking catfish, blind catfish, and crucifix catfish.

PREVIEW WORDS

catfish	scales	whisker-like
feelers	weigh	Africa
electric	volts	Egypt
cousin	piranha	crucifix

PRIOR TO THE LESSON

Make the necessary arrangements for a field trip to an aquarium. If there are no aquariums in your area, arrange for a field trip to a local pet store that sells fish.

BOOKS TO READ

A Closer Look at Fish, Keith Banister (Gloucester Press, 1980).

The Walking Catfish, David Day (Macmillan, 1991).

The Amateur Zoologist, May Dykstra (Franklin Watts, 1994).

Weird Animals, Tammy Everts and Bobbie Kalman (Crabtree Publishing, 1995).

Fishes and How They Live, George S. Fichter (Golden Press, 1960).

Peterson First Guide to Fishes of North America, Michael Filisky (Houghton Mifflin, 1989).

Fishes That Hide, Alan Mark Fletcher (Addison-Wesley, 1973).

Fishes and Their Young, Alan Mark Fletcher (Addison-Wesley, 1974).

Animals: A Picture Book of Facts and Figures, Tibor Gergely (McGraw-Hill, 1974).

Fish Do the Strangest Things, Leonora and Arthur Hornblow (Random House, 1966).

The World Book Encyclopedia of Science: The Animal World, (World Book, 1985).

Aquarium Fish, Know Your Pet, Joan Palmer (Bookwright Press, 1989).

Amazing Science: Armadillos and Other Unusual Animals, Q.L. Pearce (Julian Messner, 1989).

A Great Aquarium Book: The Putting-It-Together Guide for Beginners, Joan Sarnoff and Reynold Ruffins (Scribner's, 1977).

What Is a Fish?, Barbara R. Stratton (Franklin Watts, 1991).

The Funny Fish Story, Joanne and David Wylie (Childrens Press, 1984).

Fishes, Herbert S. Zim and Hurst H. Shoemaker (Golden Press, 1956).

VIDEOS

Stories at Sundown with Joe Hayes, Santa Fe, NM: Trails West Publishing, 1988. Includes the story *The Pet Catfish.* Length: 45 minutes.

The Wondrous World of Weird Animals, Oak Forest, IL: MPI Home Video, 1993. Length: 32 minutes.

CDS, RECORDS, AND CASSETTES

Tales of Humor and Wit, Jonesborough, TN: The National Association for the Preservation and Perpetuation of Storytelling, 1991. Includes the story *The Walking Catfish* told by Doc McConnell.

INTRODUCTORY ACTIVITIES

DAY ONE

Objective: The students will visit an aquarium or a pet store that sells fish. They will make a list of the types of catfish they see.

Curriculum subject: Science

Teacher: This week we'll learn about catfish. It's hard to imagine spending a lot of time learning about catfish; however, there are more varieties of catfish than you can imagine. Today we're going to visit an aquarium (or pet store that sells fish). As you walk from tank to tank, look for catfish. Write down the names of the catfish as you see them. When we get back, we'll compare our lists, and see who found the largest variety of catfish.

Guide the students through the aquarium. Help them locate the catfish. When you return to class, review their lists. Write the names of the catfish on chart paper. Where in the tanks did the students find the catfish, at the top, in the center of the tank, or at the bottom? Why do catfish live on the bottom of tanks? Who made the longest list of catfish?

DAY TWO

Story Lesson

Follow the *Presenting the Story Lesson* instructions in the Introduction. Each story lesson follows the same procedure; however, say the following in step 4:

"The title of the story we're reading today is *The Many Faces of the Catfish.* What do you think the story is about? What do you already know about catfish?"

EXTENSION ACTIVITIES

1. Read the story *The Walking Catfish* to the class. Next, read a description of a walking catfish from a nonfiction book such as *Peterson First Guide to Fishes of North America* by Michael Filisky, pages 46–47. How is the description of the walking catfish in the fictional story like real walking catfish? How are they different?

2. The students will write about a catfish, and make a model of the catfish. This activity continues over several days.

Catfish Models
Materials

◆ one shoe box per student
◆ clay
◆ construction paper
◆ pebbles
◆ glue
◆ white paper
◆ crayons
◆ reference books that tell about every catfish on the list

Procedure

◆ Give each student a name of a catfish. Catfish varieties include:

walking	blind	crucifix
flathead	gafftopsail	blue
white	marine	brindled madtom
electric	stonecat	glass
upside-down	bullhead	wels

◆ The students will write a paper about their catfish. Where does it live? What does it eat? How is the catfish like other catfish? How is it different? How did it get its name?

◆ Using the clay, the students make a model of the catfish. The model must be small enough to fit in a shoe box.

◆ Line the inside of a shoe box with white paper. Lay the box on end, facing the opening forward. Draw the background of a fish tank on the paper. Color the background.

◆ Glue a layer of pebbles on the floor of the tank.

◆ Cut out construction paper plants. Glue the plants into the pebbles.

◆ Set the clay catfish into the tank.

◆ Make a label for the tank that includes the name of the catfish, its length, its weight and its habitat.

◆ Display the Catfish Aquariums in the library or science room.

THE MANY FACES OF THE CATFISH

All catfish look about the same. They don't have scales. Catfish grow whisker-like feelers at the ends of their mouths. Most catfish live at the bottom of the water.

Catfish come in many sizes. Some are only one inch long. Others can grow up to ten feet and weigh 600 pounds.

One kind of catfish is the electric catfish of Africa. Electric catfish can give shocks of up to 400 volts. Hundreds of years ago in Egypt, fishermen called this kind of catfish "he who frees many." If a fisherman caught an electric catfish in his net, he often got a shock. He would drop his net, freeing all the fish.

The "walking catfish" of Florida can live on land for a long time. Be careful if you see a walking catfish. These catfish are so mean that even their famous cousin, the piranha, leaves them alone.

There are many kinds of catfish. Read about the blind catfish, the crucifix catfish, and many others.

QUESTIONS FOR THE MANY FACES OF THE CATFISH

1. Name two ways most catfish are alike.

   _____

   _____

2. What is the weight of the heaviest catfish?

   _____

   _____

3. Where does the electric catfish live?

   _____

   _____

4. Where can you find a walking catfish?

   _____

   _____

5. What is the name of the first kind of catfish described in the story?

   _____

   _____

6. What did the fishermen of Egypt usually do after an electric catfish shocked them?

   _____

   _____

7. Why are there so many kinds of catfish?

   _____

   _____

8. If you see a walking catfish, should you try to catch it? Why do you think so?

   _____

   _____

9. Animals change to fit in the environment. For example, the blind catfish did not need to see once it lived in dark caves. It did not need its eyes anymore. If catfish live under the ice of the North Pole, what changes might they make to live there?

_____

_____

10. Why is it good for a catfish to be electric?

_____

_____

11. Write a title that best describes this story. Use as few words as possible.

_____

_____

12. How is an electric catfish like a walking catfish? How are they different?

_____

_____

13. In your own words, tell about what would happen if a fisherman caught an electric catfish in his net.

_____

_____

14. We have seen that catfish change to fit into their environment. How might a catfish need to change to live in water filled with sharks?

_____

_____

15. The story said, "Electric catfish can give shocks of up to 400 volts." Is this a fact or someone's opinion? How can you prove your answer?

_____

_____

16.

_____

_____

Name _____   Date _____

THE RUNESTONE

ABOUT THE STORY

The story tells about the Heavener Runestone State Park in Oklahoma. In 1912, a group of hikers discovered the runestone on Poteau Mountain just outside the town of Heavener (hee' vener), Oklahoma. It is believed that the Vikings carved runes, letters from their alphabet, onto the stone in 1012. Some historians believe that the Vikings sailed to the Arkansas River hundreds of years before Columbus discovered America.

PREVIEW WORDS

runestone	Poteau Mountain	runes
Heavener, Oklahoma	Arkansas River	Vikings
historians	Columbus	
Heavener Runestone State Park		

ABOUT HEAVENER RUNESTONE STATE PARK

Address:

> Heavener Runestone State Park
> Route 1, Box 1510
> Heavener, OK 74937
> (918)653-2241

The park is located 2.5 miles northeast of Heavener, off U.S. 59 and 270. The facilities include two group shelters, an interpretive center, picnic areas, hiking trails, and a playground. You can contact the park in writing or by phone to order postcards.

For other information about parks throughout the United States, refer to:

Smith, Darren L., *Parks Directory of the United States,* Detroit, MI: Omnigraphics, 1994.

BOOKS TO READ

Snorri and the Strangers, Nathaniel Benchley (Harper & Row, 1976).

The Story of Writing: From Cave Art to Computer, William and Rhoda Cahn (Harvey House, 1963).

Living History: The Vikings, edited by John D. Clare (Harcourt Brace Jovanovich, 1992).

Stolen Thunder: A Norse Myth, Shirley Climo (Clarion Books, 1994).

Norse Gods and Giants, Ingri and Edgar Parin D'Aulaire (Doubleday, 1967).

How They Lived: A Viking Sailor, Christopher Gibb (Rourke Enterprises, 1987).

The Mystery of the Vikings in America, Morton J. Golding (J.B. Lippincott, 1973).

The Story of a Castle, John S. Goodall (M. K. McElderry Books, 1986).

The Vikings, James Graham-Campbell and Dafydd Kidd (William Morrow, 1980).

Explorers of America: Leif Ericson: Explorer of Vinland, Matthew G. Grant (Creative Education, 1974).

Signs, Letters, Words: Archaeology Discovers Writing, W. John Hackwell (Scribner's, 1987).

The Curse of the Ring, Michael Harrison (Oxford University Press, 1987).

Leif the Unlucky, Erik Christian Haugaard (Houghton Mifflin, 1982).

Baldur and the Mistletoe: A Myth of the Vikings, Margaret Hodges (Little, Brown, 1973).

Writing: The Story of Alphabets and Scripts, Georges Jean (Harry N. Abrams, 1992).

Explorers of the Americas Before Columbus, George deLucenay Leon (Franklin Watts, 1989).

Canute and the Vikings, Life and Times, Robin May (Bookwright Press, 1985).

William the Conqueror and the Normans, Robin May (Bookwright Press, 1985).

Writing: Man's Great Invention, J. Hambleton Ober (Peabody Institute, 1965).

Vikings, Anita Ganeri (Gloucester Press, 1992).

Let's Discover People of Long Ago, a series, (Raintree Publishers, 1986).

Thor's Visit to the Land of the Giants, Nancy Wilson Ross (Random House, 1959).

The World's Great Explorers: Leif Eriksson and the Vikings, Charnan Simon (Childrens Press, 1991).

Elfwyn's Saga, David Wisniewski (Lothrop, Lee & Shepard Books, 1990).

CDS, RECORDS, AND CASSETTES

Children of Odin: The Book of Northern Myths (cassette), Padraic Colum (Caedmon, 1975).

INTRODUCTORY ACTIVITIES

DAY ONE

Objective: The students will listen to the story *Elfwyn's Saga.* They will look for references to runes carved on boulders.

Curriculum subject: Language Arts

Teacher: Throughout the week, we'll learn about people called the Vikings. Vikings were also called Northmen because they lived in the northern land we now call Scandinavia. (Locate Scandinavia on the map. Note that the countries in Scandinavia include Denmark, Norway, and Sweden.)

Vikings explored and settled in many regions of the world. The Vikings who settled in France were called Normans. The Normans went on to conquer and settle in England. The famous Norman who defeated England was named William. He is known as William the Conqueror.

Leif Ericson is another famous Viking. He and Eric the Red explored land in the New World hundreds of years before Columbus landed in America.

Today you'll listen to the Viking story *Elfwyn's Saga* by David Wisniewski. While I read the story, look for clues that tell you about the Viking people. How did they travel? What did they call their alphabet? What type of clothes did they wear? Were they a superstitious people? Why do you think so?

Read the story *Elfwyn's Saga* by David Wisniewski. After the story, address the questions presented earlier. Place special emphasis on page 4 in which Gorm "carved hateful runes deep in a boulder overlooking the valley..."

DAY TWO

Objective: The students will listen to a short passage about the Viking alphabet, or runes.
Curriculum subject: History
Teacher: What is an alphabet? Can you name the letters in the English alphabet? English is
            an old language that people still use today; however, there are languages and their
            letters that people don't use anymore. Runes make up one type of alphabet that is
            no longer used. Vikings wrote with runes hundreds of years ago.
            Listen to this passage about Viking runes. After I read the passage, tell me where
            and why the Vikings left rune graffiti.

Read page 30 of the book *Living History: The Vikings*. Be sure to read the photograph descriptions written in italics. Reread the last paragraph. Ask the students, "Where and
why did the Vikings leave rune graffiti?" (Answer: The Vikings left rune graffiti on rocks and
buildings. The runes showed how far the Vikings traveled.)

DAY THREE

Story Lesson

> ***Note:** Before reading the story, help the students locate Heavener, Okla-
> homa, and the Arkansas River on a map.

Follow the *Presenting the Story Lesson* instructions in the Introduction. Each story lesson follows the same procedure; however, say the following in step 4:

> "The title of the story we're reading today is *The Runestone*. What do you think the
story is about? What do you already know about runes?"

EXTENSION ACTIVITIES

1. The students will make a runestone.

Make Your Own Runestone
Materials

◆ clay—Each student needs a piece of clay that will make a rock shape about the size of the
   child's opened hand.
◆ toothpicks
◆ chart of the runes with the English alphabet

Procedure

◆ Copy and display the chart in front of the class. For more information about the runic alphabet, see *Writing: Man's Great Invention: Cave Art to English Letters*, page 158.
◆ The students form their clay into rock shapes about the size of their opened hands.
◆ Using a sturdy toothpick, the students etch the runic alphabet into the clay stone. They write
   the runes along the long side of the clay.

f u þ a r k g w h n i j E p z s t b e u l ng o d

◆ Set the clay stones onto wax paper so that the runes face forward. The clay will flatten to make the base of the stone. Let the stones dry. Example:

ᚠᚢᚦᛅᚱᚲᚷᚹ:ᚺᛏᛁᚼᛉᛐᚴᛦᛋ:ᛏᛒᛗᛅᚱᛧᛦᛟ

2. In front of the class, flip through the pages of the book *Living History: The Vikings*. Notice the clothes the Vikings are wearing. Their clothes look like T-shirts tied with a woven belt over pants.

The students will make their own Viking shirt to wear at the Viking Festival (Extension Activity 4). Ask the students to bring plain, colored T-shirts, preferably with long sleeves, to class. If the students cannot afford the shirts, ask for donations at local stores.

The students will make belts for their shirts. They will braid thick yarn or cord for the belts.

Materials

◆ thick yarn or cord of various colors

◆ two large wooden beads per student

◆ masking tape

Procedure

◆ The students choose the color of yarn or cord to match their shirts. It is best if they use three different colors.

◆ Cut three lengths of cord or yarn 3 yards long.

◆ Hold the ends of the three cords together. Tie a strong knot about 2 inches from the end of the cords.

◆ Slide one large wooden bead over the long end of all three cords until it reaches the knot.

◆ Tie another knot on the other side of the bead to hold it in place.

◆ Tape the bead end of the cords to your desk.

◆ Braid the three cords together until it is long enough to tie around your waist.

◆ Tie a strong knot where you stopped braiding.

◆ Slide one wooden bead over the unbraided ends until you reach the knot.

◆ Tie another knot behind the wooden bead to hold it in place.

◆ Cut off any excess cord about two inches from the bead.

The students will put on the T-shirts. They wrap the braided belts around their waists, and tie them in the front. Remember to remove the belts when the students leave the classroom, especially when they are playing on the playground, as a safety precaution.

3. The students will make Viking shields.

Materials

◆ one poster board for each student
◆ poster paints
◆ books showing Viking shields

Examples:

Living History: The Vikings
How They Lived: A Viking Sailor

◆ precut circle stencils cut from poster board (Cut the stencil as wide as a poster board. Make one stencil for every five students.)
◆ aluminum foil
◆ glue
◆ black markers

Procedure

◆ Trace around the stencil on the poster board to make the shield. Cut it out.
◆ Cut a five-inch circle of aluminum foil.
◆ Glue the aluminum circle in the exact center of the shield.
◆ Look at the designs on the Viking shields found in the books. You can copy a design, or make a similar design of your own.
◆ Draw the lines of the designs in pencil.
◆ Paint in the design with poster paints.
◆ After the paint dries, draw over the pencil lines with a black marker.
◆ Hang the shields along the chalk board railings the way the Vikings hung their shields along the edges of their ships.

4. Hold a Viking Festival, now that the room is decorated with Viking shields.
◆ The students wear their T-shirts and belts over pants.
◆ Read stories about Thor, Odin, and other Viking legends.
◆ Serve a Viking lunch. Vikings ate the following foods:
   * hard rye bread
   * cheese
   * porridge
   * dried fish
   * salted meat
   * seasonings: mustard, horseradish, and garlic
   * buttermilk
◆ Write story problems for Math on the Viking theme.
◆ Practice map skills by tracing the Vikings' sea voyages and travels.
◆ Build models of Viking villages, using empty pint milk cartons.

◆ Hold a Viking ship building party. Provide the students with a variety of materials such as milk cartons, plastic bottles, construction paper, and tongue depressors. The students design and build Viking ships with whatever materials they choose. Pictures of Vikings ships can be found in several of the books in the Books to Read list.

THE RUNESTONE

In 1912, a group of hikers explored the Poteau Mountain just outside the town of Heavener, Oklahoma. Little did they know that they would make a discovery that would rewrite history books.

Halfway up the mountain, the hikers found a large, flat rock. The rock was 12 feet tall, 10 feet wide, and 16 inches thick. Someone had carved eight strange letters on the face of the rock. Who wrote on the rock? How old were the markings?

Historians who looked at the rock couldn't believe what they saw. The letters were from an alphabet, used by Vikings, called <u>runes</u>. The date on the carving said 1012.

Why were the historians surprised? Columbus came to the Americas in 1492. The runes tell us that the Vikings came hundreds of years earlier.

Some historians don't believe the Vikings traveled so far from home. Others say the Vikings could have sailed to the Arkansas River. There they carved the runes on the rock to mark their voyage. You can see the runestone at the Heavener Runestone State Park.

QUESTIONS FOR THE RUNESTONE

1. When did the hikers discover the runestone?

    _____

    _____

2. Where did the hikers find the runestone?

    _____

    _____

3. What is the name of the alphabet used by the Vikings?

    _____

    _____

4. Where can you see the runestone?

    _____

    _____

5. Who came to America first: Columbus or the Vikings?

    _____

    _____

6. What did the historians learn after they looked at the rock?

    _____

    _____

7. Why is the runestone important to historians?

    _____

    _____

8. Was it hard for the Vikings to make the runestone? Why do you think so?

    _____

    _____

9. Would you like to become a historian? Why do you think so?

_____

_____

10. Why did the historians read the runes on the stone?

_____

_____

11. Write a title for the story. Use as few words as possible.

_____

_____

12. Look at a picture of Viking runes. Now look at a picture of Egyptian hieroglyphics. How are the runes and hieroglyphics alike? How are they different?

_____

_____

13. In your own words, explain what the historians learned from the runestone.

_____

_____

14. How does the runestone change the way you think about American history?

_____

_____

15. The story says, "The rock was 12 feet tall, 10 feet wide, and 16 inches thick." Is this a fact or someone's opinion? How can you prove your answer?

_____

_____

16.

_____

_____

Name _____ Date _____

BONE HUNTER

ABOUT THE STORY

The story tells about Howard Wilson, a teenager who liked to collect old bones. In 1933, Howard found a human skull. No one thought it was an important find; however, in 1970, Rainer Berger tested the skull. It was 4,000 years older than any human bone found in America.

PREVIEW WORDS

Howard Wilson	collection	human
museums	America	Europe
scientist	Rainer Berger	rewrote
Laguna Beach, California	humankind	

PRIOR TO THE LESSON

Prepare for a trip to a museum of anthropology, or an archaeological site or museum with displays of ancient human history in the Americas. Collect permission slips from the students. For more information, refer to:

Folsom, Franklin, *America's Ancient Treasures: Guide to Archaeological Sites and Museums.* Chicago: Rand McNally, 1971.

BOOKS TO READ

From Map to Museums: Uncovering Mysteries of the Past, Joan Anderson (Morrow Junior Books, 1988).

Mysteries From the Past, Thomas G. Aylesworth (American Museum of Natural History, 1971).

Beginner's Guide to Archaeology, Louis A. Brennan (Stackpole Books, 1973).

She Never Looked Back: Margaret Mead in Samoa, Sam Epstein (Coward, McCann & Geoghegan, 1980).

America's Ancient Treasures: Guide to Archaeological Sites and Museums, Franklin Folsom (Rand McNally, 1971).

Ancient Indians: The First Americans, Roy A. Gallant (Enslow Publishers, 1989).

Early Man, F. Clark Howell (Time-Life Books, 1968).

The Value of Understanding: The Story of Margaret Mead, Spencer Johnson (Value Communications, 1979).

Ancient America, Jonathan Norton Leonard (Time-Life Books, 1967).

Women and Science, Valjean McLenighan (Raintree Publishers, 1979).

An Interview with Santa Claus, Margaret Mead (Walker, 1978).

Evolution, Ruth Moore (Time-Life Books, 1968).

Margaret Mead: World's Grandmother, Ann Morse (Creative Education, 1975).

Women of Courage, Dorothy Nathan (Random House, 1964).

Mesa Verde National Park, David Petersen (Childrens Press, 1992).

The Earliest Americans, Helen Roney Sattler (Clarion Books, 1993).

The Native American Book of Knowledge, White Deer of Autumn (Beyond Words Pub., 1992).

Introduction to American Archaeology, vol. 1, Gordon Randolph Willey (Prentice Hall, 1966).

VIDEOS

Indians of the Northwest: The Legacy of the American Indian, Los Angeles, CA: Camera One, 1995. Length: 60 minutes.

Indians of the Southwest: The Legacy of the American Indian, Los Angeles, CA: Camera One, 1995. Length: 60 minutes.

Odyssey: Margaret Mead—Taking Note, PBS Video, 1988. Length: 58 minutes.

MAGAZINES

Faces: The Magazine About People, Petersborough, NH: Cobblestone Publishing, 1996. Subject: Anthropology.

INTRODUCTORY ACTIVITIES

DAY ONE

Objective: The students will listen to a story about Margaret Mead. They will learn what it means to be an anthropologist.

Curriculum subject: Science

Read the story *The Value of Understanding: The Story of Margaret Mead.* While you read the story, ask the students to listen closely, and learn what it means to be an anthropologist.

Teacher: Margaret Mead was an anthropologist. What is an anthropologist? (Answer: "Anthropologists are scientists who try to understand persons from all over the world and from every time.")

Over the next several days, we will try to understand the first people to live in this area of the country. We will try to understand these people the way Margaret Mead tried to understand the people of Samoa. We'll become anthropologists.

DAY TWO

Story Lesson

Review yesterday's lesson.

Teacher: What is an anthropologist? We're going to be anthropologists this week and try to understand the first people who lived in this area of the country. Before we can try to understand them, we must look for clues they left behind. The scientists who will help us find these clues are archaeologists. Archaeologists dig in the earth to look for things that people left behind long ago.

Today we'll read a story about a teenager who found a clue about the first people who lived in California. What was his clue? How would his clue help anthropologists understand the first people to live in California?

Follow the *Presenting the Story Lesson* instructions in the Introduction. Each story lesson follows the same procedure; however, say the following in step 4:
"The title of the story we're reading today is *Bone Hunter.* What do you think the story is about?"

After completing the Questions sheet, discuss the story with the entire class. Explain that the people who look for and study human artifacts are called archaeologists. How can these bones and artifacts help anthropologists understand the people from long ago?

EXTENSION ACTIVITIES

1. Visit a museum of natural history, an archaeological museum, or an archaeological site. Depending on where you live, you might visit ancient Native American rock drawings. Some cities have museums with replicas of ancient Native American villages.

◆ Learn about the people who first lived in your area. Were they farmers, hunters, or nomads? Did they live in igloos, caves, or grass houses? What was their diet like? What have archaeologists found that would help an anthropologist understand the people's habits, customs, and mythology?

2. Working in groups, the students will learn about a specific aspect of the people who first lived in your area. One group might learn about what these people ate. Another group might learn about the customs or mythology. Ask a local anthropological society to guide the students in their work. Many societies have volunteers who will come to your class.

3. Build a replica of a village where these people lived. A piece of plywood makes a good base. The students can use their imaginations to determine what materials they will need to build the replica. Label the parts of the replica. Donate the model to the school library or local children's museum.

BONE HUNTER

Howard Wilson was a teenager in 1933. He lived in Laguna Beach, California. Howard called himself a bone hunter because he dug for old bones to put in a collection.

One day, Howard saw machines digging in the ground. A new building was going up.

"What a great place to look for bones," he thought.

In the dirt, Howard found a very old human skull. No one thought the skull was important. Still, museums displayed the skull in America and Europe.

It was not until 1970 that Rainer Berger saw the skull. Berger was a scientist. He tested the skull to learn how old it was. To his surprise, the skull was 17,000 years old. It was 4,000 years older than any human bone found in America.

Howard's find was now very important. The skull showed that people have lived in America a long time. A teenage boy and his bone collection rewrote the history of humankind in America.

QUESTIONS FOR BONE HUNTER

1. Why did Howard Wilson call himself a bone hunter?

   _____

   _____

2. Where did Howard Wilson find the human skull?

   _____

   _____

3. In what year did Howard Wilson find the human skull?

   _____

   _____

4. When did Rainer Berger test the skull?

   _____

   _____

5. What happened to the skull before 1977?

   _____

   _____

6. What did Rainer Berger learn about the skull after he tested it?

   _____

   _____

7. How did the skull change the way historians thought about human history in America?

   _____

   _____

8. Why did the skull become important after it was tested by Rainer Berger?

   _____

   _____

9. Will people continue to look for old human bones in America? Why do you think so?

_____

_____

10. Why do you think Rainer Berger studied the skull when no one else thought it was important?

_____

_____

11. Write a title that best describes the story. Use as few words as possible.

_____

_____

12. How was Howard Wilson's interest in the skull like Rainer Berger's? How was it different?

_____

_____

13. In your own words, tell about Howard Wilson's contribution to the study of ancient people in America.

_____

_____

14. Does Howard Wilson's discovery affect you and your understanding of who we are as Americans? Why do you think so?

_____

_____

15. The story said, "The skull was 17,000 years old. It was 4,000 years older than any human bone found in America." Is this a fact or someone's opinion? How can you prove your answer?

_____

_____

16.

_____

_____

Name _____ Date _____

WHO IS UNCLE SAM?

ABOUT THE STORY

This story tells about the origins of the name Uncle Sam. Some historians believe the name comes from a meat packer named Sam Wilson. Wilson sold meat to the United States troops during the War of 1812.

PREVIEW WORDS

Sam Wilson	Elber Anderson	barrels
meat-packing plant	nickname	taxes
Uncle Sam		

THROUGHOUT THE WEEK—Decorate the classroom with American flags; photographs of important American symbols and monuments; and red, white, and blue banners. Play patriotic music as the students enter and leave the classroom, and as they work. Examples are:

Wee Sing America: Songs of Patriots and Pioneers (book and cassette set), Pamela Conn Beall and Suzan Hagen Nipp, Los Angeles, CA: (Price/Stern/Sloan, 1987).

Acappella. *Acappella America: The Series.* New York: Word, Incorporated, 1992.

BOOKS TO READ

A Grateful Nation: The Story of the Arlington National Cemetery, Brent K. Ashabranner (Putnam, 1990).

A Memorial for Mr. Lincoln, Brent K. Ashabranner (Putnam, 1992).

A New Flag for a New Country: The First National Flag (a play), June Behrens (Childrens Press, 1975).

Miss Liberty: First Lady of the World, June Behrens (Childrens Press, 1986).

Ring in the Jubilee: The Epic of America's Liberty Bell, Charles Michael Boland (Chatham, 1973).

Bicentennial Plays and Programs, Aileen Fisher (Plays, Inc., 1975).

The Flag of the United States, Dennis B. Fradin (Childrens Press, 1988).

From Sea to Shining Sea: Washington, D.C., Dennis Brindell Fradin (Childrens Press, 1992).

A Statue for America: The First 100 Years of the Statue of Liberty, Jonathan Harris (Four Winds Press, 1985).

A Capital City, 1790–1814, Suzanne Hilton (Atheneum, 1992).

Our National Symbols, Linda Carlson Johnson (Millbrook Press, 1992).

The Star-Spangled Banner, Francis Scott Key (Doubleday, 1973).

America the Beautiful: Stories of Patriotic Songs, Robert Kraske (Garrard Publishing, 1972).

Story of Mount Rushmore, Marilyn Prolman (Childrens Press, 1969).

Our National Anthem, Stephanie St. Pierre (Millbrook Press, 1992).

Casey Over There, Staton Rabin (Harcourt Brace Jovanovich, 1994).

Star-Spangled Fun! Things to Make, Do, and See From American History, James Razzi (Parents' Magazine Press, 1976).

How They Built the Statue of Liberty, Mary J. Shapiro (Random House, 1985).

The Story of the Burning of Washington, R. Conrad Stein (Childrens Press, 1985).

Magnificent Bald Eagle: America's National Bird, John F. Turner (Random House, 1971).

The Story of the White House, Kate Waters (Scholastic, 1991).

The Story of the Vietnam Veterans Memorial, David K. Wright (Childrens Press, 1989).

VIDEOS

"An ABC News Presentation": Liberty Weekend, Commemorative Edition, the 100th birthday of the Statue of Liberty (Vestron Video, 1986). Length: 40 minutes.

Rand McNally Videotrip Guide to Washington D.C., with Willard Scott (Videotrip Corporation, 1986). Length: 60 minutes.

Sing Out, America! (Warner Reprise Video, 1986). Length: 25 minutes.

"Tell Me Why": Americana, (Penguin Productions, 1987). Length: 30 minutes.

Uncle Sam Magoo (Paramount: UPA Pictures, 1970). Length: 53 minutes.

CDS, RECORDS, AND CASSETTES

Acappella America: The Series (CD), Acappella (Word, Incorporated, 1992).

Wee Sing America: Songs of Patriots and Pioneers (cassette and book set), Pamela Conn Beall and Susan Hagen Nipp (Price/Stern/Sloan, 1987).

INTRODUCTORY ACTIVITIES

DAY ONE

Objective: The students will watch a patriotic video. They will define the word "patriotic."
Curriculum subject: History or Social Studies
Teacher: Can someone tell me a sentence using the word "patriotic?" What does "patriotic" mean? What do you think about when you hear the word "patriotic?"
          This week we'll look at patriotic symbols and monuments of the United States. Today we'll watch a video with a patriotic theme. While you watch the video, think about how you're feeling. How do the music and the story make you feel? Why do they make you feel this way?

Show the video *Sing Out, America!*. After the video, discuss the feelings the students had as they listened to the music and story. Did they have a "patriotic" feeling? Ask the students to draw a picture of how the video made them feel.

DAY TWO

Story Lesson

Follow the *Presenting the Story Lesson* instructions in the Introduction. Each story lesson follows the same procedure; however, say the following in step 4:

"The title of the story we're reading today is *Who Is Uncle Sam?*. What do you think the story is about? What do you already know about Uncle Sam?"

EXTENSION ACTIVITIES

1. Before the lesson, contact your local military public relations office. Request an address where the students can send letters to service men and women stationed overseas.

◆ Read the story *Casey Over There*. Why did Aubrey write to Uncle Sam when he became concerned about his brother? Why did the president write to Aubrey instead of Uncle Sam? Why is Uncle Sam called a patriotic symbol of the United States?

◆ The students will write letters to service men and women overseas. If they are serving in military action, the students can send a care package of gum, cookies, or other goodies, like the one Aubrey sent to his brother.

2. Show a video tour of Washington, D.C., such as the *Rand McNally Videotrip Guide to Washington D.C.* As the students watch the video, they will list and draw pictures of the monuments and buildings they see. Ask them to look closely at the area called the Mall. What are the famous monuments in or near the Mall? Where are Capitol Hill, the Supreme Court Building, the Smithsonian Institution, and the White House located?

3. After watching the video, the students will make a model of the Mall. Cover a piece of plywood with model railroad grass or paint the plywood green. The students will use simple maps of Washington, D.C., to guide them. A good map is found in the book *From Sea To Shining Sea: Washington D.C.,* pages 4 and 5.

◆ Divide the students into groups. Assign a monument or building to each group. Allow the students to use their own creativity to build the monuments. They can use pint milk cartons as a base, or make their models from clay. Give the students an idea of the scale of the entire model, however. The Lincoln Memorial should not be taller than the Washington Monument.

◆ Display the model in the school library or other visible location. Surround the model with books about Washington, D.C., patriotic symbols, and monuments of the United States.

WHO IS UNCLE SAM?

When it's time to pay taxes, you might hear your parents say, "It's time to pay Uncle Sam." Or maybe you saw an army poster that said, "Uncle Sam Wants You!" Who is Uncle Sam?

During the War of 1812, Sam Wilson owned a meat-packing plant. One day Elber Anderson came to the plant. Anderson worked for the army. His job was to buy supplies for the United States government.

Elber Anderson needed to buy meat for the troops. Sam Wilson sold 300 barrels of beef and pork to the United States. Wilson marked each barrel with the letters "EA-US." This meant that Elber Anderson bought meat for the United States.

When a workman asked Anderson what the letters U.S. stood for, he joked and said, "Uncle Sam Wilson." The nickname spread across the country, and soon the U.S. of United States also stood for Uncle Sam.

QUESTIONS FOR WHO IS UNCLE SAM?

1. When did Sam Wilson own a meat-packing plant?

   _____

   _____

2. What was Elber Anderson's job?

   _____

   _____

3. What did Elber Anderson say the letters U.S. stood for?

   _____

   _____

4. How many barrels of beef and pork did Sam Wilson sell to the United States?

   _____

   _____

5. What did Elber Anderson buy for the United States government after he went to Wilson's meat-packing plant?

   _____

   _____

6. What did Anderson say after the workman asked what the letters U.S. stood for?

   _____

   _____

7. The story tells us that Anderson was joking when he said the U.S. stood for Uncle Sam Wilson. Why was his answer a joke?

   _____

   _____

8. The United States army often uses the words "Uncle Sam Wants You!" What do these words mean?

   _____

   _____

9. Will people continue to use the nickname "Uncle Sam" when talking about the U.S. government? Why do you think so?

_____

_____

10. Why didn't Elber Anderson give the correct answer to the workman when he asked what the letters *U.S.* stood for?

_____

_____

11. Write a title for the story. Use as few words as possible.

_____

_____

12. How were Sam Wilson's and Elber Anderson's jobs alike? How were they different?

_____

_____

13. In your own words, tell how the letters *U.S.* became known as *Uncle Sam.*

_____

_____

14. How did the nickname *Uncle Sam* change the way people talked about the U.S. government?

_____

_____

15. The story said, "During the War of 1812, Sam Wilson owned a meat-packing plant." Is this statement a fact or an opinion? How can you prove your answer?

_____

_____

16.

_____

_____

Name _____   Date _____

THEY STOOD ON TOP OF THE WORLD

ABOUT THE STORY

The story tells about Robert Peary and Matthew Henson's historical expedition to the North Pole on April 6, 1909. Peary received many honors, however, while no one recognized Henson's work. It was not until 1954 that President Eisenhower honored the black man who reached the top of the world.

PREVIEW WORDS

Robert Peary	Matthew Henson	Eskimo
language	honors	recognized
temperature	President Eisenhower	North Pole

BOOKS TO READ

Sled Dogs, Bridgid Casey and Wendy Haugh (Dodd, Mead, 1983).

The White Caps, Jacques Yves Cousteau (World Pub., 1974).

Arctic Explorer: The Story of Matthew Henson, Jeri Ferris (Carolrhoda Books, 1989).

Tundra: The Arctic Land, Bruce Hiscock (Atheneum, 1986).

A Passion for Danger: Nansen's Arctic Adventure, Francine Jacobs (Putnam, 1994).

Arctic Animals, Bobbie Kalman (Crabtree Publishing, 1988).

The Story of Admiral Peary at the North Pole, Zachary Kent (Childrens Press, 1988).

Polar Regions, David Lambert (Silver Burdett Press, 1988).

Peary to the Pole, Walter Lord (Harper & Row, 1963).

Arctic Lands, edited by Henry Pluckrose (Gloucester Press, 1982).

Sled Dogs: Arctic Athletes, Elizabeth Ring (Millbrook Press, 1994).

How and Why Wonder Book of the Polar Regions, Irving Robbin (Wonder Books, 1965).

The Iceberg Hermit, Arthur J. Roth (Four Winds Press, 1974).

Arctic and Antarctic Regions, Francene Sabin (Troll Associates, 1985).

North to the Pole, Will Steger (Times Books, 1987).

The Arctic, Lynn M. Stone (Childrens Press, 1985).

Animals of the Arctic, Bernard Stonehouse (Holt, Rinehart and Winston, 1971).

The Haunted Igloo, Bonnie Turner (Houghton Mifflin, 1991).

Ann Bancroft: On Top of the World, Dorothy Wenzel (Dillon Press, 1989).

The Discovery of the North Pole, Donald W. Whisenhunt (Wayne Enterprises, 1987).

VIDEOS

The Living Planet: The Frozen World, Time-Life Video, 1991. Length: 60 minutes.

INTRODUCTORY ACTIVITIES

DAY ONE

Objective: The students will list facts about the North Pole. They will discuss why people go to the North Pole. They will begin to listen to the story *Arctic Explorer: The Story of Matthew Henson* by Jeri Ferris.

Curriculum subject: Science or History

Teacher: Throughout the week we will learn about the first people to walk on the North Pole. Before we can understand this accomplishment, we must learn about the North Pole.

(Display a blank chart paper page in front of the class. Write the title "North Pole" at the top of the page.)

Let's make a list of facts about the North Pole. Who can tell me a fact.

Examples of facts are:

◆ The North Pole is cold. How cold is it? (Ask a student to find the information in a reference book.)

◆ The North Pole is in the Arctic region of the world. Unlike Antarctica, there is no land under the ice.

◆ Although it is cold, animals live in the Arctic.

Why would someone go to the North Pole? In 1909, no one had stood on the North Pole. Several people hoped to be the first to stand on the top of the world. Two men claimed to reach the North Pole first, Robert Peary and Dr. Frederick Cook. We'll look at this argument later in the week.

First, let's listen to a story about Robert Peary and the men who accompanied him on the first trip to the North Pole.

Read the Foreword, Introduction, and Chapter 1 of *Arctic Explorer: The Story of Matthew Henson*. Discuss what the students learned in the story. Continue to read from the book throughout the week.

DAY TWO

Story Lesson

Follow the *Presenting the Story Lesson* instructions in the Introduction. Each story lesson follows the same procedure; however, say the following in step 4:

"The title of the story we're reading today is *They Stood on Top of the World*. What do you think the story is about?" If the students mention the North Pole, ask, "What do you already know about the North Pole?"

EXTENSION ACTIVITIES

1. Divide the students into two groups. One group will study the claims of reaching the North Pole presented by Dr. Cook. The other group will study the claims of Robert Peary. Provide reference books for the students. Your local library might have newspapers from the period on microfiche that the students can read.

◆ After they gather their information, hold a debate. Each group will argue its point of view.

◆ In the end, conduct a vote to determine which person, Cook or Peary, the students believe was the first to reach the North Pole.

2. On a large piece of white bulletin board paper, the students will make a mural of the Peary expedition.

◆ Divide the students into groups. Each group will draw a section of the mural that tells about a phase of the trip. Begin with the *Roosevelt,* Peary's ship, and end with President Eisenhower honoring Matthew Henson.

3. The students will make polar bear toys.

◆ Read to the class from the book *Arctic Animals.* Read only the chapter entitled The Polar Bear on pages 8–11.

Polar Bear Toy
Materials

◆ white fake fur

◆ white thread

◆ large, blunt sewing needles

◆ bear pattern

◆ buttons

◆ old stockings collected from parents and teachers

◆ pink thread

Procedure

◆ Cut up the stockings into 2-inch sections.

◆ Using a dark pencil, trace the bear pattern onto the back of the white fake fur.

◆ Cut out the bear, cutting ¾ inch outside the pencil line.

◆ Cut out two bear shapes.

◆ With right sides together, use a long stitch to sew along the pencil line of the bear. Leave a 2-inch opening on the side of the bear.

◆ Turn the bear right side out.

◆ Stuff the stocking pieces into the opening. Do not overstuff the bear.

◆ Stitch up the hole after turning in the raw edges.

◆ Sew on buttons for the eyes and nose.

◆ The students can stitch on mouths with pink thread if they have the skill.

◆ Donate the bears to a women's shelter, homeless shelter, or similar places. *The toys are not appropriate for tiny children, who might swallow the buttons.*

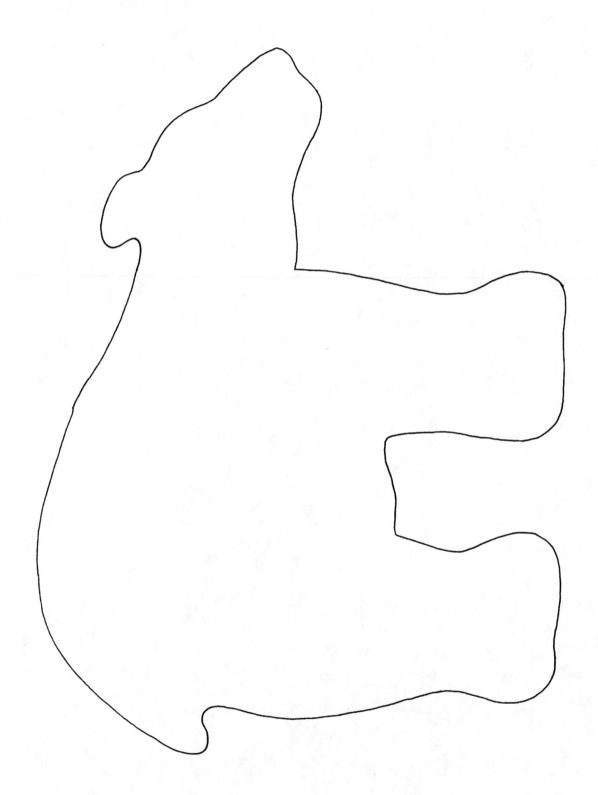

THEY STOOD ON TOP OF THE WORLD

In 1909, two Americans and four Eskimos did something no one had done before. They stood on the North Pole.

Robert Peary had tried to reach the North Pole for 20 years. At the age of 52, he was taking his last chance to make his dream come true.

Matthew Henson was the only man who could help. He worked with Peary for many years. Henson learned the Eskimo language, and he knew how to train sled dogs.

Peary and Henson began their trip on February 28, 1909. On many days the temperature dropped to 57° below zero. They reached the pole over a month later, on April 6, 1909. Matthew Henson proudly planted the American flag on the top of the world.

When they returned home, Peary received many honors, yet no one recognized Henson's work. It was not until 1954 that President Eisenhower honored him. The black man who so proudly raised his country's flag on the North Pole died in 1955.

QUESTIONS FOR
THEY STOOD ON TOP OF THE WORLD

1. Name the two Americans who first reached the North Pole.

   _____

   _____

2. How many years had Peary tried to reach the North Pole?

   _____

   _____

3. What day and year did they reach the North Pole?

   _____

   _____

4. Who planted the American flag at the North Pole?

   _____

   _____

5. What happened to Peary after he returned home?

   _____

   _____

6. What happened to Henson the first years after he returned home?

   _____

   _____

7. What one word best describes Matthew Henson?

   _____

   _____

8. Could Peary have reached the North Pole without Henson? Why do you think so?

   _____

   _____

9. Do you think a person's work will continue to be considered important, or not, based on the person's skin color or race? Why do you think so?

_____

_____

10. Why do you think Henson's work was not recognized?

_____

_____

11. Write a title for the story. Use as few words as possible.

_____

_____

12. Reread the last paragraph of the story. Compare how the two men, Peary and Henson, felt when they returned home from their historic experience.

_____

_____

13. In your own words, describe Henson's contributions to the first trip to the North Pole.

_____

_____

14. Henson's work on the first trip to the North Pole was not recognized until the end of his life. What effect do you think the lack of recognition had on Henson and his life?

_____

_____

15. The story said, "They (Henson and Peary) reached the pole over a month later, on April 6, 1909." Is this a fact or an opinion? How can you prove your answer?

_____

_____

16.

_____

_____

Name _____   Date _____

STEPHEN HAWKING

ABOUT THE STORY

This story tells about the life of Stephen Hawking. Stephen Hawking is a renowned theoretical physicist. His ideas about the universe have greatly influenced modern science as well as science fiction. He continues his work despite his inability to speak or write due to ALS (Lou Gehrig's disease).

PREVIEW WORDS

Stephen Hawking	Star Ship Enterprise
android	Lou Gehrig's disease
Speech Plus	best-selling

THROUGHOUT THE WEEK—Decorate the classroom in pictures of the universe. NASA calendars are good sources for such photographs. If possible, display pictures of famous scientists such as Hawking, Einstein, Newton, and Galileo.

During the next two weeks, read the science fiction book *My Trip to Alpha I* by Alfred Slote (Philadelphia: J.B. Lippincott Company, 1978). *My Trip to Alpha I* is a Junior Literary Guild book. As you read the story, ask the students if the author studied space science before writing the book. Why do the students think so?

BOOKS TO READ

How Was the Universe Born?, Isaac Asimov (Gareth Stevens, 1988).

The Universe: Think Big!, Jeanne Bendick (Millbrook Press Inc., 1991).

You and Relativity, Mary Lou Clark (Childrens Press, 1965).

The New Astronomy: Probing the Secrets of the Universe, Fred D'Ignazio (Franklin Watts, 1982).

Famous Experiments and How to Repeat Them, Brent Filson (Julian Messner, 1986).

Famous Experiments You Can Do, Robert Gardner (Franklin Watts, 1990).

Galaxies, Michael George (Creative Education, 1992).

Stars, Michael George (Creative Education, 1991).

Isaac Newton: Reluctant Genius, D.C. Ipsen (Enslow Publishers, 1984).

The Physics of Star Trek: With a Foreword by Stephen Hawking, Lawrence Maxwell Krauss (Basic Books, 1995).

Astronomy: From Copernicus to the Space Telescope, A First Book, Christopher Lampton (Franklin Watts, 1987).

Albert Einstein, Ibi Lepscky (Barron's, 1982).

Space Science, Projects for Young Scientists, David W. McKay and Bruce G. Smith (Franklin Watts, 1986).

Albert Einstein, Scientist of the 20th Century, Catherine Reef (Dillon Press, 1991).

How Far Is a Star?, Sydney Craft Rosen (Carolrhoda Books, 1992).

Stephen Hawking: Unlocking the Universe—A People in Focus Book, Sheridan Simon (Dillon Press, 1991).

I Can Be a Physicist, Paul P. Sipiera (Childrens Press, 1991).

My Trip to Alpha I, Alfred Slote (J.B. Lippincott, 1978).

The World Book Encyclopedia of Science: Physics Today (World Book, 1985.)

MAGAZINES

Odyssey: Science That's Out of This World, "Stephen Hawking: Probing the Universe," January 1995, vol. 4, no. 1.

INTRODUCTORY ACTIVITIES

DAY ONE

Objective: The students will guess the contents of a sealed container. They will develop a theory about the contents and conduct experiments to prove their theories.

Curriculum subject: Science

Materials

◆ one coffee can with lid per three to four students

◆ packing tape

◆ objects of various shapes

Examples:

◆ tennis ball

◆ metal whistle

◆ pencil

◆ five marbles

Procedure

1. Put one object into each coffee can. You can put five marbles in one can. Cover the clear plastic lid of the coffee can with paper, and seal it with packing tape. This prevents the students from peeking in the can.

Teacher: Today we're going to do an experiment. Break up into groups of three to four people. I'll give each group a coffee can. The coffee can has one or more objects inside. It is sealed with packing tape. If there is more than one object, all the objects are of the same type.

Your job is to guess what is in the can. Your guess will be your theory. A theory is a conclusion that has not been proven. Your idea will be a theory until you open the can and prove your theory is a fact.

On a piece of paper, write what you think is in your can. For example: Theory - There is a toy mouse in our coffee can. Next, begin experiments to try to prove your theory. List your experiments on your paper. For example, if you shake the can, write that down as experiment number one. Then write the results of your experiment. Conduct as many experiments as you can to try to prove your theory. Write every experiment and result down on your paper.

(Allow the students time to develop a theory and conduct their experiments.)

Teacher: (Display a map of the solar system that indicates the distance between the planets.) If you wanted to learn the distance from your home to school, what would you do? How would you measure the distance?

How far away is Venus? Scientists can't stretch a yardstick across space to measure this distance. They have to do experiments from Earth without ever going to Venus. This is what you did with your coffee cans. You could not touch the object of your experiment, so you worked in other ways to try to prove your theory.

One type of scientist who does this is called a theoretical physicist. A theoretical physicist might do experiments from Earth to learn about black holes in the universe. No one has seen a black hole, so a theoretical physicist conducts experiments from Earth to prove they exist. How do you think these scientists will feel if their ideas about black holes are proven to be true?

Now let's see how your experiments worked. Open your coffee can. Write what you found at the bottom of your paper. Was your theory right? (Discuss the results.) How did you feel when you learned your theory was wrong? How did you feel when you learned your theory was right?

This week we will learn about scientists who study the universe by conducting experiments on Earth and by using their imaginations.

DAY TWO

Story Lesson

Follow the *Presenting the Story Lesson* instructions in the Introduction. Each story lesson follows the same procedure; however, say the following in step 4:

"The title of the story we're reading today is *Stephen Hawking*. What do you think the story is about?"

EXTENSION ACTIVITIES

1. The students will learn about objects in the universe. They will discuss how scientists learned about these objects without visiting them.

◆ Teacher:

Today we'll read a book that tells us what scientists have learned about the universe. Stephen Hawking is a scientist who has written many theories about black holes. What does it mean when I say Stephen Hawking has written many theories about black holes? How does he come up with these theories if he has never visited a black hole?

◆ Read *How Far Is a Star?* by Sidney Rosen (Minneapolis: Carolrhoda Books, Inc., 1992) to the class. Point out the information in the book that scientists learned from Earth without ever visiting these objects in space.

◆ Teacher:

In the book *How Far Is a Star?* we learned about light speed. We measure the large distances between objects in space by how fast light travels from Earth to the distant stars. Before this could be done, someone had to do experiments to learn how fast light travels. It took many years and many experiments to prove how fast light moves through space. Many other scientists conducted experiments to measure the distance between stars.

Over the next two days, we'll learn about these scientists. We'll do some of the experiments these scientists conducted many years ago. These experiments were the beginning of a long search to learn about the universe around us.

2. Read the book *Albert Einstein* by Ibi Lepscky (Woodbury, NY: Barron's, 1982) to the class. Discuss how Einstein wrote many theories about our universe.

3. Divide the students into groups. Refer to *Famous Experiments and How to Repeat Them* by Brent Filson (New York: Julian Messner, 1986) and *Space Science Projects For Young Scientists* by David W. McKay and Bruce G. Smith (New York: Franklin Watts, 1986) for space science experiments. Assign each group an experiment.

4. The students will conduct the experiment for the class. They will discuss how the experiment leads to a better understanding of the universe. How was this experiment a stepping stone to the exploration of space?

STEPHEN HAWKING

Aboard the Star Ship Enterprise, the android Data joins Isaac Newton, Albert Einstein, and a thin man in a wheelchair in a game of poker. Who is this man who speaks through a computer?

His name is Stephen Hawking. When Hawking was only 21 years old, he developed an illness many call Lou Gehrig's Disease. Slowly, this disease would take away his ability to walk and talk. The doctors said the disease would kill him in a few years.

At first, Hawking was very sad. Why should he stay in school? Why shouldn't he just give up? Then he met a young boy who later died of cancer. Hawking realized there were other people with problems, too. If he was going to die, he wanted his life to count for something.

Hawking went back to school and finished his education. He became a scientist. Someone gave him a computer called Speech Plus to help him talk. Now he teaches other scientists. Hawking even wrote best-selling books called A Brief History of Time and Black Holes and Baby Universes.

QUESTIONS FOR STEPHEN HAWKING

1. Who were the three men playing poker with Data on the Star Ship Enterprise?

   _____

   _____

2. How old was Stephen Hawking when he developed Lou Gehrig's disease?

   _____

   _____

3. Name the best-selling books written by Stephen Hawking.

   _____

   _____

4. What is the name of the computer that helps Stephen Hawking talk?

   _____

   _____

5. How did Stephen Hawking feel before he met the young boy who died of cancer?

   _____

   _____

6. What did Stephen Hawking do after the young boy died of cancer?

   _____

   _____

7. What one word best describes Stephen Hawking?

   _____

   _____

8. Why did the writers of <u>Star Trek</u> want Stephen Hawking on their television show? Why would Data want to play poker with Stephen Hawking, Isaac Newton, and Albert Einstein?

   _____

   _____

9. Stephen Hawking can no longer speak. He uses a computer called Speech Plus to talk. What other ways might computers help someone like Stephen Hawking in the future?

_____

_____

10. The story says that Stephen Hawking wanted his life to count for something. He went back to school and finished his education. How can an education help you do more with your life?

_____

_____

11. Write a title for the story. Use as few words as possible.

_____

_____

12. Imagine your future. How do you hope your life will be like Stephen Hawking's? How will it be different?

_____

_____

13. In your own words, tell how Stephen Hawking changed his life after he met the young boy who died of cancer.

_____

_____

14. Imagine that Stephen Hawking gave up on life after he developed Lou Gehrig's disease. What effect would this have had on the people of the world? What would we have missed?

_____

_____

15. The story said, "Hawking went back to school and finished his education. He became a scientist." Is this a fact or an opinion? How can you prove your answer?

_____

_____

16. _____

_____

Name _____   Date _____

BLACK HOLES

ABOUT THE STORY

This story defines a black hole. At the center of a black hole is a collapsing star. The collapsing star creates a gravitational field strong enough to pull in light. (Stephen Hawking contributed to the development of the theory of black holes.)

PREVIEW WORDS

scientists	collapse	fuel
layers	black hole	Isaac Newton

THROUGHOUT THE WEEK—Continue reading *My Trip to Alpha I* by Alfred Slote (Philadelphia: J.B. Lippincott Company, 1978). Look for science facts in the story. Did the author base any of his story on science fact?

BOOKS TO READ

SCIENCE FACT

World of Tomorrow: Fact or Fantasy?, Neil Ardley (Franklin Watts, 1982).

Colonizing the Planets and Stars, Isaac Asimov (Gareth Stevens, 1989).

How Did We Find Out About Black Holes?, Isaac Asimov (Walker, 1978).

How Was the Universe Born?, Isaac Asimov (Gareth Stevens, 1988).

Quasars, Pulsars and Black Holes, Isaac Asimov (Gareth Stevens, 1988).

The Universe: Think Big! (an Earlybird Book), Jeanne Bendick (Millbrook Press, 1991).

Journey Through Space, Tim Furniss (Gallery Books, W.H. Smith Publishers, 1991).

Galaxies, Michael George (Creative Education, 1992).

Stars, Michael George (Creative Education, 1991).

The NOVA Space Explorer's Guide: Where to Go and What to See, Richard Maurer (Clarkson N. Potter, 1985).

How Far Is a Star?, Sydney Craft Rosen (Carolrhoda Books, 1992).

SCIENCE FICTION

The Black Hole: Discovery of the Mystery Ship, Walt Disney Productions, (Golden Press, 1979).

Walt Disney Productions Presents The Black Hole (Random House, 1979).

Strange Tomorrow, Jean Karl (Dutton, 1985).

My Trip to Alpha I, Alfred Slote (J.B. Lippincott, 1978).

Danny Dunn, Invisible Boy, Jay Williams and Raymond Abrashkin (McGraw-Hill, 1974).

◆ Other Danny Dunn books (not a complete list):

Danny Dunn, Time Traveler

Danny Dunn and the Anti-Gravity Paint

Danny Dunn and the Voice From Space

VIDEOS

New Explorers: Science of Star Trek, a PBS series, Kurtis Productions, 1994. Available through Public Media Inc., 1-800-621-0660. Teacher's guides are also available.

INTRODUCTORY ACTIVITIES

DAY ONE

Objective: The students will listen to the book *Quasars, Pulsars and Black Holes* by Isaac Asimov. They will discuss how this information would help science fiction writers develop interesting stories.

Curriculum subject: Science and Language Arts

Teacher: Last week we learned about scientists who studied the universe without leaving Earth. This week we'll learn about some of their discoveries. Stephen Hawking has spent a great deal of time forming the theory of black holes. Remember, Stephen Hawking can't travel to a black hole. He has to use his imagination, and think about what he knows about space. Then he guesses what a black hole might be. This guess is his theory or idea.

This week we'll learn about his ideas about black holes and other objects in the universe. We'll look at how science fiction writers use these science facts to create an exciting story.

Today I'll read the book *Quasars, Pulsars, and Black Holes* by Isaac Asimov. As you listen to the book, think about how this information would help you write an interesting science fiction story.

Read *Quasars, Pulsars, and Black Holes* by Isaac Asimov. As you read, discuss how this information would help a writer develop an exciting science fiction story.

Teacher: During the next few days, think about what you learned in this book. Read other books about the universe. Think about a science fiction story you could write. Remember, a science fiction story is a story someone made up. It's not true or factual, but the story involves an understanding of science. Usually, a science fiction story is a space adventure.

DAY TWO

Story Lesson

Follow the *Presenting the Story Lesson* instructions in the Introduction. Each story lesson follows the same procedure; however, say the following in step 4:

"The title of the story we're reading today is *Black Holes*. What do you think the story is about? What do you already know about black holes?"

EXTENSION ACTIVITIES

1. The students will listen to the science fiction story *The Black Hole*. They will discuss how science influenced the author.

◆ Teacher:

On Days One and Two we learned about black holes. We learned how gravity is so strong in some collapsing stars that it even pulls in light. It looks like a black hole in space.

When scientists like Stephen Hawking began to talk about black holes, writers were fascinated. They knew black holes would be exciting locations for science fiction stories. Why do you think science fiction writers felt this way?

Today I'll read the science fiction story *The Black Hole: Discovery of the Mystery Ship*. Listen to how science fiction writers use science fact in their stories. Later, you'll write a science fiction story of your own.

◆ Read *The Black Hole: Discovery of the Mystery Ship*. After the story, discuss how the writer uses science fact to write a science fiction story.

2. Read the book *World of Tomorrow: Fact or Fantasy?* to the class. Neil Ardley points out the fact and fantasy of space science, and describes how science fantasy can become science fact. He covers topics such as time travel, traveling faster than light, and alien life.

3. Watch the video *New Explorers: Science of Star Trek*. This entertaining film shows how the writers of Star Trek work to develop stories and props according to science fact. Teacher's guide are available.

4. Break the class into groups of four to five students. Each group will write a science fiction story. Encourage them to look for ideas in nonfiction books about the universe. Their stories can revolve around quasars, pulsars, the planets, and the like. If time allows, the students will illustrate their stories. The students share their science fiction stories with the class.

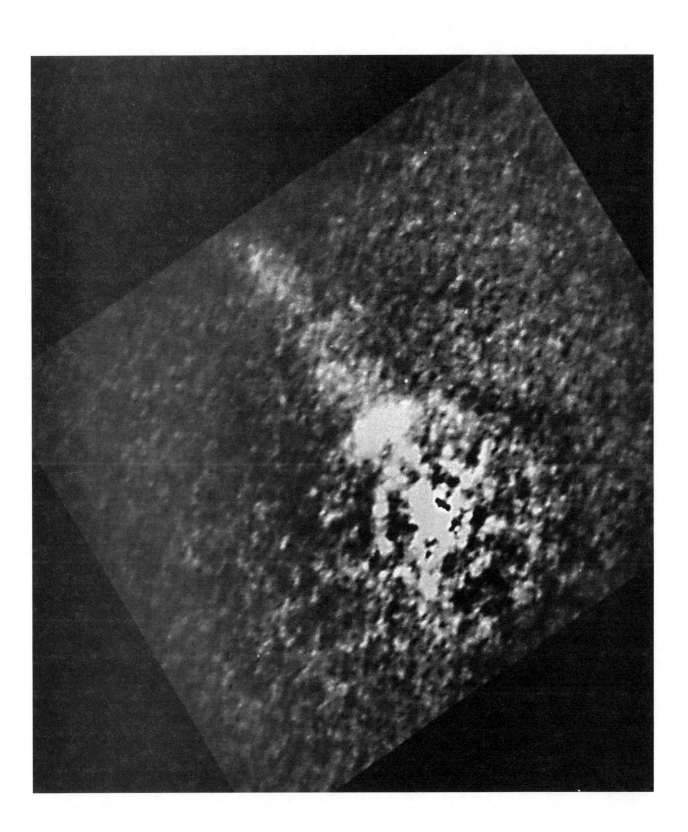

BLACK HOLES

Cars need fuel to go. If a car runs out of gas, it will stop. Stars need fuel, too. The fuel is what makes the star's fire burn. Stars also run out of fuel. When a star uses up all of its fuel, it dies. What happens to a star when it dies?

Scientists think that very large stars might become black holes after they die. They believe that when a star runs out of fuel, it collapses.

A scientist named Isaac Newton learned that gravity increases as objects get closer together. When a star collapses, the layers fall toward the star's center. As the layers fall closer and closer together, the gravity of the star gets stronger.

Finally, the material of the star gets so close together that the gravity pulls very hard. The gravity is so strong that it even pulls in light. Without light coming from the star, it looks like a black hole in space.

QUESTIONS FOR BLACK HOLES

1. What makes a star's fire burn?

   _____

   _____

2. What happens when a star runs out of fuel?

   _____

   _____

3. What happens to the gravity around a dying star as it collapses?

   _____

   _____

4. What is the name of the scientist who said gravity increases as objects get closer together?

   _____

   _____

5. What happens to a star before it collapses?

   _____

   _____

6. What happens to the light around a star after it becomes a black hole?

   _____

   _____

7. What one word best describes a black hole?

   _____

   _____

8. Why do you think scientists say that small stars, like our Sun, cannot become black holes?

   _____

   _____

9. Do you think people will ever travel into a black hole? If you said no, why do you think so? If you said yes, how might people live in such strong gravity?

_____

_____

10. Astrophysicists study matter and energy in space. They study objects in the universe like black holes. Would you like to be an astrophysicist? Why do you think so?

_____

_____

11. Write a title for the story. Use as few words as possible.

_____

_____

12. Scientists believe that black holes were once large stars that have died. Compare a star, like our Sun, to a black hole. How are they different? How are they alike?

_____

_____

13. Briefly explain why black holes look like holes in space.

_____

_____

14. What do you believe would happen to a soda can if it were pulled into a black hole? Why do you think so?

_____

_____

15. Is the theory of what black holes are and how they occur fact or opinion? Why do you think so?

_____

_____

16.

_____

_____

Name _____   Date _____

TO CLEAN OR NOT TO CLEAN

ABOUT THE STORY

The story tells how air pollution is destroying the world's art treasures. Should works, like Leonardo da Vinci's *Last Supper,* be cleaned to prevent further erosion of the paint? Or, would the cleaning process itself do more damage than the dirt?

PREVIEW WORDS

pollution	scientists	artists
treasures	priceless	Ice Age

stained glass

Michelangelo's Sistine Chapel

Leonardo da Vinci's *Last Supper*

Canterbury Cathedral

PRIOR TO THE LESSON

Prepare for a field trip to an art museum, a historical church with stained glass or an older mural, or a historical site with outdoor statuary. The students will look for and ask about pollution damage to the works of art. Tell the curator or guide the purpose of your visit. Collect parent permission slips.

BOOKS TO READ

Signs of Life, Jean Ferris (Farrar, Straus & Giroux, 1994).

If the Sky Could Talk, Stuart A. Kallen (Abdo & Daughters, 1993).

Air Pollution, Gary Lopez (Creative Education, 1992).

Michelangelo, Richard B. K. McLanathan (H.N. Abrams, 1993).

Voices From the Stone Age: A Search for Cave and Canyon Art, Douglas Mazonowicz (Thomas Crowell, 1974).

Save the Earth!: An Ecology Handbook for Kids, Betty Miles (Knopf, 1974).

Fables of Leonardo da Vinci, interpreted and transcribed by Bruno Nardini (Hubbard Press, 1973).

Eco-Solutions: It's in Your Hands, Oliver S. Owen (Abdo & Daughters, 1993).

Who Will Clean the Air?, Thomas Biddle Perera (Coward, McCann & Geoghegan, 1971).

A Weekend With Leonardo da Vinci, Rosabianca Skira-Venturi (Rizzoli, 1993).

Air Pollution, Darlene R. Stille (Childrens Press, 1990).

The Lorax, Dr. Suess (Random House, 1971).

Clean Air, Beulah Tannenbaum and Myra Stillman (McGraw-Hill, 1973).

Michelangelo's World, Piero Ventura (Putnam's, 1988).

Michelangelo, Mike Venezia (Childrens Press, 1991).

INTRODUCTORY ACTIVITIES

DAY ONE

Objective: The students will listen to a story about air pollution. They will talk about local historical and artistic sites damaged by pollution.

Curriculum subject: Science

Teacher: During this week, we'll learn how pollution not only causes health problems, but also damages ancient works of art. We'll look at historical sites in our area, and check for pollution damage.

Today, we'll begin by listening to a story about air pollution. As I read the story, look for information about damage to old churches and statues. What does air pollution do to these treasured works of art?

Read the book *Air Pollution* to the class. After the story, talk about how air pollution is damaging works of art, from the ruins of the Roman Empire to limestone statues outside local churches. Ask the students if they know of any such damage occurring in their community. Is air pollution damaging the stained glass at their church? Have they noticed decay on statuary in a local historical district? How does this damage make them feel?

DAY TWO

Story Lesson

Follow the *Presenting the Story Lesson* instructions in the Introduction. Each story lesson follows the same procedure; however, say the following in step 4:

"The title of the story we're reading today is *To Clean or Not to Clean.* What do you think the story is about?" If the students mention cleaning objects damaged by pollution, ask, "What do you already know about the damaging effects of air pollution?"

EXTENSION ACTIVITIES

1. Visit a local art museum, a historical church with stained glass or an older mural, or a historical site with outdoor statuary. Look for damage due to air pollution. Ask the curator or guide about the effects of air pollution on the art. What can be done to prevent or reduce the damage caused by air pollution? Should the items be cleaned? Why does the curator or guide think so? What would it cost to repair the artwork? Who is in charge of seeing that the cleaning is done?

2. Investigate solutions for damage to local historical sites caused by air pollution. Adopt one historical site. Work to have it cleaned or protected. The historical site needing protection might be your school building. (Your local historical society can offer guidance.)

◆ In an ideal situation, what needs to be done to protect, clean, or preserve the items? How much money would this cost? Who or what organization is in charge of the site?

◆ Educate the community about the damage caused by air pollution. Contact local news media, and ask them to do a story on the damage.

◆ Devise a plan to raise funds to help restore the site. Some businesses might offer matching funds. Hold bake sales, car washes, and so on. Involve as much of the community as possible in the project.

3. Write letters to local, state, and federal officials about the students' concerns and actions. The letters should inform the representatives of the problem. Educate them on the need for the repairs and the need to clean our air.

4. Check the levels of air pollution around the school. Plan this activity during a time when the weather is relatively calm. Iron several coffee filters until they are flat circles. Stitch them to the strings of several old, unwanted tennis rackets.

◆ Break the students into groups. Give each group a racket. The groups will choose an outdoor site for their racket. Some examples are the parking lot, the playground, near the street, or near a smokestack.

◆ Bury the handle of each racket in the ground at the selected site. Rocks can prop the racket up. Leave the racket for several days.

◆ Bring the rackets back to the room, and remove the filters. Each group will mount their filter on typing paper, and label the filter with the name of the site where it stood. The teacher mounts a new filter on typing paper, and labels it "New Filter."

◆ Compare the filters. Which one is the dirtiest? What caused it to become dirty? How does this make you feel?

◆ Display the filters in a prominent place in the school.

5. You can find other air pollution activities in *Save the Earth!: An Ecology Handbook for Kids* by Betty Miles.

TO CLEAN OR NOT TO CLEAN

Air pollution and dirt are destroying the world's art treasures. Artworks as old as the Ice Age are dirty. The dirt is eating away at these priceless works. Should we clean our artwork?

Some scientists and artists say no. If we clean away the dirt, how will we keep from cleaning away some of the paint? They want the work to stop until we understand what we are doing.

Other people want to clean the artwork now. If we wait, we might not be able to repair the damage. Special scientists and artists believe they can safely clean the cave, glass, and wall paintings.

Whether you agree or not, work has begun. It is good to know that people care enough to save the world's art for future generations.

Cleaned Art Work

Ice Age cave drawings
Michelangelo's Sistine Chapel
Leonardo de Vinci's Last Supper
Canterbury Cathedral (stained glass)

QUESTIONS FOR TO CLEAN OR NOT TO CLEAN

1. What is destroying the art treasures of the world?

    _____

    _____

2. Why do some people think we <u>should not</u> clean the artwork?

    _____

    _____

3. Why do some people think we <u>should</u> clean the artwork?

    _____

    _____

4. Name two pieces of art that have been cleaned.

    _____

    _____

5. Whose side of the argument was given first—those against the cleaning or those for the cleaning?

    _____

    _____

6. What happens to the artwork after it becomes dirty?

    _____

    _____

7. Based on what you have read, do you think the artwork should or should not be cleaned?

    _____

    _____

8. Why do you think the author refers to the artwork as "ours?"
    For example: "Should <u>we</u> clean <u>our</u> artwork?"

    _____

    _____

9. Do you think other works of art might be damaged by pollution in the future?
   What can be done to protect the artwork?

   _____

   _____

10. Why are so many people concerned about saving these works of art?

    _____

    _____

11. Write a title for the story. Use as few words as possible.

    _____

    _____

12. The story presented two opinions about the cleaning of the world's art treasures.
    Compare the two opinions, explaining how the concerns are alike and how they
    are different.

    _____

    _____

13. In your own words, summarize the concerns of the people who do not believe the
    artwork should be cleaned.

    _____

    _____

14. Some people believe that cleaning the world's artwork will damage it. If this is
    true, how will this affect later generations who wish to study the artwork?

    _____

    _____

15. The story said, "The dirt is eating away at these priceless works." Is this a fact or
    someone's opinion? How can you prove your answer?

    _____

    _____

16. _____

    _____

    _____

Name _____   Date _____

CHIEF SEATTLE

ABOUT THE STORY

This story tells about the life of Chief Seattle. Chief Seattle held a great respect for the land. He coupled this respect with Christian beliefs he developed after meeting missionaries.

PREVIEW WORDS

Chief Seattle (Seathl)

Catholic

Duwamish Indian Confederacy

Christian

missionaries

preached

Port Elliott Treaty

spirit

THROUGHOUT THE WEEK—Decorate the classroom with Native American art. Notice how the art is based on motifs of nature. Set up a Native American museum of pottery, dolls, and other artifacts.

As the students work, play Native American music such as *Dream Catchers* by Tokeya Inajin (Kevin Locke) (Redway, CA: EarthBeat! Records, 1992). Sounds of the wind and birds are heard behind the music.

BOOKS TO READ

Games of the American Indian, Gordon Cortis Baldwin (Norton, 1969).

Lightning Inside You: Riddles of the American Indians, edited by John Bierhorst (William Morrow, 1992).

Native American Crafts Workshop, Bonnie Bernstein and Leigh Blair (Fearon Teacher Aids, 1982).

American Indian Games and Crafts, Charles L. Blood (Franklin Watts, 1981).

Flying With the Eagle, Racing the Great Bear: Stories From Native North America, told by Joseph Bruchac (Bridgewater Press, 1993).

Keepers of the Animals: Native American Stories and Wildlife Activities for Children, Michael J. Caduto and Joseph Bruchac (Fulcrum Publishing, 1991).

Keepers of the Earth: Native American Stories and Environmental Activities for Children, Michael Caduto and Joseph Bruchac (Fulcrum Publishing, 1988).

Keepers of Life: Discovering Plants Through Native American Stories and Earth Activities for Children, Michael J. Caduto and Joseph Bruchac (Fulcrum Publishing, 1994).

Keepers of the Night: Native American Stories and Nocturnal Activities for Children, Michael J. Caduto and Joseph Bruchac (Fulcrum Publishing, 1994).

American Indian Fairy Tales, Margaret Compton (Dodd, Mead, 1971).

American Indian Music and Musical Instruments: With Instructions for Making the Instruments, George S. Fichter (David McKay, 1978).

Book of American Indian Games, Allan A. Macfarlan (Association Press, 1958).

Dances and Stories of the American Indian, Bernard S. Mason (A. S. Barnes, 1944).

Chief Seattle: Great Statesman, Elizabeth Rider Montgomery (Garrard Publishing, 1966).

Brother Eagle, Sister Sky!: The Words of Chief Seattle, Chief Seattle (Dial Books, 1991).

George Catlin: Painter of the Indian West, Mark Sufrin (Atheneum, 1991).

The Native American Book of Knowledge, Native People, Native Ways Series, vol. I, White Deer of Autumn (Beyond Words Publishing, 1992).

The Native American Book of Life, Native People, Native Ways Series, vol. II, White Deer of Autumn (Beyond Words Publishing, 1992).

VIDEOS

Pocahontas, Walt Disney Home Video (1995). Length: 81 minutes.

CDS, RECORDS, AND CASSETTES

Myth, Music, and Dance of the American Indian: An Activity-Oriented Sourcebook of American Indian Tradition, Based Upon the Music and Culture of 21 Tribes (book and cassette set), collected, edited, and adapted by Ruth De Cesare, Ph.D. (Alfred Publishing, 1988).

Dream Catchers (CD), Tokeya Inajin (Kevin Locke) (EarthBeat! Records, 1992).

INTRODUCTORY ACTIVITIES

DAY ONE

Objective: The students will read a letter written by Chief Seattle (1790–1866). They will discuss the meaning of the letter.

Curriculum subject: Language Arts or History

Begin the lesson by asking the students to close their eyes and lay down their heads. Play the song "Whispers on the Wind" by Tokeya Inajin (Kevin Locke) on the CD *Dream Catchers.* How did the music make you feel? Did the music sound like whispers on the wind? Why do you feel this way?

Teacher: Chief Seattle was a Native American who lived from 1790 to 1866. He was Chief of the Duwamish Indian Confederacy. The people of the Confederacy lived in the Pacific Northwest Coast.

White settlers began to move into the land where the Duwamish Indian Confederacy lived. The settlers needed more land to live in. The President of the United States, President Pierce, wanted to buy the land the Native Americans lived on. This is Chief Seattle's response.

As I read this letter, think about what Chief Seattle is saying. What is he trying to tell President Pierce? What kind of a person was Chief Seattle? Is his message important for us to listen to today? Why do you think so?

Read the book *Brother Eagle, Sister Sky: The Words of Chief Seattle* by Chief Seattle. The letter written by Chief Seattle is at the mid- to upper-fourth grade reading level. Students can read the story to the class.

DAY TWO

Story Lesson

Follow the *Presenting the Story Lesson* instructions in the Introduction. Each story lesson follows the same procedure; however, say the following in step 4:

"The title of the story we're reading today is *Chief Seattle*. What do you think the story is about? What do you already know about Chief Seattle?"

EXTENSION ACTIVITIES

1. Show the video *Pocahontas*. Before the movie begins, tell the students they will discuss these questions after the movie:

How does Pocahontas feel about owning land?

How do Pocahontas and her people feel about the land and animals? How do you know?

◆ After the movie, discuss the questions. Continue to contrast the attitude of the sailors to that of Pocahontas' tribe. What do the characters say that tells you how they feel? How do their actions tell you how they feel?

2. Throughout the week, practice the dances and music in *Myth, Music, and Dance of the American Indian: An Activity-Oriented Sourcebook of American Indian Tradition, Based Upon the Music and Culture of 21 Tribes*. This book and cassette set gives clear instructions in the music and dance of Native Americans. Practice a dance to perform for other classes.

3. *Native American Crafts Workshop* contains simple recipes for Native American foods. The students can make dried fruit and nut butter for snacks.

4. During Physical Education, play Native American games. *Book of American Indian Games* has a large selection of games requiring no equipment in Chapter 7. *American Indian Games and Crafts* also has many easy-to-play games.

5. For an art and music lesson, make a drum from an oatmeal box. Decorate the outside of the box with designs found in *American Indian Music and Musical Instruments: With Instructions for Making the Instruments,* pages 100–109. More advanced and older children might make some of the instruments described in the books.

CHIEF SEATTLE

Chief Seattle, or Seathl, was chief of the Duwamish Indian Confederacy. He was born in 1786.

Chief Seattle's father was also a chief. He taught Seattle to be peace-loving. As a young boy, Seattle learned to respect nature.

Chief Seattle saw the value of the Catholic religion preached by missionaries near his home. In the 1830s, Chief Seattle became a Christian.

One day the President of the United States asked Chief Seattle to sell his land. White settlers needed a place to live. The Chief agreed, and was the first to sign the Port Elliott Treaty. In the treaty, Chief Seattle promised to move his tribe to a reservation.

The settlers thanked Chief Seattle by naming a city after him; however, the Chief believed that people should not say the names of the dead. This would disturb their spirits. The settlers gave Chief Seattle many gifts. These gifts paid for all the times we say the name Seattle, and disturb the great Chief's spirit.

QUESTIONS FOR CHIEF SEATTLE

1. In what year was Chief Seattle born?

   _____

   _____

2. What did Seattle's father teach him?

   _____

   _____

3. What treaty did Chief Seattle sign?

   _____

   _____

4. How did the settlers thank Chief Seattle?

   _____

   _____

5. What did Chief Seattle's tribe do after he signed the Port Elliott Treaty?

   _____

   _____

6. What did the settlers give Chief Seattle before he died?

   _____

   _____

7. What one word best describes Chief Seattle?

   _____

   _____

8. According to the story, Chief Seattle became a Christian in the 1830s; however, at the end of his life he still held beliefs about the afterlife accepted by his people. What does this tell you about Chief Seattle's religious beliefs?

   _____

   _____

9. According to the story, Chief Seattle's father "taught Seattle to be peace-loving. As a young boy, Seattle learned to respect nature." Chief Seattle lived by the values taught to him by his father. Although he peacefully left his land to the settlers, he urged the white man to appreciate nature.
   Is what a father teaches his children important? Will children carry what they learn from their fathers into adulthood? Why do you think so?

   _____

   _____

10. Chief Seattle believed that to speak the name of the dead disturbs their resting spirits, but most of the settlers did not think that way.
    With this in mind, why do you think the settlers gave Chief Seattle gifts to gain permission to use his name for their city?

   _____

   _____

11. Write a title for the story. Use as few words as possible.

   _____

   _____

12. Imagine you are a chief of a large group of Native Americans. The President of the United States offers to buy your land for settlers.
    What would you do? How would your actions be like Chief Seattle's? How would they be different?

   _____

   _____

13. In your own words, give a brief summary of Chief Seattle's life.

   _____

   _____

14. What effect did Chief Seattle have on the attitudes of the settlers toward Native Americans? Why do you think so?

   _____

   _____

15. The story said, "Chief Seattle's father was also a chief." Is this a fact or an opinion? How can you prove your answer?

   _____

   _____

16. _____

   _____

Name _____   Date _____

BIBLIOGRAPHY

Alexander, Jane D., ed., "The Great Glass Controversy," *Nature/Science Annual* (1978), 106–115. Alexandria, Virginia: Time-Life Books, 1977.

"Art Restoration," *The Americana Annual* (1987), 119. Canada: Grolier Incorporated, 1987.

Alexander, Tom, "Mystery of Gravity Waves: Space Signals Hint at Black Holes Where Stars Vanish," *Nature/Science Annual* (1971), 116–124. New York: Time-Life Books, 1970.

"America's Oldest Skull," *Nature/Science Annual* (1970), 167. New York: Time-Life Books, 1969.

"An Aquatic Menace Spread by Canals," *Nature/Science Annual* (1975), 126–127. Alexandria, Virginia: Time-Life Books, 1974.

Asimov, Isaac, *Quasars, Pulsars and Black Holes.* Milwaukee: Gareth Stevens Publishing, 1988.

Bader, Barbara, *Aesop and Company: With Scenes From His Legendary Life.* Boston: Houghton Mifflin Company, 1991.

Calkins, Carroll C., project ed., *Reader's Digest: America From the Road,* pp. 270–271. Pleasantville, New York: The Reader's Digest Association, Inc., 1982.

Coates, C.W., "Catfish," *Encyclopedia Americana* (1963), 6, 49–50.

Dempewolff, Richard F., "Roadeo: No Cowboys Allowed," *Our Wonderful World: An Encyclopedic Anthology for the Entire Family* (1962), 10, 314–316.

"Fables of Aesop," *Encyclopedia Americana* (1963), 10, 692–693.

Ferris, Jeri, *Arctic Explorer: The Story of Matthew Henson.* Minneapolis, Minnesota: Carolrhoda Books, Inc., 1989.

Hawking, Stephen, *Black Holes and Baby Universes.* New York: Bantam Books, 1993.

Kemp, Peter, *The Oxford Companion to Ships and the Sea,* p. 744. New York: Oxford University Press, 1976.

Kingman, Lee, ed., *Newbery and Caldecott Medal Books: 1976–1985.* Boston, Mass.: Horn Book, 1986.

Peterson, Linda Kauffman, and Marilyn Leathers Solt, *Newbery and Caldecott Medal and Honor Books: An Annotated Biography.* Boston, Mass.: G.K. Hall, 1982.

Reader's Digest Editorial Staff, *Strange Stories, Amazing Facts of America's Past,* p. 59. Pleasantville, New York: Reader's Digest Association, 1989.

"Seattle (Seathl)," *People Who Made America,* 16, 1242. Skokie, IL: United States History Society, Inc., 1973.

"What Causes Earthquake Warning Lights?," *Nature/Science Annual* (1978), 176. Alexandria, Virginia: Time-Life Books, 1977.

READING LEVEL 5

ROBERT J. ACOSTA: TEACHER

ABOUT THE STORY

The story tells about Robert J. Acosta, who helped improve the education of the blind. Acosta founded The Blind College Students of Southern California, The Blind Teachers of California, and Future Teachers of America.

PREVIEW WORDS

Robert J. Acosta   blind   handicapped
United States Junior Chamber of Commerce
America's Ten Outstanding Young Men
Future Teachers of America

PRIOR TO THE LESSON

Look for a blind volunteer to visit the class. The volunteer might be from the Light House for the Blind, or a representative of the school district's Special Education Department. Ask the volunteer to bring equipment used by the blind to help them read and write.

THROUGHOUT THE WEEK—Read the following books to the class:

Martin, Jr., Bill, and John Archambault, *Knots on a Counting Rope.* New York: Henry Holt, 1987. A Reading Rainbow Book.

Gellman, Ellie, *Jeremy's Dreidel.* Rockville, MD: Kar-Ben Copies, 1992.

BOOKS TO READ

Mom Can't See Me, Sally Hobart Alexander (Collier Macmillan, 1990).

Seeing in Special Ways: Children Living With Blindness, Thomas Bergman (Gareth Stevens, 1988).

The Velveteen Rabbit or How Toys Become Real, Margery Williams (New York: Grosset & Dunlap, 1993). Text in braille and in clear black type.

Maggie by My Side, Beverly Butler (Dodd, Mead, 1987).

The Man Who Sang in the Dark, Eth Clifford (Houghton Mifflin, 1987).

Patrick, Yes You Can, Patricia Dendtler Frevert (Creative Education, 1983).

Jeremy's Dreidel, Ellie Gellman (Kar-Ben Copies, 1992).

Jenny's Magic Wand, Helen and Bill Hermann (Franklin Watts, 1988).

The Value of Determination, Ann Donegan Johnson (Value Communications, 1976).

Louis Braille, Stephen Keeler (Bookwright Press, 1986).

Naomi Knows It's Springtime, Virginia L. Kroll (Caroline House, Boyds Mills Press, 1993).

Knots on a Counting Rope, Bill Martin (Henry Holt, 1987). A Reading Rainbow Book.

"Seeing" in the Dark, Elizabeth Rider Montgomery (Garrard Publishing, 1979).

Dear Dr. Bell ... Your Friend, Helen Keller, Judith St. George (Putnam's, 1992).

The Power of Overcoming: Featuring the Story of Helen Keller, Virginia Swenson and Lawrence Tamblyn (Eagle Systems International, 1981).

Valiant Companions, Helen Elmira Waite (Macrae Smith Co., 1959).

Blindness, Malcolm E. Weiss (Franklin Watts, 1980).

Connie's New Eyes, Bernard Wolf (Lippincott, 1976)

Perkins: The Cat Who Was More Than a Friend, Linda Yeatman (Barron's, 1988).

VIDEOS

The Miracle Worker, Culver City, CA: MGM/UA Home Video, 1992, 1962. Length: 107 minutes.

CDS, RECORDS, AND CASSETTES

Look in your local library in the juvenile section for talking books. Many children's stories are on tape. The students can listen to the stories without pictures, and still enjoy the stories. Blind students also enjoy these tapes.

INTRODUCTORY ACTIVITIES

DAY ONE

Objective: The students will listen to a speaker explain what it is like to be blind. The speaker will demonstrate equipment that helps the blind read and write.

Curriculum subject: Social Studies

Before the speaker arrives, help the students make a who, what, when, where, and why question list to ask the speaker. Write the questions on chart paper. Such questions might include:

Who is called legally blind?

What do the blind use to read and write?

When do you use a seeing eye dog?

Where do you go to learn to read braille?

Why do you use a white cane?

Ask the speaker to demonstrate special equipment used by the blind to read and write. Also, ask the speaker to talk about her or his education, work, and daily life. Did he or she go to a special school? How did the sighted children treat him or her? How does this person get to work? Is it hard to have a job without sight? How does the speaker dress in the morning and match his or her clothes? End the class with a question-and-answer session.

DAY TWO

Story Lesson

Follow the *Presenting the Story Lesson* instructions in the Introduction. Each story lesson follows the same procedure; however, say the following in step 4:

"The title of the story we're reading today is *Robert J. Acosta: Teacher.* What do you think the story is about? What do you already know about teachers?"

EXTENSION ACTIVITIES

1. Contact a teacher who works with blind students. Arrange a pen pal correspondence between the students. Ask the teacher how to send the messages. Could you use computers, audiotapes, any other means? Use the best system for the students involved.

2. Send audiocassette letters to blind personalities. The public library can help you find the mailing addresses. Some personalities might be:

   ◆ Robert J. Acosta

   ◆ Stevie Wonder

   ◆ José Feliciano

   ◆ Ray Charles

3. The students will record audiotapes of picture books.

   ◆ Check out several picture books from the library.

   ◆ The students close their eyes and lay down their heads.

   ◆ Read each story. After each story, ask the students which books drew pictures in their imagination, and did not require pictures to understand the story.

   ◆ Break the students into groups. Assign each group a book.

   ◆ Play a recording of an old radio show that uses sound effects to help tell the story. Tell the students to listen to how the storyteller uses these sounds.

   ◆ The students will practice reading the story. They add sound effects as they practice. For example, they can tap their shoes when a character in the story walks across the room.

   ◆ After they practice, each group records its story, with sound effects.

   ◆ Play the tape for the class.

   ◆ Donate the tape to the Light House for the Blind or a class for young blind students.

ROBERT J. ACOSTA: TEACHER

In 1939, Robert J. Acosta was born blind. When he grew up, his love for education would touch every teacher and student in America.

Robert worked hard to live in a world that called a blind man handicapped. He knew he needed a good education. He finished high school and college. He earned degrees in English and social studies. Robert became a teacher.

Robert began groups for blind teachers and students. In these groups, blind teachers and students could reach out to one another and share their ideas. In 1968, the United States Junior Chamber of Commerce named Robert J. Acosta one of America's Ten Outstanding Young Men.

Robert did not stop there. He went on to start a group called the Future Teachers of America. Any student in the United States who wanted to become a teacher followed her or his dreams by joining Future Teachers. Little did they know that a blind man was leading the way.

QUESTIONS FOR ROBERT J. ACOSTA: TEACHER

1. When was Robert J. Acosta born?

   _____

   _____

2. Could Robert J. Acosta see when he was born?

   _____

   _____

3. Name the degrees Acosta earned in college.

   _____

   _____

4. When was Acosta named one of America's Ten Outstanding Young Men?

   _____

   _____

5. What did Acosta become after college?

   _____

   _____

6. What group did Acosta start after he was named one of America's Ten Outstanding Young Men?

   _____

   _____

7. What one word best describes Robert J. Acosta?

   _____

   _____

8. How did Robert Acosta feel about earning an education? Why do you think so?

   _____

   _____

9. How would joining Future Teachers of America help a student who wanted to be a teacher?

_____

_____

10. Why did Acosta begin groups for blind teachers and students?

_____

_____

11. Write a title for the story. Use as few words as possible.

_____

_____

12. How is teaching blind students like teaching sighted students? How is it different?

_____

_____

13. In your own words, tell how Acosta's love for education touched every teacher and student in America.

_____

_____

14. How does the story about Robert J. Acosta change your ideas about the blind? Why do you feel this way?

_____

_____

15. The story said, "He (Robert Acosta) knew he needed a good education." Is this a fact or someone's opinion? How can you prove your answer?

_____

_____

16.

_____

_____

Name _____   Date _____

COLUMBUS'S MYSTERIOUS LIGHT

ABOUT THE STORY

On Thursday, October 11, 1492, Columbus and his crew searched the night for any sign of land. At ten o'clock, Columbus saw a light to the west. It looked like a candle flame slowly rising and falling. Was this someone walking along the beach waiting to welcome Columbus ashore? The next morning, Columbus's men reached land; however, there were no candles. What was Columbus's mysterious light?

PREVIEW WORDS

Columbus   Caribbean   Pinta

THROUGHOUT THE WEEK—The students will follow Christopher Columbus's log throughout the week. They will prepare a daily news report on his voyage. Each day, read to the students from Columbus's log, but do not read the entry of Thursday, October 11, 1492, until the story lesson day. Both of the following books are excellent children's books. *I, Columbus: My Journal—1492–93* contains more details and longer passages, however.

Roop, Peter and Connie, editors, *I, Columbus: My Journal—1492–93.* New York: Walker, 1990.

Columbus, Christopher, *The Log of Christopher Columbus* (selections by Steve Lowe). New York: Philomel Books, 1992.

PRIOR TO THE LESSON

Make a bulletin board depicting a large map of the Atlantic Ocean between Spain and the Caribbean. Make a dotted line along the path Columbus took on his voyage. Copy, cut out, and color the drawing of the Santa Maria. Pin the ship at Palos, Spain. As the students follow Columbus's log each day, move the ship along the dotted line. Maps can be found in:

Roop, Peter and Connie, editors, *I, Columbus: My Journal—1492–93,* inside front cover.

Pelta, Kathy, *Discovering Christopher Columbus: How History Is Invented.* Minneapolis: Lerner Publications, 1991, page 85.

Anderson, Joan, *Christopher Columbus: From Vision to Voyage.* New York: Dial Books for Young Readers, 1991, page 42–43.

Santa Maria:

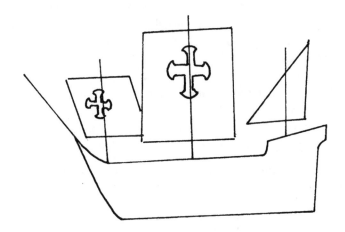

BOOKS TO READ

A Picture Book of Christopher Columbus, David A. Adler (Holiday House, 1991).

Christopher Columbus: From Vision to Voyage, Joan Anderson (Dial Books for Young Readers, 1992).

Christopher Columbus: Navigator to the New World, Isaac Asimov (Gareth Stevens Children's Books, 1991).

The Log of Christopher Columbus: The First Voyage, Spring, Summer, and Fall 1492, Christopher Columbus (Philomel Books, 1992).

Pedro's Journal: A Voyage With Christopher Columbus, Pam Conrad and Peter Koeppen (Caroline House, 1991).

Westward With Columbus, John Dyson and Peter Christopher (Scholastic, 1991).

Where Do You Think You're Going, Christopher Columbus, Jean Fritz (Putnam's, 1980).

Christopher Columbus: A Great Explorer, Carol Greene (Childrens Press, 1989).

The Tainos: The People Who Welcomed Columbus, Francine Jacobs (Putnam's, 1992).

The Value of Curiosity: The Story of Christopher Columbus, Spencer Johnson. (Value Communications, 1977).

In 1492, Jean Marzollo (Scholastic, 1991).

Discovering Christopher Columbus: How History is Invented, Kathy Pelta (Lerner Publications, 1991).

Christopher Columbus: Recognizing Stereotypes, Bonnie Szumski (Greenhaven Press, 1992).

INTRODUCTORY ACTIVITIES

DAY ONE

Objective: The students will prepare to write their news reports on Columbus's voyage.

Curriculum subject: Language Arts

Teacher: Throughout the week, we'll learn about the voyage of Christopher Columbus. Look at the map on the bulletin board. It took many days to sail from Spain to the New World. No one knew if Columbus would find land or fall off the end of the earth.

Imagine living in the time of Columbus. Would people be as interested in his voyage as we are in the voyages of our space program? When the astronauts landed on the moon, everyone around the world watched their televisions for the latest news. How is the way people felt about Columbus's voyage in 1492 like the way people feel today about space exploration?

Imagine if there had been television news in 1492. What would the news stories about Columbus sound like? Every day we'll give a news report on Columbus's voyage as if it were happening today.

Break into groups. I'll give each group a news assignment. You will prepare your report, and be ready to give your report like a television reporter.

Assign each group one of the following stories. The students will update their stories each day of the voyage.

1. How It All Began: Why Columbus Thinks the World Is Round.

2. An Interview with Queen Isabella and King Ferdinand.

3. Today's Weather: How the Weather Is Affecting the Voyage.

4. A Man-on-the-Street Report: How Do the People of Spain Feel about Columbus and His Voyage?

5. An Interview with Christopher Columbus.

6. An Interview with the Crew: The Voyage from the Crew's Viewpoint.

7. An Editorial (Students will write their own title).

8. How Are the Crew's Family Holding Up?

The students begin by organizing their report, and planning the presentation. Give the students time each day to prepare their reports. End the day with a news report on the latest developments of the voyage of Columbus.

DAY TWO

Story Lesson

Before beginning the story lesson, read Thursday, October 11, 1492, from Columbus's log.

Follow the *Presenting the Story Lesson* instructions in the Introduction. Each story lesson follows the same procedure; however, say the following in step 4:

"The title of the story we're reading today is *Columbus's Mysterious Light*. What do you think the story is about? What do you already know about Columbus and the light?"

EXTENSION ACTIVITIES

1. The students will make a model of the Niña, Pinta, or Santa Maria.

◆ Let the students look at books about Columbus that have detailed pictures of Columbus's ships. A picture of the Niña is in *Christopher Columbus: Navigator of the New World* by Isaac Asimov, pages 18–19.

◆ Make several art mediums available to the students, such as clay, paper, paint, or construction paper.

◆ Using the material of their choice, the students will use their imagination and creativity to make a model of one of Columbus's ships.

2. According to Columbus's log, Tuesday, September 4, 1492, Columbus loaded the ship with water and "dried meat and salted fish, and some fruits." Bring these foods to class. The students will sample the menu from Columbus's ship. They will imagine what it would be like to eat these foods every day of the voyage.

3. In the voice of a crew member, the students will write a letter home on Monday, September 24, 1492. Read this entry for Columbus's log to the students. What would the crew members tell their loved ones in their letters? The students can address their letters to a wife, child, friend, or parent.

COLUMBUS'S MYSTERIOUS LIGHT

Columbus and his crew almost gave up hope of surviving the voyage. Nearly a month passed, and land was nowhere in sight.

On the night of October 11, 1492, Columbus thought he saw the light of a candle flame in the distance. The candle slowly rose up and down. Was this the light of a fisherman waiting to greet the tired crew?

Four hours later, the cannon of the Pinta fired. "Land!" cried the men. Columbus believed the light he saw in the night was from the land.

The next morning Columbus went ashore, but found no candles. No one had stood on the shore during the night. What was the light he saw just the night before? Was it a spirit guiding them to safety?

Some people believe the light was a fireworm. Fireworms live in the waters of the Caribbean. Forty minutes after sunset, and before the rising of the moon, fireworms swim to the surface and glow in the night. In the darkest hours, their shining bodies float on the rippling water.

QUESTIONS FOR COLUMBUS'S MYSTERIOUS LIGHT

1. What did Columbus think he saw on the night of October 11, 1492?

   _____

   _____

2. Did Columbus find candles when he went ashore the next morning?

   _____

   _____

3. What do some people believe made the light Columbus saw that night?

   _____

   _____

4. Where do fireworms live?

   _____

   _____

5. Which happened first: the cannon on the Pinta fired, or Columbus saw a mysterious light?

   _____

   _____

6. What do the fireworms do forty minutes after sunset?

   _____

   _____

7. How do you think Columbus felt about the light when he learned that no one had stood on shore with a candle?

   _____

   _____

8. Columbus thought the light on the shore was a candle. Why didn't he realize it was a fireworm?

   _____

   _____

9. Astronauts see strange lights from the space shuttle. In the future, do you think people will learn a simple explanation for these lights? Why do you think so?

_____

_____

10. Why do you think fireworms glow?

_____

_____

11. Write a title for the story. Use as few words as possible.

_____

_____

12. How are fireworms and fireflies alike? How are they different?

_____

_____

13. In as few words as possible, tell what fireworms do at night.

_____

_____

14. How would the fireworms' behavior change if someone shined bright lights on the water all night long?

_____

_____

15. The story said, "Columbus believed the light he saw in the night was from the land." Is this a fact or Columbus's opinion? Why do you think so?

_____

_____

16.

_____

_____

Name _____   Date _____

THE REMARKABLE LIFE OF HOWARD HUGHES

ABOUT THE STORY

Howard Hughes, Jr., was born in 1905. At the age of nineteen, Howard Hughes took over his father's small family business. After years of hard work, the business grew into the multimillion-dollar Hughes Aircraft Company. Howard Hughes also wrote, produced, and directed hit movies. He set records flying in his own planes. At the end of his life, Howard Hughes all but disappeared. Rumors of his secret life ended with his death in 1976.

PREVIEW WORDS

Howard Hughes, Jr.   mechanics   Spruce Goose

multimillion-dollar

THROUGHOUT THE WEEK—Read the Newbery Award book *Lincoln: A Photobiography* by Russell Freedman (New York: Clarion Books, 1987) to the class. When someone asks us to name any president, we usually say the name Abraham Lincoln. Something about Lincoln's personality, as well as his place in history, puts him in a class by himself. As you read the story, ask the students to think about the question, "What made Lincoln such an interesting and memorable person and president?"

BOOKS TO READ

The Amazing Paper Cuttings of Hans Christian Andersen, Beth Wagner Brust (Ticknor & Fields, 1994).

Abraham Lincoln, Ingri and Edgar Parin D'Aulaire (Doubleday, 1987).

Lincoln: A Photobiography, Russell Freedman (Clarion Books, 1987).

George Washington: A Picture Book Biography, James Giblin (Scholastic, 1992).

The Will and the Way, Karen E. Hudson and Paul R. Williams (Rizzoli, 1994).

General H. Norman Schwarzkopf, Robert Italia (Rockbottom Books, 1992).

Martin Luther King, Jr.: A Man and His Dream, Stuart A. Kallen (Abdo & Daughters, 1993).

Princess Diana: Royal Ambassador, Renora Licata (Blackbirch Press, 1993).

Nolan Ryan: Strikeout King, Howard Reiser (Childrens Press, 1993).

Deion Sanders: Prime Time Player, Stew Thornley (Lerner Publications, 1993).

Anne Frank, Beyond the Diary: A Photographic Remembrance, Rian Verhoeven (Viking, 1993).

A Weekend With Leonardo da Vinci, Rosabianca Skira-Venturi (Rizzoli, 1993).

INTRODUCTORY ACTIVITIES

DAY ONE

Objective: The students will list famous people of the past and present who have qualities that set them above others in their field. They will list the attributes that all these people share.

Curriculum subject: Social Studies

Teacher: During the week, we'll read biographies about famous people. We'll focus on people of the past and present who have qualities that set them above others in their field. Name a president. (More than likely the students will name Lincoln and Washington.) No one named William McKinley, yet—like Abraham Lincoln and John F. Kennedy—McKinley was killed by an assassin. Why do we remember Lincoln and Kennedy, but not McKinley?

Let's make a list of famous people from the past or present. Remember, they must have qualities that set them above others in their fields.

(Help the students by naming general topics such as athletes, authors, artists, teachers, presidents, scientists, royalty. Write the names the students list on chart paper.) Now look closely at our list. All these people must have something in common that allows them to be on the same list. What common characteristics do these people have? (Write the list of characteristics on another piece of chart paper.)

Think about someone you'd like to learn about who has qualities that set him or her above others in the same field. You might choose a person on this list, or you might want someone else. In a few days, you'll write a biography about the person you choose.

DAY TWO

Story Lesson

Follow the *Presenting the Story Lesson* instructions in the Introduction. Each story lesson follows the same procedure; however, say the following in step 4:

"The title of the story we're reading today is *The Remarkable Life of Howard Hughes*. What do you think the story is about? What do you already know about Howard Hughes?"

EXTENSION ACTIVITIES

1. The students will choose a subject for a biography. The person must meet the criteria the students listed on Day One.

◆ The students will write an outline of the events of their subject's life. They will write the events in chronological order.

2. In the voices of their subjects, the students will write biographies of the people they chose. For example:

My name is Howard Hughes. My life has been full of adventure, fortune, and fame. It wasn't easy, but it was fun. Life should be fun.

◆ The subject should not only tell about the events of his or her life, but also tell about how he or she felt during his or her life. How did Lincoln feel when he won the election to become president? How did he feel when he had to send troops into battle? The final biography should give insight into the subject's reactions to his or her life.

3. Hold a "Living Hall of Fame."

◆ Each student will dress like the subject of his or her biography. They can use their parents' old clothes, or they can make paper hats and other accessories.

◆ Send groups of four students to the front of the class. They will strike a pose, and freeze like wax figures.

◆ The students will take turns coming out of their poses and reading their biographies. When each student finishes the biography, he or she will return to the pose and freeze.

◆ If possible, send the groups of four students to other classes in lower grades to perform the "Living Hall of Fame."

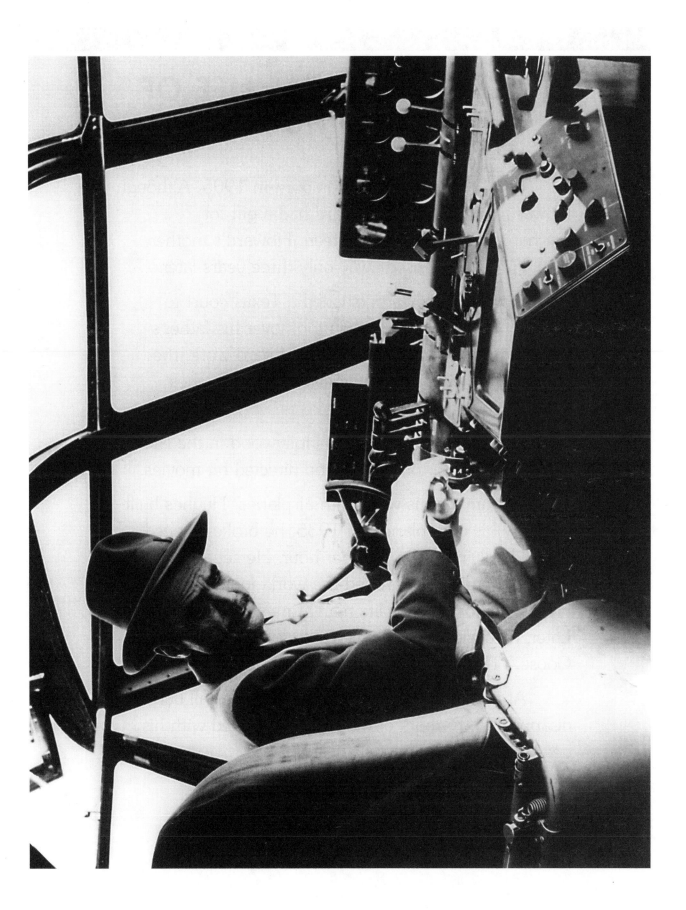

THE REMARKABLE LIFE OF HOWARD HUGHES

Howard Hughes, Jr., was born in 1905. Although he was a poor student, Howard had a gift for mechanics. When he was sixteen, Howard's mother died. His father passed away only three years later.

Howard Hughes persuaded a Texas court to declare him an adult. He then took over his father's small family business. After years of hard work, the business grew into the multimillion-dollar Hughes Aircraft Company.

Howard Hughes went to Hollywood in the late 1920s. He wrote, produced, and directed hit movies.

Continuing his work with airplanes, Hughes built and flew his own planes. In 1935, he broke a speed record by flying 352 miles per hour. He set another record when he flew around the world in 91 hours. Hughes almost lost his life many times as a test pilot. Later, he designed and built the famous "Spruce Goose." This huge plane flew only once.

At the end of his life, Howard Hughes all but disappeared. Rumors of his secret life ended with his death in 1976.

QUESTIONS FOR
THE REMARKABLE LIFE OF HOWARD HUGHES

1. In what year was Howard Hughes, Jr., born?

   _____

   _____

2. What was the name of Howard Hughes's company?

   _____

   _____

3. What did Howard Hughes do in Hollywood?

   _____

   _____

4. How many hours did it take Howard Hughes to fly around the world?

   _____

   _____

5. What happened to his father's small family business after Howard Hughes took it over?

   _____

   _____

6. What did Howard Hughes do first: write, produce, and direct hit movies, or break a speed record by flying 352 miles per hour?

   _____

   _____

7. What one word best describes Howard Hughes? Why do you think so?

   _____

   _____

8. Was Howard Hughes an intelligent man? Why do you think so?

   _____

   _____

9. Howard Hughes led a remarkable life. Will his life and accomplishments continue to interest people in the future? Why do you think so?

_____

_____

10. Why do you think Howard Hughes tried to break so many flying speed records?

_____

_____

11. Write a title for the story. Use as few words as possible.

_____

_____

12. How is breaking a speed record by flying 352 miles per hour like setting a record by flying around the world in 91 days? How is it different?

_____

_____

13. In your own words, tell about the speed records set by Howard Hughes.

_____

_____

14. Howard Hughes was only nineteen years old when the courts declared him an adult. He then took over his father's business. How do you think this affected Howard Hughes's life?

_____

_____

15. The story said, "Howard had a gift for mechanics." Is this a fact or an opinion? How can you prove your answer?

_____

_____

16.

_____

_____

Name _____   Date _____

THE BATTLE OF THE IRONCLADS

ABOUT THE STORY

America's iron ships are famous throughout the world. However, America's first ironclad ships turned their guns on each other. During the Civil War, the South built the Merrimack, and the North built the Monitor. The story tells about the battle between America's ironclads which ended in a draw.

PREVIEW WORDS

ironclad	Merrimack	Monitor
Abraham Lincoln	John Ericsson	crewman

THROUGHOUT THE WEEK—Read the book *Bull Run* by Paul Fleischman (New York: HarperCollins Publishers, 1993) to the class. The book tells the story of the battle of Bull Run through the eyes of sixteen different people, each with his or her own personal insight.

Play music from the original soundtrack recording *The Civil War: A Film by Ken Burns* (New York: Elektra Entertainment, 1990) as the students enter and leave the classroom, and as they do their seat work.

BOOKS TO READ

Ironclads of the Civil War, Frank R. Donovan (American Heritage, 1964).

Runaway Balloon: The Last Flight of Confederate Air Force One, Burke Davis (Coward, McCann & Geoghegan, 1976).

Duel Between the First Ironclads, William C. Davis (Doubleday, 1975).

Addy's Cookbook: A Peek at Dining in the Past, With Meals You Can Cook Today, Jodi Evert, Susan Mahal, and Mark Salisbury (Pleasant Co. Publications, 1994).

Bull Run, Paul Fleischman (HarperCollins, 1993).

Across Five Aprils, Irene Hunt (Follett, 1964). Newbery Medal Honor Book.

The Civil War to the Last Frontier: 1850-1880's, William Loren Katz (Raintree Steck-Vaughn, 1993).

The Story of John Brown's Raid on Harpers Ferry, Zachary Kent (Childrens Press, 1988).

Honest Abe, Edith Kunhardt (Greenwillow Books, 1993).

Unconditional Surrender: U.S. Grant and the Civil War, Albert Marrin (Maxwell Macmillan International, 1994).

Christmas in the Big House, Christmas in the Quarters, Pat McKissack (Scholastic, 1994).

Voices From the Civil War, edited by Milton Meltzer (Thomas Crowell, 1989).

The Long Road to Gettysburg, Jim Murphy (Clarion Books, 1992).

A Naval History of the Civil War, Howard P. Nash, Jr. (A.S. Barnes, 1972).

The 290, Scott O'Dell (Houghton Mifflin, 1976).

Pink and Say, Patricia Polacco, (Philomel Books, 1994).

Changes for Addy: A Winter Story, Connie Rose Porter (Pleasant Co., 1994).

Addy Learns a Lesson: A School Story, Connie Rose Porter (Pleasant Co., 1993).

Behind Rebel Lines: The Incredible Story of Emma Edmonds, Civil War Spy, Seymour Reit
 (Harcourt Brace Jovanovich, 1988).

The Story of the Monitor and the Merrimac, R. Conrad Stein (Childrens Press, 1983).

VIDEOS

Random House Video: Newbery Video Collection: Across Five Aprils, Irene Hunt (Newbery
 Award Records, 1986). Length: Part 1 - 14:35 minutes, Part 2 - 14:45 minutes.

CDS, RECORDS, AND CASSETTES

The Civil War: A Film by Ken Burns, Original Soundtrack (CD) (Elektra Entertainment, 1990).

INTRODUCTORY ACTIVITIES

DAY ONE

Objective: The students will watch a video of the Newbery Medal Honor book *Across Five Aprils.*
Curriculum subject: Language Arts or History
Teacher: Throughout the week we'll learn about the Civil War. The Civil War is the only time
 in our history when Americans entered into war against one another. Family members living in the North went into battle wondering if the person they were shooting
 at was a relative living in the South. What was once a country joined together to
 fight for a common cause in the American Revolution was suddenly divided by a war
 that killed a staggering number of fellow countrymen.

 Before we learn about some of the interesting events of the war, we'll listen to a story
 about a family caught between family loyalty and loyalty to their country. After the
 film, we'll talk about the problems created by the Civil War. How were the problems
 faced by families during the Civil War like those of wars fought against other countries, like World War II? How were the problems of the families different in the Civil
 War? We'll talk about these comparisons after the movie.

Show the movie *Across Five Aprils* by Irene Hunt (Random House Video: Newbery
Video Collection, 1986) or read the Newbery Honor Book *Across Five Aprils* by Irene Hunt
(Chicago: Follett Publishing Co., 1964). After the story, discuss how the Civil War affected the
families of soldiers. Next, compare the problems faced by these families to those faced by families during the time of World War II.

DAY TWO

Story Lesson
Follow the *Presenting the Story Lesson* instructions in the Introduction. Each story lesson follows the same procedure; however, say the following in step 4:

"The title of the story we're reading today is *The Battle of the Ironclads.* What do you
think the story is about?" If the students mention the Civil War, ask, "What do you already know
about the Civil War?"

EXTENSION ACTIVITIES

1. Read *The Story of the Monitor and the Merrimac* to the class.

◆ The story said, "The first clash between armored ships became one of history's most important sea battles." Why was this an important battle? How can we see the effects of this battle when we look at modern warships?

2. The students will exchange letters, taking on the personas of the characters in *Bull Run* by Paul Fleischman.

◆ Divide the students into pairs (Student A and Student B). If there is an odd number of students, take one student as your partner.

◆ Assign each person a character from *Bull Run*. Although a character might be repeated in the class, each student in the pair must have a different character.

◆ On the first day, Student A will write a letter to Student B in the voice and personality of his or her character as homework. Student A will tell Student B about the Battle of Bull Run as he or she experienced it.

◆ On the second day, Student B will respond to Student A's letter in the voice and personality of his or her character.

◆ Continue the correspondences over several days.

3. The students will sample recipes from the time of the Civil War.

◆ Read pages 1–3 from *Addy's Cook Book: A Peek at Dining in the Past, With Meals You Can Cook Today*. Compare Addy's kitchen and cooking utensils with modern kitchens and utensils. How are they alike? How are they different?

◆ Prepare foods from the cook book, and serve them during an Emancipation Party (*Addy's Cook Book,* pages 42–44).

THE BATTLE OF THE IRONCLADS

America's iron ships are famous throughout the world; however, America's first ironclad ships turned their guns on each other.

During the Civil War, the South built the Merrimack. The Merrimack was a wooden ship 275 feet long. To protect the ship, they covered its body with iron, and armed it with ten guns.

In concern for the Northern fleet, Abraham Lincoln asked John Ericsson to make an ironclad ship. Ericsson built a 172-foot-long ship with a round, rotating gun house. He named his ironclad the Monitor.

The Merrimack and Monitor met on March 9, 1862. The fight began at 8 A.M., and lasted all morning. Every crewman lived, and each ship suffered only a few injuries after four hours of fighting. The first battle of the ironclads ended without a winner.

On May 11, 1862, the South burned the Merrimack after losing the war. The Monitor sank in a storm on December 31, 1862.

QUESTIONS FOR THE BATTLE OF THE IRONCLADS

1. What were the names of the ironclad ships that were the first to meet in battle?

   _____

   _____

2. In what war does the story take place?

   _____

   _____

3. Whom did Abraham Lincoln ask to make the ironclad ship for the North?

   _____

   _____

4. What day did the Merrimack and Monitor meet in battle?

   _____

   _____

5. Which ship was built first, the Monitor or the Merrimack?

   _____

   _____

6. What did Abraham Lincoln do after he learned about the Merrimack?

   _____

   _____

7. Reread paragraph four. How well did the iron protect the ships? Why do you think so?

   _____

   _____

8. The Monitor was built with a round, rotating gun house. How would this help the ship in battle?

   _____

   _____

9. Searchers found the Monitor in 1974. What do you think will happen to the Monitor? Why do you think so?

_____

_____

10. Why do you think the South burned the Merrimack after losing the war?

_____

_____

11. Write a title for the story. Use as few words as possible.

_____

_____

12. How were the Monitor and Merrimack alike? How were they different?

_____

_____

13. In your own words, tell about the battle of the Merrimack and the Monitor.

_____

_____

14. What effect did the Monitor and Merrimack have on modern warship design?

_____

_____

15. The story said, "America's iron ships are famous throughout the world." Is this a fact or the author's opinion? Why do you think so?

_____

_____

16.

_____

_____

Name _____   Date _____

HOW FAST THE TREES GROW

ABOUT THE STORY

Oliver L. Phillips and Alwyn H. Gentry watch trees in tropical forests. Since the 1950s, Phillips and Gentry have watched for forests to thicken or thin out. Phillips and Gentry found that the life cycle of trees in tropical forests is speeding up. They found faster life cycles in trees around the world. The speed with which seedlings grow to adults and die has doubled over the past thirty-eight years.

PREVIEW WORDS

Oliver L. Phillips	Alwyn H. Gentry	seedlings
tropical	life cycle	carbon dioxide
oxygen	inhale	exhale

THROUGHOUT THE WEEK—Read the book *Julie's Tree* by Mary Calhoun (New York: Harper & Row, Publishers, 1988) to the class. The story tells about a shy girl who speaks out to save an old tree that the city wants to cut down.

PRIOR TO THE LESSON

Contact a volunteer from the National Arbor Day Foundation in your area. Contact the National Arbor Day Foundation at 100 Arbor Avenue, Nebraska City, NE 68410, to find your local chapter. Ask the volunteer to talk to your class about the purpose of the National Arbor Day Foundation, and the activities the Foundation is involved in. Discuss the content of the lesson with the volunteer so that you can prepare an introduction.

BOOKS TO READ

Giants in the Land, Diana Karter Appelbaum (Houghton Mifflin, 1993).

Julie's Tree, Mary Calhoun (Harper & Row, 1988).

Ring of Tall Trees, John Dowd (Alaska Northwest Books, 1992).

The Birthday Tree, Paul Fleischman (Harpertrophy, 1991, c1979).

Trees, Linda Gamlin (Dorling Kindersley, 1993).

If the Trees Could Talk, Stuart A. Kallen (AbDO & Daughters, 1993).

Be a Friend to Trees, Patricia Lauber (HarperCollins, 1994).

Trees of North America, David More, Alan Mitchell, and Angela Royston (Thunder Bay Press, 1994).

Yosemite National Park, David Petersen (Childrens Press, 1993).

The Tree Almanac: A Year-Round Activity Guide, Monica Russo (Sterling, 1993).

The Oak, Andrienne Soutter-Perrot (Creative Education, 1993).

VIDEOS

Dawn Saves the Trees, Tina Stern, Gina Scheerer, Noel Black, and Mary Pleshette (Distributed by Kid Vision, 1993). Length: 30 minutes.

INTRODUCTORY ACTIVITIES

DAY ONE

Objective: The students will photograph, map, and take leaf samples from trees around and near the school.
Curriculum subject: Science

Before the lesson, draw a map outlining the layout of the school and surrounding area. Draw and label the buildings, sidewalks, play areas, and parking lots. Do not include drawings of the trees. The students will fill in the trees as they go for their walk.

Teacher: This week we'll learn about trees and the important role trees play in our environment. Trees not only provide shade and beauty but also help to clean our air, provide shelter for wildlife, and tell us when air pollution is becoming a danger.
Today we'll photograph trees around our school. We'll count the number of trees, take a leaf sample from each tree, and mark their locations on a map.

1. Take the students for a walk around the school.
2. Let the students take turns photographing each tree, using a Polaroid camera.
3. Clip off one leaf from the tree, and put it in an envelope with the photograph. Label the envelope Tree 1.
4. The students will draw a circle on the map of the school at the location of the tree, and label the circle Tree 1.
5. Repeat steps 1 to 4 for every tree in the area.

DAY TWO

Objective: The students will make a catalogue of the trees around their school.
Curriculum subject: Science

Tree Catalogue
Materials

◆ Envelopes collected on Day One
◆ Construction paper
◆ Notebook paper
◆ Flower press
◆ Glue stick
◆ Map drawn on Day One
◆ *Picture Guide to Tree Leaves* by Raymond Wiggers (New York: Franklin Watts, 1991)

Procedure

1. Display the map drawn on Day One at the front of the class.
2. Break the students into groups. There should be one group for each envelope collected yesterday.

3. Using the *Picture Guide to Tree Leaves* the students will identify their trees.

4. At the top of a piece of white paper, the students will write their tree name and number. For example:

Sugar Maple
Tree 4

5. The students will set their leaf on the paper.

6. Starting with Tree 1, set the paper into the flower press. Set the next leaf from Tree 2 on its paper, and stack it on the leaf from Tree 1. Continue stacking so that each leaf is between sheets of paper. Finally, place a blank page on the last leaf. Set the top of the flower press on top of the last page, and tighten the screws.

7. The students will mount the picture of their tree on the top half of the construction paper, leaving space to glue in the leaf after it dries. Label the page according to the name of the tree, the tree number, and the date of the photograph.

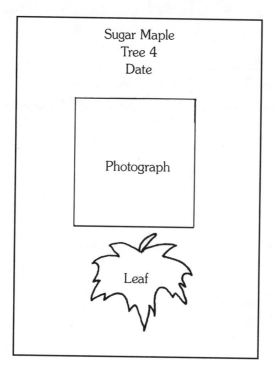

8. The students will write a short description of the tree on a piece of notebook paper. They will include the height at maturity, the expected life span, insect problems, and so on.

9. The students will write in the names of the trees in the circle on the map with their tree number.

10. After the leaves remain in the press for the required time period, glue the leaves under their photographs.

11. Punch notebook holes into the right side of the construction paper on which the photographs are mounted. Insert the pages into a notebook, facing the photograph page toward the notebook paper page.

12. The students will work together to write a title for the notebook.

13. At the end of the lesson week, store the map in the notebook. This activity is repeated each year with your next class. Next year's students will enter and identify any new trees planted in the map area. They will photograph every tree in the area, and make photograph and leaf pages. After several years, you will have not only a catalogue of the trees, but a record of their yearly development for classes to follow for many years to come. This activity promotes a continuing study of the growth, health, and number of trees around the school.

DAY THREE

Story Lesson

Follow the *Presenting the Story Lesson* instructions in the Introduction. Each story lesson follows the same procedure; however, say the following in step 4:

"The title of the story we're reading today is *How Fast the Trees Grow*. What do you think the story is about? What do you already know about trees?"

EXTENSION ACTIVITIES

1. Invite a volunteer from the National Arbor Day Foundation to the class.

◆ Before the volunteer arrives, help the students make a who, what, when, where, and why question list. Write the list on chart paper. For example:

   ◆ Who can become involved in Arbor Day activities?

   ◆ What is the National Arbor Day Foundation?

   ◆ When is Arbor Day?

   ◆ Where can you go to become involved in Arbor Day activities?

   ◆ Why is Arbor Day important?

◆ End the session with a question-and-answer session.

◆ On the following day, the students will write thank-you notes to the volunteer. They must give specific examples of what they enjoyed about the lesson.

2. The students will plant a tree around the area of the school. Photograph the tree and enter it into the notebook.

HOW FAST THE TREES GROW

Oliver L. Phillips and Alwyn H. Gentry watch trees in tropical forests. They count dead trees, and look for seedlings. Since the 1950s, Phillips and Gentry have watched as forests thickened or thinned out.

Phillips and Gentry found that the life cycle of trees in tropical forests is speeding up. After counting trees in nineteen places untouched by man, they noticed that trees are dying off. If many trees die, forests should have fewer trees. Phillips and Gentry's studies show that this is not the case. Seedlings quickly replace the dead trees.

Phillips and Gentry found faster life cycles in trees around the world. The speed with which seedlings grow to adults and die has doubled over the past thirty-eight years.

Why is this happening? No one knows for sure. Scientists point to the increase of carbon dioxide in the air. Plants take in carbon dioxide and give off oxygen. People and animals inhale oxygen and exhale carbon dioxide. Some types of pollution also add carbon dioxide to the air.

QUESTIONS FOR HOW FAST THE TREES GROW

1. Who are the two men watching trees in tropical forests?

   _____

   _____

2. What do Phillips and Gentry count?

   _____

   _____

3. What did Phillips and Gentry learn about the life cycle of trees in tropical forests?

   _____

   _____

4. What do scientists point to as a possible cause for the faster life cycles in trees?

   _____

   _____

5. What did Phillips and Gentry do before they discovered that the life cycle of trees is speeding up?

   _____

   _____

6. What replaces the trees after they die?

   _____

   _____

7. Is the study of trees conducted by Phillips and Gentry important? Why do you think so?

   _____

   _____

8. Are scientists concerned about the shortened life cycle of trees? If so, why are they concerned?

   _____

   _____

9. Will scientists continue to study the life cycle of trees for many years in the future? Why do you think so?

_____

_____

10. Why do you think Phillips and Gentry began their study?

_____

_____

11. Write a title for the story. Use as few words as possible.

_____

_____

12. Acid rain develops when pollution mixes with clouds. The pollution turns into acid within the clouds. When it rains, the acid falls on trees. The trees in the famous Black Forest in Germany are dying. The acid poisoned the soil so new trees cannot grow. How is the increase in the life span of trees like the problem of acid rain in the Black Forest? How is it different?

_____

_____

13. In your own words, tell about the findings of the Phillips and Gentry study.

_____

_____

14. Does the information learned in the Phillips and Gentry study affect your life? Why do you think so?

_____

_____

15. The story said, "The speed with which seedlings grow to adults and die has doubled over the past thirty-eight years." Is this statement a fact or an opinion? How can you prove your answer?

_____

_____

16.

_____

_____

_____

Name _____   Date _____

BEETHOVEN

ABOUT THE STORY

Beethoven was born in Bonn, Germany. He played the violin and piano. He liked playing other people's music, but he liked making his own music even more. A friend found a publisher for his work when he was only seventeen. One day, Beethoven heard humming in his ears. He was losing his hearing; however, he did not give up. Beethoven went on to write some of the finest music of all time

PREVIEW WORDS

Beethoven	Bonn, Germany	piano
violin	publisher	musicians
deaf	choir	orchestra
violent	thunderstorm	

THROUGHOUT THE WEEK—Play music by Beethoven as the students enter and leave the classroom. *Beethoven Lives Upstairs: Classical Kids* (BMG Music, 1989) is on CD, and is designed for children. The CD includes *Moonlight Sonata,* Symphony no. 6, *The Storm,* and Symphony no 9, IV.

Read the story *Beethoven's Cat* by Elisabet McHugh (New York: Atheneum, 1988) to the class. Ask the students to look for information about the real life of Beethoven within the fictional story.

BOOKS TO READ

Ludwig van Beethoven: Musical Pioneer, Carol Green (Childrens Press, 1989).

Beethoven, Nancy Loewen (Rourke Enterprises, 1989).

Beethoven's Cat, Elisabet McHugh (Atheneum, 1988).

What Makes Musicians So Sarcastic?, Charles M. Schulz (Holt, Rinehart and Winston, 1976).

Schroeder: Music Is My Life, Charles M. Schulz (Sparkler Books, 1988).

VIDEOS

Beethoven, MCA/Universal Home Video, 1992. Length: 87 minutes.

Beethoven Lives Upstairs, Library Video Co., BMG Distribution, 1992. Length: 52 minutes.

Fantasia, Walt Disney Productions, Buena Vista Home Video. Length: 120 minutes.

CDS, RECORDS, AND CASSETTES

Piano Concerto no. 3, op. 37; Piano Sonata no. 18 in E-Flat, op. 31, no. 3 op. (CD), Ludwig van Beethoven, 1770–1827 (Philips Classic Productions, 1992, P1986).

String Quartets, op. 18, no. 1 and op. 132 (CD), Ludwig van Beethoven, 1770–1827 (Sony, 1992).

The Classical Child, vol. 1 (cassette), Ernie Mavrides, (Sophia Sounds, 1989).

The Classical Child, vol. 2 (cassette), Ernie Mavrides (Sophia Sounds, 1989).

Beethoven Lives Upstairs (CD), Barbara Nichol (Classical Kids, 1989).

INTRODUCTORY ACTIVITIES

DAY ONE

Objective: The students will watch the movie *Beethoven Lives Upstairs*. They will look for information about the real life of Beethoven within the fictional story.

Curriculum subject: Music or Language Arts

Teacher:　During the week we'll learn about the life of Ludwig van Beethoven. Beethoven's life has inspired many people in many different fields. Charlie Brown's friend, Schroeder, uses Beethoven as his role model. Walt Disney animated Beethoven's Symphony no. 6 in his movie *Fantasia*. Even today, people continue to write about the very interesting personality of Beethoven.

As we learn about Beethoven, look for reasons why people continue to be fascinated by a man who was born in 1770. What is special about his music? What is special about his personality? Why do people consider him such an interesting character?

Today we'll watch the film *Beethoven Lives Upstairs*. Think about these questions as you watch the film.

Show the video *Beethoven Lives Upstairs* (BMG Distribution, 1992). After the film, help the students to explore the questions presented before the movie. What is in Beethoven's music and personality that makes him such a fascinating character nearly 200 years after his death?

DAY TWO

Story Lesson

Follow the *Presenting the Story Lesson* instructions in the Introduction. Each story lesson follows the same procedure; however, say the following in step 4:

"The title of the story we're reading today is *Beethoven*. What do you think the story is about? What do you already know about Beethoven?"

After the students finish the story lesson, ask them to lay their heads down and close their eyes. Tell them that you will play music Beethoven wrote after he lost his hearing. Play Beethoven's Symphony no. 9, IV. Do not ask questions after the tape. Watch for the students' reactions in the quiet of the room after the music stops.

EXTENSION ACTIVITIES

1. The students will discuss how Beethoven's Symphony no. 9, IV made them feel. They will make finger paintings while they listen to Beethoven's music.

◆ Ask the students to discuss how they felt when they heard Beethoven's Symphony no. 9. Beethoven never heard this music. After hearing the symphony, how would they describe Beethoven's music?

◆ Next, the students will listen to other pieces by Beethoven. Tell them to think about the colors and feelings they imagine as they listen to the songs.

- Give the students finger paints and paper. Tell them to listen to the music, then choose the colors they want to use in their paintings. The paintings should reflect how the music makes them feel.

- Play Beethoven's *Moonlight Sonata* as the students paint. After the music is over, ask the students to share their paintings. What colors did they choose and why? How did the music make them feel? How are these feelings reflected in the paintings?

- Repeat the activity with Beethoven's Symphony no. 6, *The Storm*.

2. The students will watch the movie *Fantasia* by Walt Disney Productions (Buena Vista Home Video, 120 minutes). Show only the section using Beethoven's Symphony no. 6. How did the music make the Disney animators feel? How are their ideas or interpretations different from the students'? How are they the same?

3. The students will look for information about Beethoven in Charles M. Schulz's *Peanuts* books.

- Hand out *Peanuts* books by Charles M. Schulz. Include the book *Schroeder: Music Is My Life*.

- The students will go on a Schroeder-Beethoven hunt. They will look for stories that tell about Beethoven. What does Schroeder teach you about Beethoven? Make a list of the facts.

4. End the week with a discussion about the personality of Beethoven. The students have seen Beethoven used in many art forms from movies, to animated film, to cartoons. Why does Beethoven fascinate us nearly 200 years after his death?

BEETHOVEN

Ludwig van Beethoven was born in 1770 in Bonn, Germany. He was a sad child, who loved his mother and music, yet his sad mood stayed with him all his life.

Beethoven played the piano and violin. Although he liked to play other people's music, he liked making his own music even more. When Beethoven was seventeen, a friend found a publisher for Beethoven's music. Now other musicians could enjoy his work.

One day Beethoven began to hear humming sounds in his ears. He was losing his hearing. Beethoven felt very frightened and sad. Sometimes his fear spilled out as anger; however, he never gave up.

Beethoven worked by listening to his music in his head. He wrote wonderful music for choirs to sing with orchestras. Beethoven never heard the music, however, many people call his work the finest music of all time. Beethoven died in 1827 during a violent thunderstorm.

QUESTIONS FOR BEETHOVEN

1. When was Ludwig van Beethoven born?

   _____

   _____

2. What instruments did Beethoven play?

   _____

   _____

3. How old was Beethoven when a friend found a publisher for his work?

   _____

   _____

4. When did Beethoven die?

   _____

   _____

5. How did Beethoven feel when he was losing his hearing?

   _____

   _____

6. How did Beethoven work after he lost his hearing?

   _____

   _____

7. What one word best describes Beethoven? Why do you think so?

   _____

   _____

8. Did the quality of Beethoven's music change after he lost his hearing?

   _____

   _____

9. What would have happened to Beethoven if he had given up?

_____

_____

10. Why did Beethoven continue to write music after he lost his hearing?

_____

_____

11. Write a title for the story. Use as few words as possible.

_____

_____

12. How did Beethoven change the way he wrote after he lost his hearing? How did he stay the same?

_____

_____

13. In your own words, tell about the life of Ludwig van Beethoven.

_____

_____

14. What effect did Beethoven's hearing loss have on his music? Why do you think so?

_____

_____

15. The story said, "Many people call his work the finest music of all time." Is this a fact or an opinion? Why do you think so?

_____

_____

16.

_____

_____

Name _____   Date _____

THE FLAGS OF THE AMERICAN COLONIES

ABOUT THE STORY

The story tells about the flags of the American colonies, and the meaning behind their design. The Liberty Tree flag depicted an elm tree in Boston. The Prime Minister of England said he would stand with "the colonists under his feet." The Southern colonists responded with a Rattlesnake flag that read, "Don't Tread on Me." Later, the two flags merged into one that said, "An Appeal to God, Don't Tread on Me."

PREVIEW WORDS

American Colonies	British	Liberty
symbolize	punish	elm tree
colonists	Prime Minister	tread
appeal	resented	ever watchful
Boston Tea Party		

PRIOR TO THE LESSON

Decorate the classroom in a patriotic theme. Include pictures of symbols of the United States, such as Uncle Sam, a bald eagle, the Statue of Liberty. The decorations will continue into the next lesson week.

BOOKS TO READ

Our Flag, Eleanor H. Ayer (Millbrook Press, 1992).

Flag, William G. Crampton (Knopf, 1989).

Flags of American History, David D. Crouthers (Hammond, 1973).

The Flag of the United States, Dennis B. Fradin (Childrens Press, 1988).

Our Country's Flag, Nicholas Georgiady and Louis Romano (Follett, 1963).

How Proudly They Wave: Flags of the Fifty States, Rita D. Haban (Lerner Publications, 1989).

The Biggest (and Best) Flag That Ever Flew, Rebecca C. Jones (Tidewater Publishers, 1988).

The Story of Old Glory, Albert I. Mayer (Childrens Press, 1970).

The American Flag, Thomas Parrish (Simon & Schuster, 1973).

State Names, Seals, Flags, and Symbols: A Historical Guide, Benjamin F. Shearer, (Greenwood Press, 1987).

I Pledge Allegiance, June Swanson (Carolrhoda Books, 1990).

VIDEOS

United States Flag, Rhonda Fabian and Jerry Baber (Schlessinger Video Productions, 1996). Length: 25 minutes.

INTRODUCTORY ACTIVITIES

DAY ONE

Objective: The students will listen to a story about the flag that inspired Francis Scott Key's
Star-Spangled Banner.

Curriculum subject: History

Teacher: During the week, we'll look at flags of the United States of America. We'll learn
about their designs, and what these designs mean.

Today I'll read the story *The Biggest (and Best) Flag That Ever Flew* by Rebecca
C. Jones. Look closely at the flag in the story. How does it look like the flag in our
classroom? How is it different? Why is it different?

Read the book *The Biggest (and Best) Flag That Ever Flew* to the class. After the
story, discuss the questions presented before the story.

DAY TWO

Story Lesson

Follow the *Presenting the Story Lesson* instructions in the Introduction. Each story lesson follows the same procedure; however, say the following in step 4:

"The title of the story we're reading today is *The Flags of the American Colonies.*
What do you think the story is about? What do you already know about the flags of the American Colonies?"

EXTENSION ACTIVITIES

1. The students will make copies of flags that flew over the United States.

◆ Give each student a name of a flag. If there are not enough flag names for each student,
they can work in pairs.

Flag names:

- ◆ Viking Banner
- ◆ Columbus's Personal Flag
- ◆ Cross of St. Andrew
- ◆ Dutch East India Company Flag
- ◆ Dutch West India Company Flag
- ◆ Lily Banner
- ◆ Edicott Flag
- ◆ Escutcheoned Jack
- ◆ Union Flag
- ◆ Royal Standard
- ◆ Washington's Cruisers Ensign

- ◆ Columbus's Standard
- ◆ Cross of St. George
- ◆ Swedish Flag
- ◆ Bourbon Banner
- ◆ Colonial Ensign
- ◆ New England Flag
- ◆ Red Ensign

- ◆ Commander-in-Chief's Personal Flag
- ◆ Commander-in-Chief's Life Guard Flag
- ◆ Rhode Island Flag
- ◆ Bunker Hill Flag
- ◆ Gadsden Flag
- ◆ Linked Hand Flag
- ◆ Bennington Flag
- ◆ Texel Flag
- ◆ Guilford Flag
- ◆ Merchant Flag
- ◆ Stars and Stripes (first)
- ◆ Continental Flag
- ◆ Grand Union Flag
- ◆ Liberty Tree Flag
- ◆ Taunton Flag
- ◆ Culpeper Flag
- ◆ Third Maryland Regiment

- ◆ Give each student a piece of 12" x 20" bulletin board paper.

- ◆ The students will use construction paper, crayons, markers, etc., to make the design. They will write the date of the use of the flag on the back with an explanation of the design.

- ◆ Hang the flags along the top of the walls around the classroom.

- ◆ REFERENCE:

  Crouthers, David D., *Flags of American History.*

2. Teach the students the meaning behind the design of your state flag. The students will make a construction paper model of their state flag.

3. Throughout the week, students learn that flags have a special meaning. The stars and stripes of the American flag tell people about our country.

- ◆ Design a flag that tells about your city or town. What colors would you choose? What special design would you put on the flag that tells the goals of the citizens in your community? Keep the design as simple as possible.

4. Make a flag for your city or town. You will need a 3' x 5' piece of fabric, hemmed around the edges.

- ◆ Draw the design in pencil onto the flag.

- ◆ Rotating in small groups, the students take turns painting the flag with fabric paint.

- ◆ Insert an eyelet in the top left corner and bottom left corner of the flag.

- ◆ Present the flag to the mayor.

THE FLAGS OF THE AMERICAN COLONIES

Before the United States became a country, it was the American Colonies. The King of England ruled over the colonies. Soon Americans resented British rule.

The colonists in the North met under an elm tree in Boston. There they planned such acts of rebellion as the Boston Tea Party. To punish the colonists, the British army cut down the tree. Later, the Americans designed a flag to symbolize the North. It showed a picture of an elm tree with the words "Liberty Tree—An Appeal to God."

The Southern colonists also disliked British rule. One day the Prime Minister of England said he would stand with "the colonists under his feet." The Southerners sent a clear message to England. Their flag showed a rattlesnake that said, "Don't Tread On Me." A rattlesnake has no eyelids, so it is ever-watchful. It never begins a fight. When a fight starts, it never gives up.

Later, the Northern and Southern colonies joined their flags together. This flag showed a pine tree with a rattlesnake wrapped around its trunk. It said, "An Appeal to God, Don't Tread on Me."

QUESTIONS FOR
THE FLAGS OF THE AMERICAN COLONIES

1. How did the Americans feel about British rule?

   _____

   _____

2. Where did the colonists in the North meet?

   _____

   _____

3. What did the British army do to punish the Northern colonies?

   _____

   _____

4. What did the flag of the Southern colonists say?

   _____

   _____

5. What was the United States before it became a country?

   _____

   _____

6. What did the Northern colonies do after the British army cut down their elm tree?

   _____

   _____

7. What did the American colonists try to tell England when they joined their flags together?

   _____

   _____

8. What was the "clear message" the Southern colonists sent to England when they made the rattlesnake flag?

   _____

   _____

9. Do you think the United States will ever use the "Pine Tree Rattlesnake" flag again? Why do you think so?

    _____

    _____

10. Why did the American colonists choose to make flags as signs of protest?

    _____

    _____

11. Write a title for the story. Use as few words as possible.

    _____

    _____

12. How were the elm tree flag and the rattlesnake flag alike? How were they different?

    _____

    _____

13. In your own words, tell about the events that led to the Northern colonists making the elm tree flag.

    _____

    _____

14. What effect, if any, do you think the flags of the American colonists had on the rulers in England?

    _____

    _____

15. The story said, "The colonists in the North met under an elm tree in Boston. There they planned such acts of rebellion as the Boston Tea Party." Is this a fact or an opinion? How can you prove your answer?

    _____

    _____

16.

    _____

    _____

Name _____   Date _____

THE FLYER

ABOUT THE STORY

On December 17, 1903, Wilbur and Orville Wright towed their clumsy machine up Kill Devil Hill. They named the 605-pound invention the Flyer. The first self-powered, heavier-than-air craft flew only twelve seconds and covered 120 feet.

PREVIEW WORDS

Wilbur Wright	Orville Wright	Flyer
Kill Devil Hill	clumsy	self-powered
Kitty Hawk, North Carolina	lighter-than-air craft	

PRIOR TO THE LESSON

Ask a model plane collector to visit your class. Perhaps the visitor has motorized planes. If you do not know someone who collects model planes, contact a local hobby shop. Many hobby shop owners know model plane enthusiasts.

When the model plane collector prepares for the visit, ask him or her to tell short histories of the planes on which the models are based. Include information about the Wright brothers' Flyer. Discuss the lesson with the visitor before class so you can prepare an introduction.

A field trip to an aviation museum can be substituted for this activity, Introductory Activity: Day One. Contact the guide before the trip. Ask him or her to focus on early planes, such as the Flyer.

THROUGHOUT THE WEEK—Read the story *And Now, a Word From Our Sponsor: The Story of the Roaring '20's Girl* by Dorothy and Thomas Hoobler (Englewood Cliffs, NJ: Silver Burdett Press, 1991) to the class. The story tells about a young girl, Fran Parker, who is trying to adapt to a changing world. Fran enters a radio contest called "The Most Important Invention of Our Time." Fran hopes to win with her essay on airplanes.

BOOKS TO READ

By the Seat of Their Pants: The Story of Early Aviation, Phil Ault (Dodd, Mead, 1978).

Flight!: Free As a Bird, Siegfried Aust (Lerner Publications, 1990).

Airplanes, Jeanne Bendick (Franklin Watts, 1982.

Before the Wright Brothers, Don Berliner (Lerner Publications, 1990).

Flight in America: From the Wrights to the Astronauts, Roger E. Bilstein (Johns Hopkins University Press, 1994).

The Smithsonian Book of Flight, Walter J. Boyne (Smithsonian Books, 1987).

The Smithsonian Book of Flight for Young People, Walter J. Boyne (Aladdin Books, 1988).

The Wright Brothers: How They Invented the Airplane, Russell Freedman (Holiday House, 1991).

Flying, Gail Gibbons (Holiday House, 1986).

Wright Brothers, Charles P. Graves (Putnam, 1973).

And Now, a Word From Our Sponsor: The Story of a Roaring '20's Girl, Dorothy and Thomas Hoobler (Silver Burdett Press, 1992).

Man With Wings, Edward Jablonski (Doubleday, 1980).

Flight: Fliers and Flying Machines, David Jefferis (Franklin Watts, 1991).

The Wright Brothers: Kings of the Air, Mervyn D. Kaufman (Garrard, 1964).

The Wright Brothers: Pioneers of American Aviation, Quentin James Reynolds (Random House, 1950).

The Story of the Flight at Kitty Hawk, R. Conrad Stein (Childrens Press, 1981).

Milestones of the Air: Jane's 100 Significant Aircraft, John W. R. Taylor (McGraw-Hill, 1969).

The Wright Brothers: Conquering the Sky, Becky Welch (Fawcett Columbine, 1992).

VIDEOS

Awesome Airplanes, (Plymouth, MN: Simitar Entertainment, 1994). Length: approx. 30 minutes.

Flight, (Marina Del Rey, Calif.: Tell Me Why, 1989). Length: approx. 30 minutes.

There Goes an Airplane, Dave Hood, presenter (Kid Vision, 1994). Length: 35 minutes.

INTRODUCTORY ACTIVITIES

DAY ONE

Objective: A model plane collector will visit the class. The students will learn about the history of the planes, particularly the Wright brothers' Flyer.

Curriculum subject: History

Before the speaker comes to class, help the students prepare a who, what, when, where, and why list. Write the list on chart paper. For example:

Who invented the first self-propelled airplane?

What do you enjoy about collecting model planes?

When did you begin collecting model planes?

Where can we learn about model planes?

Why do you enjoy planes?

Emphasize information about early airplanes. End the lesson with a question-and-answer session.

DAY TWO

Story Lesson

Follow the *Presenting the Story Lesson* instructions in the Introduction. Each story lesson follows the same procedure; however, say the following in step 4:

"The title of the story we're reading today is *The Flyer*. What do you think the story is about?" If the students mention the Wright brothers, ask, "What do you already know about the Wright brothers?"

EXTENSION ACTIVITIES

1. Read the Caldecott Medal Book *The Glorious Flight: Across the Channel with Louis Bleriot, July 25, 1909* by Alice and Martin Provensen (New York: Puffin Books, 1987) to the class.

◆ Before reading the book, ask the students to locate the English Channel on a map.

◆ Ask the students to imagine living in the year 1909. As you read the story, the students will imagine what it would be like to see an airplane for the first time. How would they feel?

◆ After the story, the students will write a narrative story. In the voice of a person living in 1909, they will tell about the experience of seeing their first airplane. What did it look like? What did it sound like? How did the people around you react? How did you feel when you saw the plane flying above your head?

◆ Later, ask the students if they have seen a space shuttle in person. If they say yes, how did they feel when they saw it for the first time? Would your feelings be like those of people in 1909 who saw an airplane for the first time? If the students have not seen the space shuttle, would they like to see it? Why do many people feel it is of personal importance to see a space shuttle?

2. The students will make a lighter-than-air craft picture.

Materials

◆ one toothbrush per student
◆ thin, black marker
◆ watercolors
◆ newspaper
◆ copies of the stencil and pattern pages
◆ paper clips
◆ white paper
◆ scissors
◆ tape
◆ cup of water
◆ aprons

Procedure

◆ Give each student copies of the stencil and pattern pages.
◆ Cut the stencil so that the cuts are inside the balloon and basket shapes.
◆ Cut out the shapes of the pattern pages so that the cuts are on the outsides of the shapes.
◆ Paper clip the stencil page (the balloon and basket) over the white paper.

◆ Cover your work area with newspaper. Lay the papers onto the newspaper.

◆ The students should wear aprons or old shirts to protect their clothing.

◆ Dip the toothbrush into water. Wipe off as much water as possible.

◆ Rub the toothbrush on the brown watercolors.

◆ Hold the brush over the basket part of the stencil about 1 inch above the paper. Rub your thumb over the brush so that the paint splatters down onto the basket stencil.

◆ Rinse off the brush. Wipe off as much water as possible. Rub the toothbrush over a bright watercolor. Rub the bristles of the brush with your thumb over the balloon stencil. Using this method, you can make stripes by alternating colors on the brush.

◆ Let the picture dry.

◆ Remove the stencil page.

◆ Gently place one piece of rolled tape onto the balloon and basket patterns. Gently tape the balloon pattern over the painted balloon, and the basket pattern over the painted basket. Tape on the cloud shapes so they overlap the balloon and basket. This protects what you have painted and what will remain white from the next layer of paint.

◆ Rub a damp toothbrush into blue watercolor. Rub your thumb over the brush. Paint all the area not covered by pattern pieces with blue splatters.

◆ Let dry.

◆ Remove the cloud patterns only.

◆ Using a thin, black marker, trace around the basket and balloon patterns.

◆ Remove the basket and balloon patterns.

◆ Using the thin, black marker, fill in details of the picture. For example, draw in the basket weave, the balloon ropes, and birds flying in the sky.

◆ Mount the picture on large, colored construction paper.

◆ The students can make airplane patterns of their own, and repeat the art activity.

3. The students will make paper airplanes, and determine which paper airplane design flies best and why.

◆ Break the students into groups. Each group will work on making the best paper airplane. The paper airplane must fly far and in a controlled pattern. The students will look at their planes, and prepare to tell the class why each plane flies well. Does the material make a difference (lighter or heavier paper)? How does the design of the plane affect the way it flies?

◆ The students can make up their own paper plane designs, or look in reference books. For example,

Churchill, E. Richard, *Fabulous Paper Airplanes*. New York: Sterling Publishing, 1992.

Ross, Frank Xavier, *Flying Paper Airplane Models*. New York: Lothrop, Lee & Shepard, 1975.

◆ Hold a paper airplane contest. Which plane flies the longest? Which has the best control? Which is the best overall plane? Why do these paper plane designs behave this way? Give awards to the best paper airplane design.

Stencil:

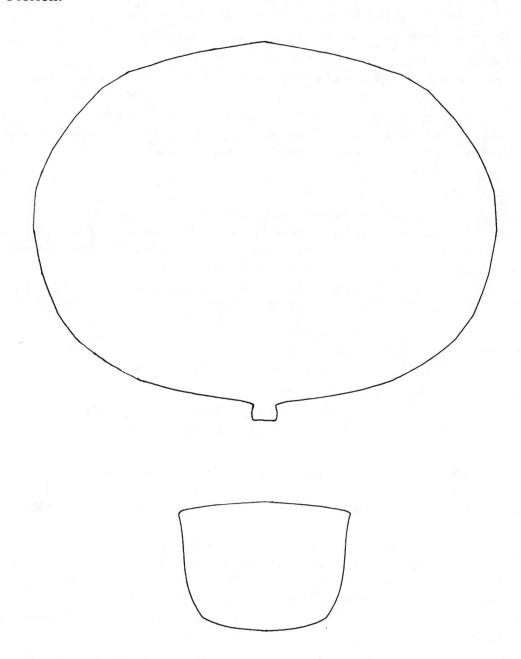

Pattern:

THE FLYER

On December 17, 1903, the wintry wind blew a bone-chilling 27 miles per hour. Just after nine o'clock in the morning, Wilbur and Orville Wright towed their clumsy machine up Kill Devil Hill. They named their 605-pound invention the Flyer.

Outside of Kitty Hawk, North Carolina, Kill Devil Hill rose up one hundred feet. Earlier, the Wright brothers built a sixty-foot rail runway up the side of the hill.

At 10:30 A.M., Orville Wright mounted the Flyer. Without a seat, he lay on his stomach with arms stretched out to the controls. Orville started the engine, and brought it to full power. Slowly, the Flyer picked up speed as it slid along the runway rail. Wilbur, steadying the Flyer with his hand on a wing, cheered on his younger brother.

Suddenly, the Flyer gracefully lifted off the rail, floating ten feet above the ground. The twelve-second flight covered 120 feet, yet this short flight placed the Flyer in history books as the first self-powered heavier-than-air craft.

QUESTIONS FOR THE FLYER

1. What day and year did the story take place?

   _____

   _____

2. Where is Kill Devil Hill?

   _____

   _____

3. What did the Wright brothers name their invention?

   _____

   _____

4. How high did Orville Wright fly?

   _____

   _____

5. What did the Wright brothers build before they took the Flyer to Kill Devil Hill?

   _____

   _____

6. What happened after the Flyer lifted off the rail runway?

   _____

   _____

7. Why is the flight of the Flyer an important event in history?

   _____

   _____

8. How did Wilbur Wright feel about his brother's flight?

   _____

   _____

9. You can see the Flyer at the Smithsonian Museum in Washington, D.C. Will Americans continue to admire and display the Flyer in the future? Why do you think so?

_____

_____

10. Why did the Wright brothers build the Flyer?

_____

_____

11. Write a title for the story. Use as few words as possible.

_____

_____

12. Look at a picture of the Flyer and a picture of a modern passenger airplane. How are they alike? How are they different?

_____

_____

13. In your own words, tell what happened at Kill Devil Hill on December 17, 1903.

_____

_____

14. How did the flight of the Flyer affect your life?

_____

_____

15. The story said, "They (the Wright brothers) named their 605-pound invention the Flyer." Is this a fact or someone's opinion? How can you prove your answer?

_____

_____

16.

_____

_____

Name _____   Date _____

THE MAGIC OF SPECIAL EFFECTS

ABOUT THE STORY

Every year movie makers work to dazzle viewers with amazing special effects. The opening scene of *Star Wars* introduced audiences to special effects unlike any seen before. Today's film makers learned about special effects from people who made movies many years ago. In the late 1890s, a Frenchman named Georges Méliès invented some of the first special effects.

PREVIEW WORDS

special effects	galaxy	Frenchman
Georges Méliès	magician	

PRIOR TO THE LESSON

Contact a local news program and ask if a cameraperson would come to your class. Ask the cameraperson to demonstrate his or her craft to your students. Can he or she demonstrate special effects? Before the cameraperson comes to your class, go over the lesson with him or her so you can make a proper introduction.

Review simple special effect techniques students can do with a camera. There are several children's books with camera activities (see Books to Read). Collect your materials, and take photographs using these techniques before the lesson.

THROUGHOUT THE WEEK—Read a children's science fiction story to the class. Ask the students why we usually see special effects in science fiction movies. Why do science fiction stories lend themselves to special effects photography more often than other types of stories? As you read the story, ask the students to make drawings of the types of special effects they would use if they were making a movie based on the story. Some suggested books are:

Saunders, Susan, *Runaway Spaceship: Skylark Choose Your Own Adventure no. 30.* New York: Bantam Books, 1985.

Montgomery, R.A., *Space and Beyond: Choose Your Own Adventure no. 4.* New York: Bantam Books, 1980.

Asimov, Isaac, Martin H. Greenberg, and Charles G. Waugh, eds., *Space Shuttles: Isaac Asimov's Wonderful Worlds of Science Fiction no. 7.* New York: Signet, 1987.

BOOKS TO READ

Space Shuttles: Isaac Asimov's Wonderful Worlds of Science Fiction no. 7, edited by Isaac Asimov, Martin H. Greenberg, and Charles G. Waugh (Signet, 1987).

Special Effects: A Look Behind the Scenes at Tricks of the Movie Trade, Rick Clise (Viking Kestrel, 1986).

Croy's Camera Trickery, Otto R. Croy (Hastings House, 1977).

The Saga of Special Effects, Ronald W. Fry and Pamela Fourzon, (Prentice Hall, 1977).

Cameras, Ian Graham (Gloucester Press, 1991).

The Book of Special Effects Photography, Michael John Langford (Random House, 1981).

Special Effects, Dan Millar (Chartwell Books, 1990).

Space and Beyond: Choose Your Own Adventure no. 4, R.A. Montgomery (Bantam Books, 1982).

Photography: Take Your Best Shot, Terri Morgan and Shmuel Thaler (Lerner Publications, 1991).

Runaway Spaceship: Skylark Choose Your Own Adventure no. 30, Susan Saunders (Bantam Books, 1985).

Camcorder Tricks and Special Effects: Over 40 Fun, Easy Tricks Anyone Can Do, Michael Stavros (Amherst Media, 1995).

Photo Fun: An Idea Book for Shutterbugs, David Webster (Franklin Watts, 1973).

VIDEOS

From Star Wars to Jedi: The Making of a Saga, Richard Schickel (CBS/Fox Video, 1992, c1983). Length: 65 minutes.

INTRODUCTORY ACTIVITIES

DAY ONE

Objective: The students will learn about the art of special effects as they watch the video *From Star Wars to Jedi: The Making of a Saga.*

Curriculum subject: Art

Teacher: During this week, we'll learn about the history and art of special effects. We'll learn how such movie makers as George Lucas produce amazing special effect scenes.

Today, we'll watch the video *From Star Wars to Jedi: The Making of a Saga.* In the video, George Lucas and others tell about the making of the three *Star Wars* films and their special effects.

As you watch the movie, take notes on the types of special effects described in the film. Do the film makers use special camera tricks, models, and computers to make imaginary scenes seem real? Would it be easy to make a movie with amazing special effects? Why do you think so?

After the movie, we'll discuss what you learned. Later in the week we'll talk to a cameraperson who will tell us about special effects he or she can create with his or her camera. Finally, we'll make still photographs of our own using simple special effect techniques.

Show the movie *From Star Wars to Jedi: The Making of a Saga.* Discuss the special effect techniques described in the story. Why do special effects make a movie more enjoyable to watch? What do the students think the next generation of special effect movies will look like? Tomorrow, they will learn about the history of special effects in motion pictures.

DAY TWO

Story Lesson

Follow the *Presenting the Story Lesson* instructions in the Introduction. Each story lesson follows the same procedure; however, say the following in step 4:

"The title of the story we're reading today is *The Magic of Special Effects*. What do you think the story is about? What do you already know about special effects?"

EXTENSION ACTIVITIES

1. The students will learn about special effects from a local news program cameraperson.

◆ Before the cameraperson arrives, help the students write a who, what, when, where, and why question list. Write the list on chart paper. For example:

   ◆ Who can become a cameraperson?

   ◆ What do you do for the news program?

   ◆ When did you become interested in cameras?

   ◆ Where did you learn how to use your camera?

   ◆ Why do you like being a cameraperson?

◆ End the lesson with a question-and-answer session.

◆ After the visitor leaves, the students will write thank-you notes. They must give specific examples of what they enjoyed about the lesson.

2. The students will use special effects to take still photographs.

◆ You can find instructions for simple camera techniques in the children's book *Photo Fun: An Idea Book for Shutterbugs* and other books about photography.

◆ Divide the students into groups. Assign each group a special effect. The students will work together to take several photographs using their special effect technique.

◆ Examples of special effect techniques from *Photo Fun* are:

   *Trick Photography:

   ◆ A trick where the subject appears to be holding tiny people or trees (page 13)

   ◆ Making the subject appear to be balancing on one finger (page 14)

   ◆ Distorting the subject by photographing it through imperfect glass (pages 16–18)

   *Using reflections as special effects (pages 20–27)

   *Compound pendulum photographs (pages 40–41)

   *Aerial photographs (pages 52–61)

   *Pictures through microscopes and binoculars (pages 67–73)

   *Underwater photography (pages 74–78)

   *Pictures without cameras (pages 79–84).

3. The students will make a poster telling how they made their special effects photographs.

◆ The students will return to the groups they were in during Extension Activity 2.

◆ Give each group a poster board. The students will write a brief explanation of their special effect technique on the poster board, and give the poster a title.

◆ Finally, they will mount their photographs on the poster around the writing.

◆ Display the posters on a bulletin board entitled "Special Effect Photography."

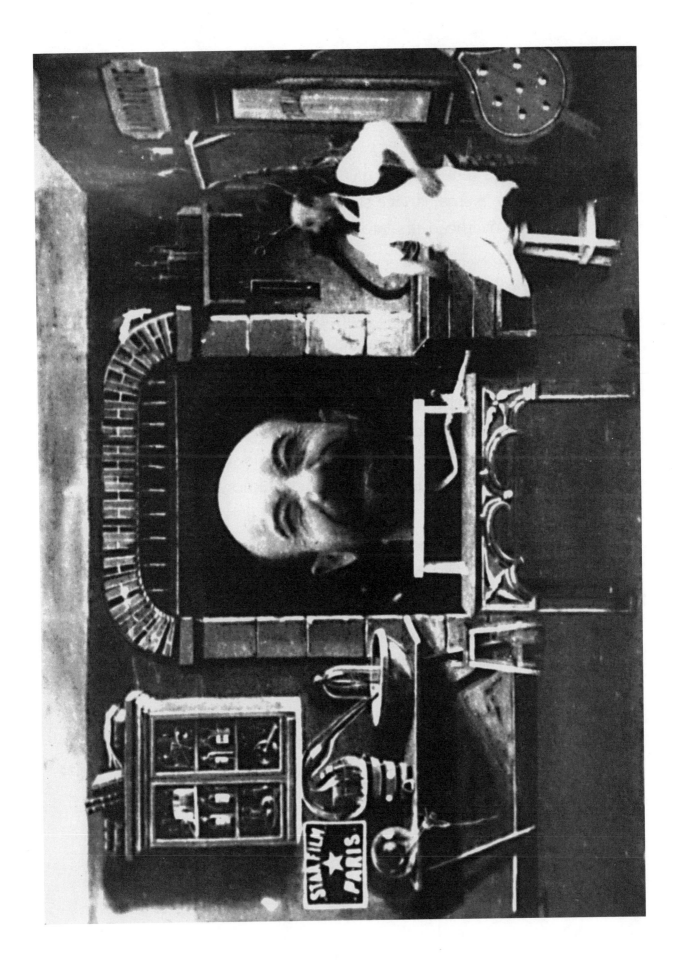

THE MAGIC OF SPECIAL EFFECTS

Stars in a faraway galaxy twinkle in the black sky. Suddenly, a small space ship dashes by. A huge ship appears overhead. Its large body slowly comes into view.

The opening scene of Star Wars was one of the first special effects of its kind. The filming took place in a studio, not in a "galaxy far, far away." The giant space ships were really small models.

These film makers learned about special effects from people who made movies many years ago. In the late 1890s, a Frenchman named Georges Mélies invented some of the first special effects. Cameras were a new idea. How did Georges Mélies know about special effects?

Before making movies, Georges Mélies was a magician. He used what he knew about magic tricks to make special effects.

When you watch movies like Star Wars, you can see that film makers are like magicians. They take us through time and space with their amazing special effects.

QUESTIONS FOR THE MAGIC OF SPECIAL EFFECTS

1. Who invented some of the first special effects?

   _____

   _____

2. What is the name of the movie described in the story?

   _____

   _____

3. When did Georges Mélìes invent his special effects?

   _____

   _____

4. What did Georges Mélìes use to make special effects?

   _____

   _____

5. What did Georges Mélìes do before he made special effects?

   _____

   _____

6. Which special effects were created first: those made by Georges Mélìes, or those made for <u>Star Wars</u>?

   _____

   _____

7. What one word best describes Georges Mélìes? Why do you think so?

   _____

   _____

8. Is Georges Mélìes an important person in the history of film making? Why do you think so?

   _____

   _____

9. What do you think special effects in movies might look like in the year 2030?

_____

_____

10. Why did the film makers use special effects in the movie <u>Star Wars</u>?

_____

_____

11. Write a title for the story. Use as few words as possible.

_____

_____

12. How are magic tricks and special effects in movies alike? How are they different?

_____

_____

13. In your own words, tell about Georges Mélìes' special effects.

_____

_____

14. How is a movie changed when the director uses very good special effects?

_____

_____

15. The story said, "Film makers are like magicians." Is this a fact or the author's opinion? Why do you think so?

_____

_____

16.

_____

_____

Name _____   Date _____

MAKING CARTOONS MOVE

ABOUT THE STORY

There are many ways to make cartoons move. Joseph Plateau invented the phenakistoscope in 1832. His invention was a simple toy that looks like a pinwheel. The viewer spins the wheel and looks through the slits in front of a mirror. The pictures on the wheel appear to move like an animated movie.

PREVIEW WORDS

phenakistoscope (phen à kis´ tō scōpe)

zoetrope (zō´ ē trōpe)

cartoons	high-tech	Joseph Plateau
pinwheel	Dr. Horner	hurdles

PRIOR TO THE LESSON

The activities in this lesson week will last longer than one week. The students will make a cartoon movie. There are several techniques described in Yvonne Andersen's book *Make Your Own Animated Movies and Videotapes: Film and Video Techniques from the Yellow Ball Workshop* (Boston: Little, Brown, 1991). Prior to the lesson week, research the technique you will use with your class based on your situation. Collect your materials, and make an animated film of your own to prepare yourself for the lesson.

BOOKS TO READ

Make Your Own Animated Movies and Videotapes: Film and Video Techniques From the Yellow Ball Workshop, Yvonne Andersen (Little, Brown, 1991).

The Art of Walt Disney: From Mickey Mouse to the Magic Kingdoms, Christopher Finch (Harry N. Abrams, 1995).

Flipbook Animation, Patrick Jenkins (Addison-Wesley, 1991).

The Animation Book: A Complete Guide to Animated Filmmaking, From Flip-Books to Sound Cartoons, Kit Laybourne (Crown Publishers, 1979).

The Animated Film, Ralph Stephenson (A. S. Barnes, 1973).

Disney's Art of Animation: From Mickey Mouse to Beauty and the Beast, Bob Thomas (Hyperion, 1991).

VIDEOS

Raymond Briggs': The Snowman (Snowman Enterprises, Ltd., 1982). Length: 26 minutes.

Computer Animation Festival (Miramar, BMG Video, C1994). Length: 58 minutes.

Stanley and the Dinosaurs (Clay Animation), (Golden Book Video, 1989, c1962). Length: 26 minutes.

State of the Art of Computer Animation (Pacific Arts Video, 1988.

Paddington's Birthday Bonanza (Goodtimes Home Video, C1992. Length: 50 minutes.

INTRODUCTORY ACTIVITIES

DAYS ONE AND TWO

Objective: The students will watch several animated films. The films will use a variety of techniques. The students will compare and contrast the films based on style and presentation.

Curriculum subject: Art

Teacher: Throughout the week, we'll learn about the art of making animated film. We'll learn about simple toys that animate only a few drawings, and we'll make an animated film of our own.

Before we make our film, we must study animated film. There are many techniques animators use in creating their animation. For example, artists who make paintings can choose from a variety of mediums. They might use watercolors or oil paints. Animators might use drawings called flat animation, computers, or three-dimensional animation (movable clay figures and toys).

Over the next two days, we'll watch animated films. Copy these words on a piece of paper. You'll make a page like this for every film.

Film Title:
Type of animation:
My opinion of the story:
My opinion of the animation:

As you watch the film, fill in the information. Give your opinion of the story. Was it funny? Was it boring? Why do you feel this way?

Next, give your opinion of the quality of the animation. Was the animation presented in a unique way? Was there a great deal of detail in the artwork? After we see all the films, we'll discuss our notes and compare the films.

The following films are suggestions of a variety of animated movies using several different techniques. After each film, discuss the student's notes. After all the films are over, compare the films. How are they alike? How are they different? Which film was the most realistic? Why did the animator choose the technique he/she used?

1. Clay animation (three-dimensional animation):

Stanley and the Dinosaurs

2. Computer animation:

Computer Animation Festival, vol. 2.0

*This video contains twenty-two award-winning computer animation shorts. Not all the films are appropriate for young students; therefore, review the film to select the animated shorts you want to show. Before reviewing the video, set the video recorder counter to zero. Make a note of the counter number for each film you choose.

3. Flat animation (drawings):

Raymond Briggs': The Snowman

*An Academy Award Nominee

4. Mixed (flat animation with puppetry or three-dimensional animation):

Paddington's Birthday Bonanza

DAY THREE

Story Lesson

Follow the *Presenting the Story Lesson* instructions in the Introduction. Each story lesson follows the same procedure; however, say the following in step 4:

"The title of the story we're reading today is *Making Cartoons Move*. What do you think the story is about? What do you already know about making cartoons move?"

EXTENSION ACTIVITIES

1. Over the next several days, the students will make their own animated movie. Yvonne Andersen has written a detailed book on animated movies and produced videotapes with instructions for children.

Andersen, Yvonne, *Make Your Own Animated Movies: Yellow Ball Workshop Film Techniques.* Boston: Little, Brown, 1991.

Anderson, Yvonne, *Make Your Own Animated Movies and Videotapes: Film and Video Techniques from the Yellow Ball Workshop.*

2. Hold an "Animated Film Festival" for your class and visiting classes. Your students will introduce the films reviewed on Days One and Two, and their own animated movies.

MAKING CARTOONS MOVE

A phenakistoscope is not a high-tech science instrument. In fact, a phenakistoscope is a toy for children.

Joseph Plateau invented the phenakistoscope in 1832. The name means "an instrument used for viewing that fools the observer."

The phenakistoscope fools the person using it by making still pictures appear to move. A phenakistoscope is a paper wheel. Eight to twelve cartoon drawings line the edge of the wheel. Plateau cut thin slits under each picture. He then mounted the wheel on a stick like a pinwheel.

The viewer faces the phenakistoscope toward a mirror. When the viewer spins the wheel and looks through the slits, the pictures appear to move like a motion picture.

In 1834, Dr. Horner invented the zoetrope or "wheel of life." A zoetrope looks like a tin cup that spins on its base. An artist drew cartoons on the inside of the cup. Horner cut slits in the side of the cup. Spin the cup, look through the slits, and you can see clowns juggle, monkeys jump hurdles, or even a boxing match.

QUESTIONS FOR MAKING CARTOONS MOVE

1. What is a phenakistoscope?

   _____

   _____

2. Who invented the phenakistoscope?

   _____

   _____

3. Who invented the zoetrope?

   _____

   _____

4. In what year was the phenakistoscope invented?

   _____

   _____

5. Which was invented first, the phenakistoscope or the zoetrope?

   _____

   _____

6. What do viewers look through after they spin the cup of the zoetrope?

   _____

   _____

7. Why did Dr. Horner call his toy the "wheel of life"?

   _____

   _____

8. Were toys that animated cartoons popular in the 1800s? Why do you think so?

   _____

   _____

9. If someone made zoetropes today, would they be popular toys? Why do you think so?

_____

_____

10. Why would a child enjoy playing with a phenakistoscope?

_____

_____

11. Write a title for the story. Use as few words as possible.

_____

_____

12. How are a phenakistoscope and a zoetrope alike? How are they different?

_____

_____

13. In your own words, explain how a child uses a phenakistoscope.

_____

_____

14. Would the name phenakistoscope make people want to buy the toy? Why do you feel this way?

_____

_____

15. The story said, "The phenakistoscope fools the person using it by making still pictures appear to move." Is this a fact or an opinion? Why do you think so?

_____

_____

16.

_____

_____

Name _____   Date _____

MAKE YOUR OWN PHENAKISTOSCOPE

ABOUT THE STORY

The story tells the students how to make a phenakistoscope. The only materials required are lightweight cardboard, a copy of the example picture, scissors, a glue stick, crayons, a pencil, a large-head thumbtack, and a mirror.

PREVIEW WORDS

phenakistoscope	Joseph Plateau	cardboard
eye-catching color	thumbtack	slits
reflection		

PRIOR TO THE LESSON

Contact a person who collects antique toys. A local antique dealer might direct you to someone who would enjoy sharing a collection with the class. Ask the collector to visit the class and bring samples of his or her toys. Tell the visitor that your students are learning about the phenakistoscope and zoetrope. Ask the collector to tell how the toys reflect the history of their time. Discuss the lecture with the collector before the lesson so you can prepare an appropriate introduction.

THROUGHOUT THE WEEK—Decorate the room with photographs of antique toys. If possible, set up a toy museum in the classroom.

BOOKS TO READ

Texas Toys and Games, Francis Edward Abernethy (Southern Methodist University Press, 1989).

Patterns for Soft Toys: Applying Soft Toy Techniques, Enid Anderson (B.T. Batsford, 1985).

American Antique Toys, 1830–1900, Bernard Barenholtz (H. N. Abrams, 1980).

Easy-to-Make Water Toys That Really Work, Mary Blocksma and Dewey Blocksma (Prentice Hall, 1984).

Action Contraptions: Easy-to-Make Toys That Really Move, Mary Blocksma (Prentice Hall Books for Young Readers, 1987).

The Little Book of Bear Care, Pauline Cockrill (Dorling Kindersley, 1992).

The Little Book of Traditional Bears, Pauline Cockrill (Dorling Kindersley, 1992).

The Little Book of Celebrity Bears, Pauline Cockrill (Dorling Kindersley, 1992).

The Collector's Book of Dolls' Clothes: Costumes in Miniature, 1700–1929, Dorothy S., Elizabeth A., and Evelyn J. Coleman (Crown Publishers, 1975).

Asian Crafts, Judith Hoffman Corwin (Franklin Watts, 1992).

Wild West Toys You Can Make, Maurice Gogniat (Sterling Publishing, 1976).

How to Make Pop-Ups, Joan Irvine (Morrow Junior Books, 1988).

The Great All-American Wooden Toy Book, Norman Marshall (Rodale Press, 1986).

Build Your Own Farmyard, Kate Petty (Franklin Watts, 1985).

A Collector's History of the Teddy Bear, Patricia N. Schoonmaker (Hobby House Press, 1981).

Teddy Bears, Judy Sparrow (Smithmark, 1993).

Antique Toys and Their Background, Gwen White (Arco, 1971).

Action Figures, Robert Young (Dillon Press, 1992).

Dolls, Robert Young (Dillon Press, 1992).

Teddy Bears, Robert Young (Dillon Press, 1992).

VIDEOS

Paper Playthings & Gifts, Pacific Arts Video, 1989. Length: 45 minutes.

████████████

INTRODUCTORY ACTIVITIES

DAY ONE

Objective: The students will listen to an antique toy collector tell about his or her collection. They will learn about the time in history in which the toys were made.

Curriculum subject: History

Tell the students that they will learn about and make a phenakistoscope during this lesson week. Help the students prepare a who, what, when, where, and why question list before the antique toy collector arrives. Write the questions on chart paper. For example:

◆ Who collects antique toys?

◆ What type of toys do you collect?

◆ When did you begin collecting antique toys?

◆ Where do you find the toys?

◆ Why do you collect antique toys?

Point out how the antique toys tell the students about the time in history that the toys were made. What will video games tell future generations about our time in history? End the lesson with a question-and-answer session.

After the speaker leaves, the students will write thank-you notes. They must include specific examples of things they enjoyed about the lesson.

DAY TWO

Story Lesson

Follow the *Presenting the Story Lesson* instructions in the Introduction. Each story lesson follows the same procedure; however, say the following in step 4:

"The title of the story we're reading today is *Make Your Own Phenakistoscope.* What do you think the story is about? What do you already know about phenakistoscopes?"

████████████

EXTENSION ACTIVITIES

1. Following the directions in the story, the students will make phenakistoscopes.

  *Help the students pin the wheel to the pencil eraser so that they do not stick themselves with the point.

◆ First, the students will make a bouncing ball phenakistoscope from the example picture. They will make the phenakistoscope by reading the directions in the lesson story. Avoid giving any oral directions. This exercise allows the students to practice following written directions.

◆ Next, the students will design their own phenakistoscope cartoon. Use correction fluid to remove the circles from a copy of the example picture. Make one copy of a blank wheel for each student.

  The students will draw pictures in the notches of the wheel. The last cartoon must end in a position that allows the first cartoon to pick up the movement. This will allow a fluid motion as the characters repeat the action of the cartoon.

2. The students will bring an old toy to class.

◆ Ask the students to bring a toy that belonged to a parent or grandparent. It would be wise to get written permission from the parents. Any student who cannot bring an old toy can bring a toy of her or his own.

◆ In a "Show and Tell" format, the students will tell about their toys. How old is the toy? Whose toy is it? What does the toy tell us about the history of the time it was made? Students who bring newer toys can also answer these questions.

3. The students will write stories about an antique toy.

◆ Allow the students to browse through books about antique toys.

◆ The students choose a toy they like, and draw a picture of it.

◆ The students write a story telling about the toy. When was the toy made? How did the toy work? What does the toy tell us about its time in history?

◆ Display the pictures and stories on a bulletin board entitled "Antique Toys."

MAKE YOUR OWN PHENAKISTOSCOPE

You can make your own phenakistoscope. You need a piece of light cardboard like the back of a note pad, a copy of the example picture, scissors, a glue stick, crayons, a pencil, a large-head thumbtack, and a mirror.

First, color the circles on the example picture a bright, eye-catching color. Use the same color on every circle. Glue that picture to the piece of cardboard. Cut out the picture and cardboard, following the dark black lines.

Finally, stick the thumbtack through the dot in the center of the wheel. Pin the picture to the side of a pencil eraser. Your finished phenakistoscope looks like a flat pinwheel.

To make your picture move, stand in front of the mirror. Face the picture on your phenakistoscope toward the mirror. Look through the slits at the top of the phenakistoscope. Hold the phenakistoscope about four inches from your nose. Spin the wheel and watch the reflection of your colored circles come to life. Now try to design your own phenakistoscope cartoon.

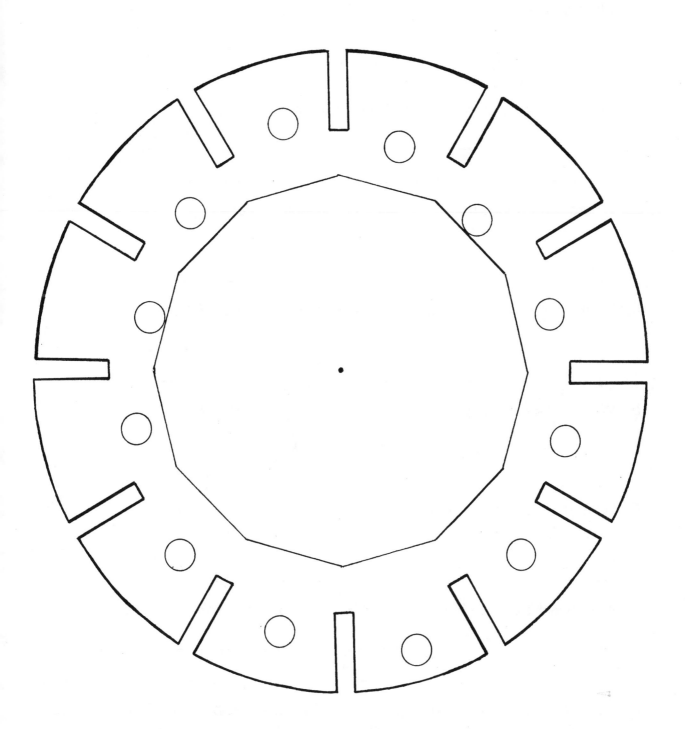

QUESTIONS FOR
MAKE YOUR OWN PHENAKISTOSCOPE

1. What do you need to make a phenakistoscope?

    _____

    _____

2. What color do you use on the circles of the example picture?

    _____

    _____

3. Where do you face the picture on your phenakistoscope?

    _____

    _____

4. How far from your nose do you hold your phenakistoscope?

    _____

    _____

5. What is the first thing you do to make your phenakistoscope?

    _____

    _____

6. What do you do after you spin the wheel of the phenakistoscope?

    _____

    _____

7. Is a phenakistoscope hard to make? Why do you think so?

    _____

    _____

8. Does the author want you to know what the circles on the phenakistoscope will do before you see it for yourself? Why do you think so?

    _____

    _____

9. Will you make your own phenakistoscope design? Why do you think so? If you said yes, what would your design look like?

_____

_____

10. Why would someone make a phenakistoscope?

_____

_____

11. Write a title for the story. Use as few words as possible.

_____

_____

12. How are the phenakistoscope and the animated cartoons you see on television alike? How are they different?

_____

_____

13. In your own words, explain how to make a phenakistoscope.

_____

_____

14. Do you think your friends will want a phenakistoscope after they see yours? Why do you think so?

_____

_____

15. The story said, "You can make your own phenakistoscope." Is this a fact or an opinion? How can you prove your answer?

_____

_____

16.

_____

_____

Name _____   Date _____

MOUNT PINATUBO ERUPTS

ABOUT THE STORY

On June 15, 1991, Mount Pinatubo erupted, blowing the mountain apart. Steam and hot gases shot sixteen miles into the air. Heavy rain washed the ash down, crushing the roofs of buildings. Millions of tons of gas reached high into the sky. This lowered Earth's temperature for nearly three years.

PREVIEW WORDS

Mount Pinatubo	volcano	eruption
Philippine Islands	ozone layer	skin cancer

PRIOR TO THE LESSON

Locate a geologist and invite him or her to visit the class to talk about volcanoes. One source for a speaker is a local university; a professor or student might volunteer to visit the class. Discuss the lecture with the speaker beforehand so you can prepare an introduction. Ask the speaker to bring samples of lava rock.

THROUGHOUT THE WEEK—Read the story *Volcano!* (New York: Bantam Books, 1986) to the class. *Volcano!* is no. 64 in a large series called Choose Your Own Adventure. These are extremely popular books. Many children read the entire series.

BOOKS TO READ

Magic Dogs of the Volcanoes, Manlio Argueta (Children's Book Press, 1990).

Volcano, Lionel Bender (Franklin Watts, 1988).

Activities in the Earth Sciences, Helen Challand (Childrens Press, 1982).

Volcanoes, Jacqueline Dineen (Gloucester Press, 1991).

Volcanoes, David Lambert (Franklin Watts, 1985).

Volcano, Christopher Lampton (Millbrook Press, 1991).

Volcano: The Eruption and Healing of Mount St. Helens, Patricia Lauber (Bradbury Press, 1986).

Earth Alive!, Sandra Markle (Lothrop, Lee & Shepard, 1990).

1001 Questions Answered About Natural Land Disasters, Barbara Tufty (Dodd, Mead, 1969).

Science in Your Backyard, William R. Wellnitz (TAB Books, 1991).

Volcanoes: Fire From Below, Jenny Wood (Gareth Stevens Children's Books, 1990).

VIDEOS

Volcano, National Geographic Video, 1992. Length: 60 minutes.

The Volcano Watchers, PBS Home Video, 1990. Length: 60 minutes.

The Tortoise and the Hare/Hill of Fire, Children's Video Library, 1987. Length: 60 minutes.

INTRODUCTORY ACTIVITIES

DAY ONE

Objective: The students will watch a video about volcanoes.

Curriculum subject: Science

Teacher: Throughout the week we'll learn about volcanoes. We'll look at the effects of volcano eruptions, and the science of predicting volcanoes.

Today we'll begin by watching a video about Mexico's Paricutin volcano and volcanoes in Hawaii. As you watch the video, listen for facts about volcanoes. Write down three facts on a piece of paper. After the video, we'll share our facts.

Show the second half of the video *The Tortoise and the Hare/Hill of Fire.* After the video, the students will share their facts about volcanoes. List the facts on a chart entitled "Volcano Facts."

DAY TWO

Story Lesson

Follow the *Presenting the Story Lesson* instructions in the Introduction. Each story lesson follows the same procedure; however, say the following in step 4:

"The title of the story we're reading today is *Mount Pinatubo Erupts.* What do you think the story is about?" If the students mention volcanoes, ask, "What do you already know about volcanoes?"

After the story, return to the photograph of Mount Pinatubo. Notice the lightning above the volcano. The eruption was so powerful, it created its own lightning storm.

EXTENSION ACTIVITIES

1. Invite a geologist to the class to talk about volcanoes.

◆ Before the lesson, prepare a who, what, when, where, and why question list. Write the question list on chart paper. For example:

   ◆ Who is involved in the study of volcanoes?

   ◆ What causes a volcano to erupt?

   ◆ When does a volcano erupt? Can you predict the eruption?

   ◆ Where are volcanoes located?

   ◆ Why do you study volcanoes?

◆ End the class with a question-and-answer session.

◆ Write thank-you notes to the speaker. The students will write about specific examples of the lesson that they enjoyed.

2. The students will demonstrate a volcanic eruption.

◆ Locate an earth science book containing projects dealing with volcanic eruptions. One such source is *Activities in the Earth Sciences.*

◆ Break the class into groups. Each group will make a model of a volcano.

◆ The students will label their volcano according to formation and rock type.

◆ When the students are ready to make their volcano erupt, the teacher should handle all chemicals involved. Some chemicals can irritate the skin. Wear protective gloves as a precaution.

3. The students will go on a "Volcano Scavenger Hunt."

Reference:

1001 Questions Answered About Natural Land Disasters, pp. 55–97.

Any reference book dealing with volcanoes can be used.

◆ Break the students into groups of five. Give each group three questions. The students will go on a "Volcano Scavenger Hunt," and look for the answers to their three questions. They can use books, ask geologists, put the question out on the Internet, or use any other means to find the answers to their questions.

◆ Reward each group to return with correct answers to all three questions.

MOUNT PINATUBO ERUPTS

A giant volcano sat quietly on the Philippine Islands for over 600 years. In 1991, Mount Pinatubo began to rumble.

Scientists watched the volcano closely. They knew something big was about to happen. A small eruption of steam and ash shook the island in April. By June the volcano gave off stronger blasts. Earthquakes sent out warnings of a major eruption. The word went out, "Get away from the volcano!"

On June 15, Mount Pinatubo erupted, blowing the mountain apart. Steam and hot gases shot sixteen miles into the air. Heavy rain washed the ash down, crushing the roofs of buildings. Over 500 people died.

Millions of tons of gas reached high into the sky. The ash and gases spread over the entire world. This lowered Earth's temperature for nearly three years.

The ashes also ate into Earth's ozone layer. This layer acts like a blanket, keeping the dangerous sun rays out. Scientists worry that skin cancer, a known killer, will increase. The impact of Mount Pinatubo's eruption reaches far into the future.

QUESTIONS FOR MOUNT PINATUBO ERUPTS

1. Where is Mount Pinatubo?

   _____

   _____

2. In what year did Mount Pinatubo begin to rumble?

   _____

   _____

3. On what day did Mount Pinatubo erupt?

   _____

   _____

4. How far in the air did steam and hot gases shoot?

   _____

   _____

5. What happened before people said, "Get away from the volcano!"

   _____

   _____

6. What happened after heavy rain washed the ash down on buildings?

   _____

   _____

7. How dangerous are volcano eruptions? Why do you think so?

   _____

   _____

8. Would so many people have died if it had not rained at the time of the eruption?

   _____

   _____

9. A person who studies volcanoes is a volcanologist. Would you like to become a volcanologist? Why do you think so?

_____

_____

10. Why did scientists watch Mount Pinatubo carefully as soon as it started to rumble?

_____

_____

11. Write a title for the story. Use as few words as possible.

_____

_____

12. How are earthquakes and volcano eruptions alike? How are they different?

_____

_____

13. In your own words, tell about the events that led up to the eruption of Mount Pinatubo.

_____

_____

14. What are some of the long-term effects of the Mount Pinatubo eruption? Will the eruption affect your life? Why do you think so?

_____

_____

15. The story said, "The ash and gases spread over the entire world. This lowered Earth's temperature for nearly three years." Is this a fact or an opinion? How can you prove your answer?

_____

_____

16.

_____

_____

Name _____   Date _____

A FOLKTALE COMES TO LIFE

ABOUT THE STORY

The story of John Chapman's life became known as the American folktale "Johnny Appleseed." Chapman was a war hero during the War of 1812. Americans remember him for a pouch of apple seeds, however. Chapman planted apple orchards from Pennsylvania to Indiana. As he traveled, he preached the Christian religion. Soon the pioneers told stories about the famous Johnny Appleseed.

PREVIEW WORDS

John Chapman	legendary	War of 1812
Mansfield, Ohio	folktale	pioneers
Christian	Pennsylvania	Indiana
preached	orchards	tin-pan

THROUGHOUT THE WEEK—Read one story a day from the book *Classic American Folk Tales,* retold by Steven Zorn (Philadelphia, Pennsylvania: Courage Books, 1992) to the class. Begin with the story of Johnny Appleseed on page 16. Read only the stories about people, such as Paul Bunyan, John Henry, Davy Crockett, Pocahontas, and Pecos Bill. After each story, ask the students if they think the story is based on a real or fictional person.

BOOKS TO READ

Story of Johnny Appleseed, Aliki (Prentice Hall, 1963).

The Quilt-Block History of Pioneer Days: With Projects Kids Can Make, Mary Cobb (Millbrook Press, 1995).

Davy Crockett, Frontier Adventurer, Matthew G. Grant (Childrens Press, 1973, c1974).

John Chapman: The Man Who Was Johnny Appleseed, Carol Greene (Childrens Press, 1991).

Lantern in the Valley, Betty Elliott Hanna (Eakin Press, 1981).

Daniel Boone: Pioneer Trailblazer, Jim Hargrove, (Childrens Press, 1985).

Better Known As Johnny Appleseed, Mabel Leigh Hunt (Lippincott, 1950).

Value of Love: Story of Johnny Appleseed, Ann Donegan Johnson (Value Communications, 1979).

Black People Who Made the Old West, William Loren Katz (Crowell, 1977).

Johnny Appleseed: A Tall Tale, Steven Kellogg (Morrow Junior Books, 1988).

Rose Wilder Lane: Her Story, Rose Wilder Lane (Stein and Day, 1977).

Johnny Appleseed: A Poem, Reeve Lindbergh (Little, Brown, 1990).

She Won the West: An Anthology of Western and Frontier Stories by Women, Marcia Muller and Bill Pronzini (Morrow, 1985).

Davy Crockett: An American Hero, Tom Townsend (Eakin Press, 1987).

The Story of Johnny Appleseed, Walt Disney Productions (Golden Press, 1969).

Classic American Folk Tales, Steven Zorn (Courage Books, 1992).

VIDEOS

Johnny Appleseed, Shelley Duval's Tall Tales and Legends (FOX Video, 1995). Length: 52 minutes.

CDS, RECORDS, AND CASSETTES

The Story of Johnny Appleseed (record), Walt Disney Productions (Walt Disney Productions, 1964).

INTRODUCTORY ACTIVITIES

DAY ONE

Objective: The students will watch a video about Johnny Appleseed. They will discuss whether Johnny Appleseed was a real person.

Curriculum subject: Language Arts

Teacher: A folktale is a legend or a myth that has been told for several generations. Many of the stories are based on real people; however, as the story is passed from one person to the next the character becomes exaggerated.

Today we'll watch a movie about a man named Johnny Appleseed. As you watch the story, decide whether you think Johnny Appleseed was a real person. Be ready to talk about your opinion after the movie is over.

Show the video *Johnny Appleseed* starring Rob Reiner, Molly Ringwald, and Martin Short. After the film, discuss whether the students believe the story of Johnny Appleseed is based on a real person. Do not give them the answer. Tomorrow they will read a biography about John Chapman (Johnny Appleseed).

DAY TWO

Story Lesson

Before reading the story, review what they discussed yesterday. Was Johnny Appleseed a real person or a fictional character? Do not give the students the answer.

Follow the *Presenting the Story Lesson* instructions in the Introduction. Each story lesson follows the same procedure; however, say the following in step 4:

"The title of the story we're reading today is *A Folktale Comes to Life.* What do you think the story is about?" If the students mention Johnny Appleseed, ask, "What do you already know about Johnny Appleseed?"

EXTENSION ACTIVITIES

1. The students will make a list of Johnny Appleseed's attributes that are fictional (exaggerated) and nonfictional based on the folktale.

◆ Divide a chart paper in half. Label one half fiction and the other half nonfiction.

FICTION	NONFICTION

◆ Compare the folktale about Johnny Appleseed with the biography of John Chapman. Which parts of the folktale are fictional? Which parts of the folktale are based on fact (nonfiction)? Enter the students' answers into the chart.

◆ Explain to the students that the story of Johnny Appleseed became a folktale when people began to pass the story from person to person. Each time the story was told the legend moved farther away from the facts. Over time, the life of John Chapman became the folktale we know as Johnny Appleseed.

2. The students will write a nonfiction biography.

◆ The students will choose a person they would like to learn about, and write a short biography about the person. The subject of the biography should be someone who has done something special. The subject might be a sports hero, a musician, a teacher, or other person who achieved something beyond what was expected.

3. The students will write a folktale.

◆ Review the facts about each student's subject (see Extension Activity 2). Can the student exaggerate the person's accomplishments? If the subject is a track star, can the student embellish his or her accomplishments? For example:

> Jackie Joyner-Kersee is the greatest track star who ever lived. When she jumps over the hurdles, thunder sounds in the stadium from the force of her strength. The rush of wind in her wake blows the hats off the spectators.

◆ The students will draw pictures to illustrate their folktales.

◆ Divide a bulletin board in half. Display the biographies on one side and the folktales on the other.

A FOLKTALE COMES TO LIFE

John Chapman, born in 1774, lived a legendary life. In fact, his life became a cherished American folktale.

Chapman met a group of settlers heading West in 1804. He joined the pioneers for a short time. Soon he left the group to begin traveling alone for over twenty-five years.

In his lifetime, Chapman had many adventures. Chapman brought more troops to Mansfield, Ohio, during the War of 1812. That night he ran thirty-six miles in the woods.

Americans remember John Chapman for a pouch of apple seeds, however. From Pennsylvania to Indiana, Chapman planted apple orchards. Soon the pioneers told stories about the famous Johnny Appleseed.

While he traveled, Chapman preached the Christian religion. Many people said Johnny Appleseed wore a tin-pan hat. One story tells how Johnny slept in the arms of a bear.

Many folktales come from true stories. In fact, you can still find many of the apple trees planted by Johnny Appleseed along the old pioneer trails.

QUESTIONS FOR A FOLKTALE COMES TO LIFE

1. In what year was John Chapman born?

   _____

   _____

2. What did Chapman do in the War of 1812?

   _____

   _____

3. What did Chapman plant from Pennsylvania to Indiana?

   _____

   _____

4. What did John Chapman preach while he traveled?

   _____

   _____

5. What did Chapman do after he left the group of pioneers?

   _____

   _____

6. What was John Chapman called after he began to plant apple seeds?

   _____

   _____

7. What one word best describes John Chapman (Johnny Appleseed)? Why do you think so?

   _____

   _____

8. Why did Johnny Appleseed's life become an American folktale?

   _____

   _____

9. Will people continue to tell the story of Johnny Appleseed in the future? Why do you think so?

_____

_____

10. Why do people remember John Chapman (Johnny Appleseed) for planting apple seeds and not for his work in the War of 1812?

_____

_____

11. Write a title for the story. Use as few words as possible.

_____

_____

12. How is the folktale about John Chapman like his real life? How is it different?

_____

_____

13. In your own words, tell what John Chapman did to help the army in the War of 1812.

_____

_____

14. What effect do the trees planted by Johnny Appleseed have on people today?

_____

_____

15. The story said, "You can still find many of the apple trees planted by Johnny Appleseed along the old pioneer trails." Is this a fact or someone's opinion? How can you prove your answer?

_____

_____

16.

_____

_____

Name _____   Date _____

FREEDOM

ABOUT THE STORY

The story describes the space station Freedom. America's NASA, Japan, Canada, and the European Space Agency agreed to work together to build Freedom. The station will cost as much as 30 billion dollars.

PREVIEW WORDS

experiments	space shuttles	equipment
space station	tunnels	Freedom
panels	European Space Agency	Canada
Japan	NASA	

THROUGHOUT THE WEEK—Read the book *Space Camp: The Great Adventure for NASA Hopefuls* by Anne Baird (New York: Morrow Junior Books, 1992) to the class. This nonfiction book follows students as they participate in the six-day NASA program, Space Camp.

PRIOR TO THE LESSON

During the week, the students will pretend they live on a space station. You will need to prepare for the week by choosing activities appropriate to your curriculum. Some of these activities require special materials.

There are many other sources for space station activities. They include:

McKay, David W., and Bruce G. Smith, *Space Science, Projects for Young Scientists*. New York: Franklin Watts, 1986.

Petty, Kate, *Build Your Own Space Station*. New York: Franklin Watts, 1985.

Simon, Seymour, *How to Be a Space Scientist in Your Own Home*. New York: J.B. Lippincott, 1982.

Wood, Robert W., *Science for Kids: 39 Easy Astronomy Experiments*. Blue Ridge Summit, PA: TAB Books, 1990.

Teacher's Companion to the Space Station: A Multi-Disciplinary Resource: A Project of Martin Marietta and the Louisiana Nature & Science Center, Lynn Purnell Hagan, Kathleen E. Beauford and Elizabeth Ann "Liz" Elsen. New Orleans, Louisiana: Michoud Aerospace Public Relations Dept., n.d.

The *Teacher's Companion to the Space Station* is an excellent resource for both elementary and secondary teachers. The book contains activities from many curriculum subjects based on the topic of a space station. The Louisiana Nature & Science Center is located at 11000 Lake Forest Blvd., New Orleans, LA 70127, (504)246-5672.

BOOKS TO READ

Space Station, Necia H. Apfel (Franklin Watts, 1987).

The World's Space Programs, Isaac Asimov, (Gareth Stevens Children's Books, 1990).

Space Camp: The Great Adventure for NASA Hopefuls, Anne Baird (Morrow Junior Books, 1991).

If You Lived on Mars, Melvin Berger (Lodestar Books, 1988).

Our Future in Space, Don Berliner (Lerner Publications, 1991).

Easy to Make Spaceships That Really Fly, Mary Blocksma (Prentice Hall, 1983).

Workshops in Space, Ben Bova (Dutton, 1974).

Space Colony: Frontier of the 21st Century, Franklin M. Branley (Elsevier/Nelson Books, 1982).

Skylab, Dennis B. Fradin (Childrens Press, 1984).

Space Exploration, Michael George (Creative Education, 1993).

Homes in Space, Graham Rickard (Lerner Publications, 1989).

Skylab Pioneer Space Station, William G. Holder and William D. Siuru, Jr. (Rand McNally, 1974).

Space Exploration, Brian Jones (Gareth Stevens Children's Books, 1989).

Space Station: Leadership for the Future, Franklin D. Martin (National Aeronautics and Space Administration, 1987).

Science Experiments for the Space Age, Sam Rosenfeld (Harvey House, 1972).

The Space Station: An Idea Whose Time Has Come, Theodore R. Simpson , ed. (Institute of Electrical and Electronics Engineers, 1985).

Space Laboratories, Gregory Vogt (Franklin Watts, 1989).

Far Out: How to Create Your Own Star World, Robin West, (Carolrhoda Books, 1987).

INTRODUCTORY ACTIVITIES

DAY ONE

Objective: The students will research designs of space stations. They will write a brief description of a space station.

Curriculum subject: Science or Language Arts

Teacher: This week we'll learn about space stations. We'll imagine we're on a space station, and do space experiments.

Before we can imagine the inside of our station, we must determine what it looks like on the outside. There are many types of space station designs. The United States built Skylab where astronauts could work in an orbiting laboratory. The Soviets share their Mir space station with visiting astronauts from other countries.

Every space station has its own unique design. What will the design of our space station look like?

Break into groups. Using our reference books, look for pictures of space stations. Choose the station that you believe is the best design. Write a brief paper telling why you prefer this design. Later, we'll listen to each group, and vote on the design for our space station.

Hold a debate on the space station designs the students chose. After the debate, the students vote for the design they would like to use.

Working together, the students will make a mural-size picture of their space station design on bulletin board paper. They will label the various sections according to their use. Display the picture in front of the class.

After the students leave for the day, decorate the room like the space station. Set up tables for experiments, rearrange the chairs, and hang space photographs around the room.

DAY TWO

Story Lesson

Follow the *Presenting the Story Lesson* instructions in the Introduction. Each story lesson follows the same procedure; however, say the following in step 4:

"The title of the story we're reading today is *Freedom*. What do you think the story is about?" If the students mention space stations, ask, "What do you already know about space stations?"

EXTENSION ACTIVITIES

1. There are many reference books containing activities in space science for use in the classroom (see Prior to the Lesson). Spend the rest of the week with the students play-acting a trip on a space station.

2. Perform activities in each curriculum subject based on the space station theme.

◆ Math: Write story problems involving your math objectives on a space theme. For example; The Soviet Mir space station is 56 feet long. NASA's Long Duration Exposure Facility (LDEF) is 30 feet long. How much longer is the Mir space station than the LDEF?

◆ Physical Education:

The students focus on astronaut training exercises like those described in *Space Camp: The Great Adventure for NASA Hopefuls* by Anne Baird, page 17. Astronauts must exercise in space to maintain muscle tone.

3. On the last day of the space station week serve a space lunch.

Menu

◆ Grilled "moon" cheese sandwiches

◆ Dried fruit

◆ "Little-Green-Men" cookies

Ingredients:

One package of chocolate drop cookies
    One can of white icing
    Green food coloring

Mix green food coloring into the white icing. Spread the icing on one chocolate drop cookie. Press another chocolate drop cookie on top of the icing. Serve.

◆ "Red Planet Juice Drink" (cranberry juice or other red drink)

◆ Also see *Teacher's Companion to the Space Station,* page 37–38, for a list of shuttle food and beverages.

FREEDOM

A giant space station orbits Earth. The people living in the station study the stars, and do science experiments. Space shuttles often make trips to the station bringing people, food, and equipment.

This story is not taking place hundreds of years from now. Today, many countries are ready to work together to build a space station. They will call the station Freedom.

Freedom will have two living spaces connected by tunnels. Each living space will be 45 feet long and 13.8 feet round. In the center of the station, large panels will collect energy from the sun.

Japan, Canada, the European Space Agency, and America's NASA agreed to work together. These countries must raise 30 billion dollars before they can build Freedom.

Should we build a space station? Is a space station a good way to spend our money? We must find the answers to these questions as America dreams of reaching for the stars.

QUESTIONS FOR FREEDOM

1. What is the name of the space station in the story?

   _____

   _____

2. How many living spaces will the station have?

   _____

   _____

3. Where will Freedom's energy come from?

   _____

   _____

4. Who has agreed to work together to build Freedom?

   _____

   _____

5. What must happen before Freedom can be built?

   _____

   _____

6. What will people do after they begin living on the space station?

   _____

   _____

7. Is it possible that Freedom will never be built? Why do you think so?

   _____

   _____

8. Why do you think NASA, Canada, Japan, and the European Space Agency agreed to build Freedom together?

   _____

   _____

9. Do you think the United States will give NASA the money needed to build Freedom? Why do you think so?

_____

_____

10. Why do you think NASA feels it is important to build Freedom?

_____

_____

11. Write a title for the story. Use as few words as possible.

_____

_____

12. How are space shuttles and space stations alike? How are they different?

_____

_____

13. In your own words, tell what the space station Freedom will look like.

_____

_____

14. How will a space station affect the lives of the American people?

_____

_____

15. The story said, "Today, many countries are ready to work together to build a space station." Is this a fact or someone's opinion? How can you prove your answer?

_____

_____

16.

_____

_____

Name _____   Date _____

THE TELEPHONE OF THE FUTURE

ABOUT THE STORY

AT&T introduced its new VideoPhone 2500 in 1992. Like the phones in science fiction movies, the VideoPhone shows the person you are talking to on a television screen. It may take several years before the cost of the VideoPhone becomes affordable for the general public, but a video-pay-phone may come to a store near you.

PREVIEW WORDS

AT&T	VideoPhone	science fiction
diameter	twitch	images

THROUGHOUT THE WEEK

Read the book *A Connecticut Yankee in King Arthur's Court* by Mark Twain (New York: William Morrow, 1988) to the class. As the students listen to the story, ask them to imagine a man from the year 2050 appearing in the classroom. What would he look like? What kind of clothes would he wear? What strange inventions would he share with us?

BOOKS TO READ

Fact or Fantasy, Neil Ardley (Franklin Watts, 1982).

Out Into Space, Neil Ardley (Franklin Watts, 1981).

Transport on Earth, Neil Ardley (Franklin Watts, 1981).

Science Fiction, Science Fact, Isaac Asimov (Gareth Stevens Children's Books, 1989).

Eureka! Its a Telephone, Jeanne Bendick (Millbrook Press, 1993).

What to Do When Your Mom or Dad Says, "Get the Phone!," Joy Wilt Berry (Childrens Press, 1983).

Alexander Graham Bell, Andrew Dunn (Bookwright Press, 1991).

World's Fairs and Expos, Allan Fowler (Childrens Press, 1991).

The Future and the Past: Life 100 Years From Now and 100 Years Ago, Robert Gardner and Dennis Shortelle (Julian Messner, 1989).

Future Cities: Homes and Living Into the 21st Century, Kenneth William Gatland (Usborne, 1979).

Great Inventions, (Dorling Kindersley, 1993).

The Visual Dictionary of Everyday Things, (Dorling Kindersley Book, 1991).

Homes in the Future, Mark Lambert (Lerner Publications, 1989).

Transportation in the Future, Mark Lambert (Bookwright Press, 1986).

Hello, Alexander Graham Bell Speaking: A Biography, Cynthia Copeland Lewis (Dillon Press, 1991).

Alexander Graham Bell, Patricia Ryon Quiri, (Franklin Watts, 1991).

Science: It's Changing Your World (National Geographic, 1985).

Get the Message: Telecommunications in Your High-Tech World, Gloria Skurzynski (Maxwell Macmillan International, 1993).

A Connecticut Yankee in King Arthur's Court, Mark Twain (Morrow, 1988).

Telephone Time: A First Book of Telephone Do's and Don'ts, Ellen Weiss (Random House, 1986).

2041: Twelve Short Stories About the Future by Top Science Fiction Writers, selected and edited by Jane Yolen (Delacorte Press, 1991).

INTRODUCTORY ACTIVITIES

DAY ONE

Objective: The students will compare objects of the past to their counterparts of the present.
Curriculum subject: History
Teacher: This week we'll imagine the world of the future. Like science fiction writers, we'll imagine the cities, homes, and schools of the year 2050. What will the buildings look like? What form of transportation will we use? What will the field of medicine offer us? What clothes will we wear?

Before we can predict the future, we must first look at the past. It is easier to predict what a bicycle will look like in fifty years if we look at bicycles designed fifty years ago. Break into groups. I'll assign each group a topic. Look for examples of the subject from the past, and examples of that same subject today. Compare the changes made in the technology and design. For example, if you're looking at the bicycle, draw a picture of an old model and a picture of the latest bicycle design. How have bicycles changed? How have they remained the same?

When you're finished, you'll share your findings with the class.

After the students finish their work, ask each group to share what they learned. Display the pictures and papers on a bulletin board entitled "Yesterday and Today."
Suggested subjects:

◆ clothing   ◆ airplanes   ◆ CDs

◆ cars   ◆ furniture   ◆ homes

◆ schools   ◆ parks   ◆ restaurants

◆ computers

DAY TWO

Story Lesson

Follow the *Presenting the Story Lesson* instructions in the Introduction. Each story lesson follows the same procedure; however, say the following in step 4:

"The title of the story we're reading today is *The Telephone of the Future.* What do you think the story is about? What do you already know about telephones?"

EXTENSION ACTIVITIES

1. The students will design items of the future.

◆ The students return to their groups from Day One.

◆ Using the same topic as Day One, they will design their subject as they imagine it in the year 2050.

◆ They will draw pictures of their design, and write a description of how the object works.

2. Remaining in their groups, the students will write letters to companies that produce their subject product. The companies might include automobile companies, clothes designers, architects, airplane manufacturers, or computer companies.

◆ The students will ask the designers about their predictions for future products in their companies.

◆ You can find the addresses for these companies at your local library.

3. The class will make a mural of the city of the future.

◆ Hold a class discussion on what a future city might look like. Each group will give input, using the information they learned about their subject.

◆ On the chalkboard, chart paper, or overhead projector, draw out a rough design of the mural based on the students' input. If you feel uncomfortable drawing, ask a student to help. This is only a rough drawing. Do not include details. Stick people and box-shaped cars will give the general idea of the mural. This plan will help avoid arguments during the activity.

◆ Roll out a long piece of bulletin board paper. The students will work together to draw their mural. The students who looked into the future of cars will draw the cars. The students who worked on clothing will draw the people, and so on.

◆ Display the mural with the title "City of the Future."

THE TELEPHONE OF THE FUTURE

AT&T introduced its new VideoPhone 2500 in 1992. Like the telephones in science fiction stories, the VideoPhone shows the person you are talking to on a television screen.

The VideoPhone is the first of its kind to use the same wires as a regular telephone. Simply unplug your telephone and plug in your VideoPhone.

Unlike the large screens in science fiction stories, AT&T's screen is only 3.3 inches in diameter. The VideoPhone also sends only two to ten pictures per second. This makes the images on the screen twitch.

To make the picture clearer, you must adjust the focus. The clearer you make the picture, however, the fewer pictures you will see per second.

You might not have a VideoPhone in your home for many years. A VideoPhone cost $1,000 in 1993. A video-pay-phone may come to a store near you, however.

QUESTIONS FOR THE TELEPHONE OF THE FUTURE

1. What company introduced the VideoPhone 2500?

   _____

   _____

2. In what year was the VideoPhone 2500 introduced?

   _____

   _____

3. How large is the screen of the VideoPhone?

   _____

   _____

4. How much did the VideoPhone cost in 1993?

   _____

   _____

5. What must you do before you plug in your VideoPhone?

   _____

   _____

6. What happens to the picture on the screen after you adjust the focus?

   _____

   _____

7. Do you think the VideoPhone will replace telephones in the future? Why do you think so?

   _____

   _____

8. Does the author expect the cost of VideoPhones to go down? Why do you think so?

   _____

   _____

9. Will people want to buy a VideoPhone? Why do you think so?

_____

_____

10. Why did AT&T make the VideoPhone 2500?

_____

_____

11. Write a title for the story. Use as few words as possible.

_____

_____

12. How is a VideoPhone like the telephone you use at home? How is it different?

_____

_____

13. In your own words, describe the images on the VideoPhone. Why do they look this way?

_____

_____

14. Imagine that everyone owned a VideoPhone. How would the way you answer the telephone change?

_____

_____

15. The story said, "You might not have a VideoPhone in your home for many years." Is this a fact or the author's opinion? Why do you think so?

_____

_____

16.

_____

_____

Name _____   Date _____

BIBLIOGRAPHY

Adler, T., "Rain-Forest Trees Exhibit High Turnover," *Science News,* 145, no. 8 (Feb. 19, 1994), 116.

Angelucci, Enzo, and Attilio Cucari, *Ships.* New York: Greenwich House, 1983, pp. 133–134.

Berrill, N.J., "Fireworm," *Encyclopedia Americana* (1963), 11, 257.

"Chapman, John (Johnny Appleseed)," *People Who Made America.* 3, 206. Skokie, IL: United States History Society, Inc., 1973.

Crouthers, David D., *Flags of American History.* Maplewood, NJ: Hammond, Inc., 1973.

Fiero, Robert, "The Video Phone," *Americana Annual* (1994), 192. Canada: Grolier Inc., 1994.

Fry, Ron and Pamela Fourzon, *The Saga of Special Effects,* pp. 5–16. Englewood Cliffs, NJ: Prentice Hall, 1977.

Greene, Carol, *John Chapman: The Man Who Was Johnny Appleseed.* Chicago: Childrens Press, 1991.

——, *Ludwig van Beethoven: Musical Pioneer.* Chicago: Childrens Press, 1989.

Jenkins, Patrick, *Animation: How to Draw Your Own Flipbooks, and Other Fun Ways to Make Cartoons Move.* Reading, Mass.: Addison-Wesley Publishing Company, Inc., 1991.

Marshall, Richard, ed., *Great Events of the 20th Century,* 12–17. Pleasantville, New York: The Reader's Digest Association, Inc., 1977.

Monastersky, Richard, "The Eruption of Mount Pinatubo," *The Americana Annual* (1992), 251. Canada: Grolier Inc., 1992.

"Robert J. Acosta," *People Who Made America,* 1, 10. Skokie, IL: United States History Society, Inc., 1973.

Sloan, Henry S., "Hughes, Howard," *Americana Annual* (1977), 374. Canada: Grolier Inc., 1977.

"Space Exploration," *Americana Annual* (1987), 470. Canada: Grolier Enterprises, Inc., 1987.

"Space Exploration," *Americana Annual* (1988), 470. Canada: Grolier Enterprises, Inc., 1988.

"Space Exploration," *Americana Annual* (1989), 472. Canada: Grolier Enterprises, Inc., 1989.

"Space Exploration, " *Americana Annual* (1992), 470. Canada: Grolier Enterprises, Inc., 1992.

"Special Effect," *The New Illustrated Science and Invention Encyclopedia* (1989), 19, 2516.

Stein, R. Conrad, *The Story of the Monitor and the Merrimac.* Chicago: Childrens Press, 1983.

Waldron, Colonel W.H., "Flags of America," *Our Wonderful World: An Encyclopedic Anthology for the Entire Family* (1962), 7, 270.

"Zoetrope: The Wheel of Life," *Our Wonderful World: An Encyclopedic Anthology* (1962), 7, 196.

READING LEVEL 6

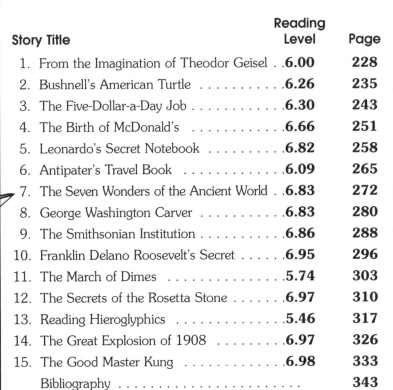

FROM THE IMAGINATION OF THEODOR GEISEL

ABOUT THE STORY

The story tells about the life and accomplishments of Theodor Geisel. The author explains why Geisel chose the pen name Dr. Seuss. Dr. Seuss won many awards for his work, including an Oscar, two Academy Awards, and a Pulitzer Prize for his lifetime of work.

PREVIEW WORDS

Theodor Geisel   Academy Award   Oscar

Pulitzer   scientific

BOOKS TO READ

Ready! Set! Read!: The Beginning Reader's Treasury, compiled by Joanna Cole and Stephanie Calmenson (Doubleday, 1990).

Wider Than the Sky: Poems to Grow Up With, collected and edited by Scott Elledge (Harper & Row, 1990).

Dr. Seuss, Ruth K. MacDonald (Twayne Publishers, 1988).

The Tough Coughs As He Ploughs the Dough: Early Writings and Cartoons by Dr. Seuss, edited by Richard Marschall (William Morrow, 1986).

Dr. Seuss, We Love You, Patricia Stone Martin (Rouke Enterprises, 1987).

Dr. Seuss From Then to Now: A Catalogue of the Retrospective Exhibition, San Diego Museum of Art (Random House, 1986).

Daisy-Head Mayzie, Dr. Seuss (Random House, 1994).

I Can Read With My Eyes Shut!, Dr. Seuss (Random House Books for Young Readers, 1978).

I Am Not Going to Get Up Today, Dr. Seuss (Random House Books for Young Readers, 1987).

Oh, the Places You'll Go!, Dr. Seuss (Random House, 1990).

Six by Seuss, Dr. Seuss (Random House, 1991).

You're Only Old Once!, Dr. Seuss (Random House, 1986).

*Ask your librarian for a complete list of books by Dr. Seuss.

VIDEOS

Dr. Seuss on the Loose, Dr. Seuss (Playhouse Video, 1989). Length: 30 minutes.

Dr. Seuss's The 5000 Fingers of Dr. T, Dr. Seuss (RCA/Columbia Pictures Home Video, 1991). Length: 88 minutes.

Pontoffel Pock, Where Are You?, Dr. Seuss (Random House Home Video, 1992). Length: 30 minutes.

It's Grinch Night, Dr. Seuss (Random House Home Video, 1992). Length: 30 minutes.

Horton Hatches the Egg, Dr. Seuss (Random House Home Video, 1992). Length: 30 minutes.

Horton Hears a Who!, Dr. Seuss (Random House Home Video, 1992). Length: 30 minutes.

CDS, RECORDS, AND CASSETTES

Dr. Seuss's ABC (cassette and book set), Dr. Seuss (Random House, 1977).

Gerald McBoing and Other Heros (CD), XTET (musical group) (Delos International, 1990).

Horton Hears a Who! (cassette and book set), Dr. Seuss (Random House, 1990).

Oh, the Thinks You Can Think (cassette and book set), Dr. Seuss (Random House, 1986).

INTRODUCTORY ACTIVITIES

DAY ONE

Objective: The students will watch a video of a Dr. Seuss story. They will listen closely to his style of writing, and discuss the unique characteristics of his work.

Curriculum subject: Language Arts

Teacher: Throughout the week, we'll listen to and look at stories by Dr. Seuss. Today we'll watch a video called *Horton Hears a Who.* (You can use any Dr. Seuss video if this one is not available.)

Every writer and illustrator has his or her own unique style. Dr. Seuss also has a unique style.

As you watch the film, you'll take notes. You'll list what you hear and see that is part of Dr. Seuss's unique style. Does he use special characters? Does he make up special rhyming words? What is the tone of his poems: sad, happy, scary? Write down specific examples of Dr. Seuss's unique style.

Watch the movie *Horton Hears a Who.* After the movie, discuss Dr. Seuss's unique style. Write a list on chart paper.

DAY TWO

Objective: The students will listen to three poems. Based on yesterday's discussion, they will identify which of the three poems was written by Dr. Seuss.

Curriculum subject: Language Arts

Display the chart listing features of Dr. Seuss's unique style. Review yesterday's discussion.

Teacher: Today we'll listen to three poems by different poets. I won't tell you the names of the poets. Listen carefully. When you think you hear a poem by Dr. Seuss, write down the title. I'll read the title at the beginning and the end of the poem. If you didn't hear the title the first time, wait to hear it again at the end. When I finish the poems, we'll see who could recognize the poem by Dr. Seuss.

Read the following three poems, or poems of your choice, from *Wider Than the Sky: Poems to Grow Up With.* Remember, do not read the name of the poet until after all the poems are read, and the students discuss their choices.

"Stopping by Woods on a Snow Evening," Robert Frost, page 16

"Too Many Daves," Dr. Seuss, page 137

"Roger the Dog," by Ted Hughes, page 41

DAY THREE

Story Lesson

Follow the *Presenting the Story Lesson* instructions in the Introduction. Each story lesson follows the same procedure; however, say the following in step 4:

"The title of the story we're reading today is *From the Imagination of Theodor Geisel.* What do you think the story is about?" If the students mention Dr. Seuss, ask, "What do you already know about Dr. Seuss?"

EXTENSION ACTIVITIES

1. The students will listen to two stories by Dr. Seuss: *I Am Not Going to Get up Today!* and *Oh, the Thinks You Can Think!*. Which story did the students enjoy the most? Why? How are the two books alike? How are they different?

2. The students will listen to the story *Oh, the Places You'll Go!*. After reading the story, discuss places the students might like to go. Would they like to see the Grand Canyon? Would they like to see a space shuttle take off?

◆ Give each student a poster board. They will cut out pictures from magazines of places they would like to go. The students will use glue sticks to mount the pictures in collage form on the poster board. Display the collages under the title "Oh, the Places You'll Go!"

3. The students will make trash monsters with available materials such as milk cartons, egg cartons, plastic cola bottles, broken ping pong balls, and so on. Encourage them to use their imaginations. The monsters can sit, stand, hang from the ceiling, or act as bookends.

◆ The students will name their monsters and write Dr. Seuss-like poems about the monsters. The students can refer to Dr. Seuss books for inspiration.

FROM THE IMAGINATION OF THEODOR GEISEL

On March 2, 1904, a boy named Theodor Geisel was born. Theodor's father ran a zoo, and the young boy often went with his father to work. The strange and unusual animals became part of Theodor's imagination.

Theodor grew up and graduated from college in 1925. In 1937, Theodor wrote and illustrated his first children's book.

He didn't like the sound of his name. Theodor thought an author of children's books should sound more "scientific," so he took his middle name and added the title Dr. Dr. Seuss soon became loved by children around the world.

Dr. Seuss created a new company to sell his books called Beginner Books. He wrote funny stories like Marvin K. Mooney Will You Please Go Now!, and stories that taught lessons (The Lorax).

Dr. Seuss also worked on movies that told true stories. Two of these films won Academy Awards. His cartoon Gerald McBoing-Boing won an Oscar in 1951. Finally, in 1984, Dr. Seuss won a special Pulitzer award for his lifetime of work. Theodor Seuss Geisel died on September 25, 1991.

QUESTIONS FOR
FROM THE IMAGINATION OF THEODOR GEISEL

1. When was Theodor Geisel born?

_____

_____

2. Where did Theodor's father work?

_____

_____

3. When did Theodor Geisel graduate from college?

_____

_____

4. When did Theodor Geisel win a special Pulitzer award for his lifetime of work?

_____

_____

5. What did Theodor Geisel do before he wrote his first children's book?

_____

_____

6. Which award did Dr. Seuss win first: an Oscar or a special Pulitzer award?

_____

_____

7. What one word best describes Dr. Seuss?

_____

_____

8. How do people feel about Dr. Seuss', work? Why do you think so?

_____

_____

9. Will children continue to enjoy the stories by Dr. Seuss in the future? Why do you think so?

_____

_____

10. Why do you think Dr. Seuss wrote children's books, worked on movies, and made cartoons?

_____

_____

11. Write a title for the story. Use as few words as possible.

_____

_____

12. Read the books <u>Marvin K. Mooney Will You Please Go Now!</u> and <u>The Lorax</u>. How are these Dr. Seuss stories alike? How are they different?

_____

_____

13. In your own words, tell how Theodor Geisel created the name he used as an author of children's books.

_____

_____

14. Read the story <u>Horton Hears a Who</u> by Dr. Seuss. How do you think visiting the zoo as a young boy affected Dr. Seuss's work?

_____

_____

15. The story said, "Dr. Seuss also worked on movies that told true stories. Two of these films won Academy Awards." Is this statement a fact or an opinion? How can you prove your answer?

_____

_____

16.

_____

_____

Name _____   Date _____

BUSHNELL'S AMERICAN TURTLE

ABOUT THE STORY

During the American Revolution, colonists had few weapons to use against the well-armed British Navy. The colonists turned to David Bushnell. Bushnell designed the first working submarine. The shape of the submarine inspired its name, Bushnell's Turtle.

PREVIEW WORDS

David Bushnell	American Revolution	British
gunpowder	submarine	hull
Eagle	torpedoes	

THROUGHOUT THE WEEK—Read fiction stories about submarines to the class. For example:

Webb, Robert N., *We Were There on the Nautilus.* New York: Grosset & Dunlap Publishers, 1961. Historical Consultant: Captain William R. Anderson, U.S.N.

Verne, Jules, *Twenty Thousand Leagues Under the Sea.* Englewood Cliffs, NJ: Globe Books, 1992.

Jones, Raymond F., *Voyage to the Bottom of the Sea.* Racine, Wisconsin: Whitman Publishing Company, 1965.

BOOKS TO READ

Nautilus 90 North, William R. Anderson, (World Publishing Company, 1959).

Run Silent, Run Deep, Edward L. Beach (Naval Institute Press, 1986).

The U-Boats, Douglas Botting (Time-Life Books, 1979).

Strange Craft, Walter Buehr (Norton, 1963).

What About? Submarines, Ron and Joyce Cave (Gloucester Press, 1982).

Submarine: A Guided Tour Inside a Nuclear Warship, Tom Clancy (Berkley Books, 1993).

Submarine Warfare: Men, Weapons, and Ships, C.B. Colby (Coward-McCann, 1967).

Two Centuries of Seapower: 1776–1976, C.B. Colby (Coward, McCann & Geoghegan, 1976).

Modern Military Techniques: Submarines, Tony Gibbons (Lerner Publications, 1987).

Ships and Submarines, Modern Technology, Michael Grey (Franklin Watts, 1986).

From the Turtle to the Nautilus, Edwin Palmer Hoyt (Little, Brown, 1963).

Voyage to the Bottom of the Sea, Raymond F. Jones (Whitman Publishing Company, 1965).

American Submarines, H.T. Lenton (Doubleday & Company, 1973).

Vessels for Underwater Exploration, Peter R. Limburg and James B. Sweeney (Crown Publishers, 1973).

Submarine Warfare: Today and Tomorrow, John E. Moore and Richard Compton-Hall (Adler & Adler, 1987).

Submarines, A New True Book, David Petersen (Childrens Press, 1984).

Who Said There's No Man on the Moon?: A Story of Jules Verne, Robert M. Quackenbush (Simon & Schuster Books for Young Readers, 1989).

Nuclear Submarine, The Inside Story, Mike Rossiter (Gloucester Press, 1983).

Looking Inside Ships Through the Ages, David Sharp (Rand McNally, 1976).

David Bushnell and His Turtle: The Story of America's First Submarine, June Swanson (Atheneum, 1991).

Submarines, Robert van Tol (Franklin Watts, 1984).

Twenty Thousand Leagues Under the Sea, Jules Verne (Globe Books, 1992).

The World of Model Ships and Boats, Guy R. Williams (Putnam's, 1971).

We Were There on the Nautilus, Robert N. Webb (Grosset & Dunlap, 1961).

VIDEOS

20,000 Leagues Under the Sea (Burbank, CA: Walt Disney Home Video, [1991?]) Length: 127 minutes.

INTRODUCTORY ACTIVITIES

DAY ONE

Objective: The students will watch the movie *Voyage to the Bottom of the Sea.* They will watch how the submarine dives and surfaces.

Curriculum subject: Science

Teacher: During the week we'll learn about submarines. We'll learn about submarine history and the science behind the operation of submarines.

Today we're going to watch a fictional story about submarines called *Voyage to the Bottom of the Sea.* Although the story is fictional, the film makers wanted the submarine to look as real as possible.

As you watch the film, look at the way the submarine operates. What do the men do to make the submarine dive? What do they do to make the submarine surface? What can you learn about the submarines when you watch the film?

Show the film *Voyage to the Bottom of the Sea.* Discuss the questions presented before the story. Make a list on chart paper of the things the students observed about submarines.

DAY TWO

Story Lesson

Follow the *Presenting the Story Lesson* instructions in the Introduction. Each story lesson follows the same procedure; however, say the following in step 4:

"The title of the story we're reading today is *Bushnell's American Turtle.* What do you think the story is about?" If the students mention submarines, ask, "What do you already know about submarines?"

EXTENSION ACTIVITIES

1. The students will learn how a submarine operates. First, review the notes the students made on Day One regarding what they noticed about submarines in the film *Voyage to the Bottom of the Sea*.

Materials

◆ a fish tank or other clear container large enough to hold a plastic cola bottle lying on its side

◆ plastic cola bottle with a black plastic bottom

◆ small, plastic toy people

Procedure

◆ Fill the fish tank with water.

◆ Carefully remove the black plastic bottom of the cola bottle. Cut about 1inch off the bottom of the bottle.

◆ Put five plastic toy people in the bottle. Replace the black bottom over the cut end.

◆ Tighten the bottle top.

Teacher: Today we'll learn how a submarine dives and surfaces. This cola bottle is a model of a submarine. There's air in our submarine so our sailors can breath.
What happens to our submarine when I put it in the water?
(Answer: The bottle floats. It tends to turn in the water.)
(Discuss these questions as you write them on the board.)

◆ How does a real submarine dive and rise in the water without taking out the air the sailors breath?

◆ How does the design of a submarine keep it from turning in the water?

◆ Remember, we saw that the submarine in *Voyage to the Bottom of the Sea* didn't go straight down when it dived. It angled slowly and gracefully into the water. Why doesn't a submarine dive straight down?

◆ What does the word buoyancy mean? If you were to talk to a submariner, he or she would tell you about three types of buoyancy: positive buoyancy, negative buoyancy, and neutral buoyancy. What do these terms mean?

Let's break into four groups. Each group will work on one of these questions. You must look for sources to answer your questions. You can use books, or ask someone who knows about submarines. Tomorrow the groups will come up to our submarine model and demonstrate what they learned.

2. The students will learn about different types of submarines.

◆ Break the students into groups.

◆ Give each group one of the following names of submarines.

◆ The students will research the submarine and write about it. They need to know when the submarine was built, who designed it, how deep it can dive, and the purpose of the submarine.

◆ They will draw a picture of the submarine, preferably a cut-away drawing, on a poster board.

◆ Display the posters and stories in the classroom.

   Submarines:

   ◆ Robert Fulton's *Nautilus*

   ◆ *The Intelligent Whale*

   ◆ *Holland*

   ◆ German U-Boat

   ◆ *U.S. Albacore*

   ◆ *HL Hunley*

   ◆ *Deep Quest*

   ◆ *Aluminaut*

   ◆ *Deepstar 4,000*

   ◆ *Trieste*

   ◆ *Archimède*

   ◆ *Alvin*

3. Read *David Bushnell and His Turtle: The Story of America's First Submarine* to the class.

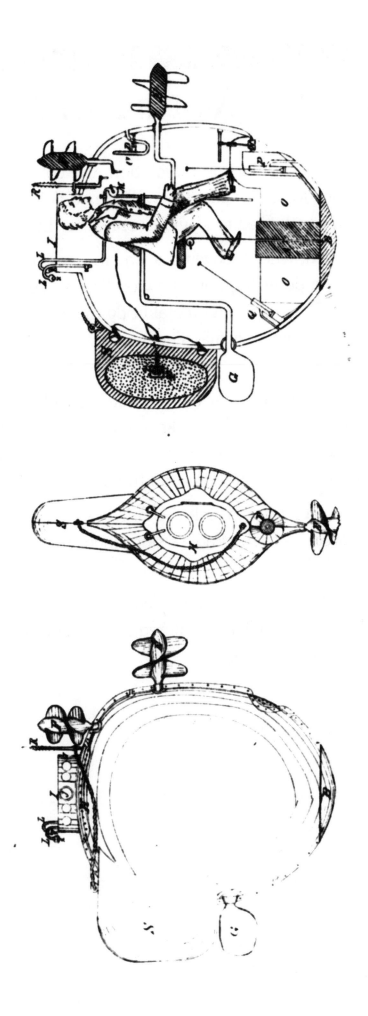

BUSHNELL'S AMERICAN TURTLE

During the American Revolution, the colonists had few weapons to use against the well-armed British Navy. The Americans turned to David Bushnell for help.

Bushnell, who discovered a way to explode gunpowder underwater, built the world's first true submarine. The shape and metal body made Bushnell's submarine look like a turtle. The Turtle was ready for action in 1775.

The Turtle had water tanks inside. To sink, the tanks filled with water. The tanks emptied and filled with air when the Turtle rose to the surface. The turtle could fire torpedoes. It also had drills on the outside of the shell.

The Turtle tried to sink the British ship Eagle. It quietly moved up to the Eagle's side, then tried to drill a hole in the hull.

All of the Turtle's attacks were unsuccessful, but Bushnell's American Turtle entered history books as the first working submarine.

QUESTIONS FOR BUSHNELL'S AMERICAN TURTLE

1. Who were the American colonists fighting against in the American Revolution?

   _____

   _____

2. Who built the world's first true submarine?

   _____

   _____

3. Why was Bushnell's submarine called the Turtle?

   _____

   _____

4. How did the Turtle try to sink the British ship, the Eagle?

   _____

   _____

5. What happened to the tanks inside the Turtle before the submarine could sink?

   _____

   _____

6. What did the Turtle do just before it tried to drill a hole in the Eagle's hull?

   _____

   _____

7. Was building the Turtle a good use of American war money during the American Revolution? Why do you think so?

   _____

   _____

8. How effective were the Turtle's drills in sinking enemy ships? How can you prove your answer?

   _____

   _____

9. Will submarines have drills on the outside in the future? Why do you think so?

_____

_____

10. Why did the American colonists want a submarine?

_____

_____

11. Write a title for the story. Use as few words as possible.

_____

_____

12. Look at a picture of the Turtle and a picture of a modern submarine. How are they alike? How are they different?

_____

_____

13. In your own words, tell how Bushnell made the Turtle sink. How did he make it rise to the surface?

_____

_____

14. How did the Turtle change the way navies fight at sea?

_____

_____

15. The story said, "The shape and metal body made Bushnell's submarine look like a turtle." Is this statement a fact or someone's opinion? How can you prove your answer?

_____

_____

16.

_____

_____

Name _____   Date _____

THE FIVE-DOLLAR-A-DAY JOB

ABOUT THE STORY

The story tells about Henry Ford and his respect for the hard work of the common people. In 1914, he more than doubled the daily wages of assembly-line workers. The five-dollar-a-day jobs caused a flood of applicants. In turn, Ford's loyal workers increased productivity and profits.

PREVIEW WORDS

Henry Ford

assembly-line

genius

revolutionized

Detroit

manufacturing

machinist

PRIOR TO THE LESSON

Contact a local historical automobile society or someone who rebuilds antique cars. Ask if someone could drive an antique car, preferably a Model T, to the school. Ask if the driver could explain the history and operation of the car.

THROUGHOUT THE WEEK—Read the book *We'll Race You, Henry: A Story about Henry Ford* by Barbara Mitchell (Minneapolis: Carolrhoda Books, 1986) to the class. Ask the students to look for passages that point to Henry Ford's drive to create a high-quality automobile.

BOOKS TO READ

Henry Ford: Young Man With Ideas, Hazel B. Aird and Catherine Ruddiman (Simon & Schuster Children's Books, 1986).

Cars and How They Go, Joanna Cole (Thomas Crowell, 1983).

Driver's Ed, Caroline B. Cooney (Delacorte Press, 1994).

The Automobile, Arthur Evans (Lerner Publications, 1985).

A Collector's Guide to Automobilia, edited by John A. Gunnell (Krause Publications, 1994).

Henry Ford, Jacqueline L. Harris (Franklin Watts, 1984).

What's Inside?: Cars, edited by Hilary Hockman (Dorling Kindersley, 1993).

Classic Cars, Robert B. Jackson (H.Z. Walck, 1973).

Waves, Wheels, and Wings: Museums of Transportation, Robert B. Jackson (H.Z. Walck, 1974).

The Story of Cars, Howard W. Kanetzke (Raintree Childrens Books, 1978).

We'll Race You, Henry: A Story about Henry Ford, Barbara Mitchell (Carolrhoda Books, 1986).

The Smithsonian Collection of Automobiles and Motorcycles, Smith Hempstone Oliver and Donald H. Berkebile (Smithsonian Institution Press, 1968).

Henry Ford, Adrian Paradis (Putnam's, 1968).

The Irrepressible Automobile: A Freewheeling Jaunt Through the Fascinating World of the Motorcar, Vernon Pizer (Dodd, Mead, 1986).

The A-to-Z Book of Cars, Angela Royston and Terry Pastor (Barron's, 1991).

Great Cars, H.R. Sheffer (Crestwood House, 1983).

The Model T Ford, Christopher Simonds (Silver Burdett Press, 1991).

Encyclopedia Brown's Book of Wacky Cars, Donald J. Sobol (Morrow, 1987).

Tin Lizzie, Peter Spier (Doubleday, 1975).

Automobiles of the Future, Irwin Stambler (Putnam's, 1966).

The Buffy-Porson: A Car You Can Build and Drive, Peter and Mike Stevenson (Scribners, 1974).

Look Out! Here Comes the Stanley Steamer, K.C. Tessendorf (Atheneum, 1984).

Automobile: From Prototype to Scrapyard, Frank Young (Gloucester Press, 1982).

Miniature Vehicles, Robert Young (Dillon Press, 1993).

VIDEOS

Henry Ford Museum and Greenfield Village, Select Video Publishing. Length: 30 minutes.

INTRODUCTORY ACTIVITIES

DAY ONE

Objective: The students will listen to the story *Tin Lizzie*. They will list ways in which Ford's automobile changed the way people live.

Curriculum subject: Languages Arts or Social Studies

Teacher: Throughout the week we'll learn about Henry Ford. Henry Ford built a car called the Model T, or Tin Lizzie. These were the first mass-produced cars. For the first time, most families could afford an automobile.

Henry Ford's cars not only changed the way people moved from place to place, but also changed the way people lived. Listen to the story *Tin Lizzie* by Peter Spier. As I read the story, look for ways the Tin Lizzie changed its owners' lives, and affected the people in the towns where the first car owners lived.

Read the story *Tin Lizzie* to the class. Emphasize how the Tin Lizzie changed society. Later in the week, the students will design cars of the future and predict how these cars will change their lives.

DAY TWO

Story Lesson

Follow the *Presenting the Story Lesson* instructions in the Introduction. Each story lesson follows the same procedure; however, say the following in step 4:

"The title of the story we're reading today is *The Five-Dollar-a-Day Job*. What do you think the story is about?" If the student's mention Henry Ford or the Model T, ask, "What do you already know about Henry Ford? What do you already know about the Model T?"

EXTENSION ACTIVITIES

1. Invite someone who owns a Model T (or other antique car) to class.

◆ Before meeting with the speaker, prepare a who, what, when, where, and why question list with the students. For example:

Who designed and built the car?

What changes did society experience after the introduction of the car?

When was the car produced?

Where was the car built?

Why did the designer or manufacturer make this particular car?

◆ End the visit with a question-and-answer session.

2. Read the book *Automobiles of the Future* to the class. If your library does not have this book, request it through interlibrary loan.

◆ Select passages to read to the students that predict changes in cars. For example, page 66 discusses a car design by the Ford Motor Company called the Nucleon. The designers at Ford predicted that future cars might run on nuclear power. This prediction was made over thirty years ago. With what we know about nuclear power and waste, will we ever see nuclear-powered cars? Why do the students think so, or think not?

◆ Ask the students to look at the cars, and imagine cars thirty years in the future. What will the cars look like? What form of energy will power the cars? What will the roads look like? How will these new cars change our society?

3. The students will design cars of the future. This activity will last several days.

◆ Break the class into groups of four to five students. Each group will design a car of the future. They will write a description of the car, and make a poster to advertise their car.

◆ The students will:

  ◆ choose a power source for the car;

  ◆ design the exterior and interior;

  ◆ consult mechanics, scientists, car designers, or collectors; and

  ◆ present their final designs and concepts to the class.

◆ Encourage the students to write to designers of major car companies. Your local library can supply the addresses. The students should inquire about the power sources for future cars. How will computers change the cars we drive?

◆ After the students present their designs, discuss how the cars will change society. Will we continue to see people driving their personal cars to work? What will the roadways look like? Will these new cars reduce or eliminate pollution? Why is the future of cars important to our personal lives?

4. After finishing the book *We'll Race You, Henry,* ask the following questions:

◆ Henry Ford said, "Most people spend more time and energy in going around problems than trying to solve them."

What does this mean?

Did Henry Ford work to solve his problems in the story?

Why do you think so?

Have you ever wasted time going around a problem instead of solving it?

What would have been a better response to the problem?

THE FIVE-DOLLAR-A-DAY JOB

In 1992, most workers in the United States earned $440 per week, or $88 a day. Imagine living in the year 1914, earning about $2 a day.

Henry Ford, the man who revolutionized automobile manufacturing, believed in the hard work of the common people. In 1914, he decided to more than double the daily wages of assembly-line workers. He advertised, "Henry Ford wants hard-working men. Earn a salary of <u>five dollars a day</u>!"

Hundreds of men flooded Detroit for a chance to work for the Ford Company. Outside Ford's factory, police kept the hopeful men in order. When it was over, hundreds went away without jobs.

Those hired by Ford became loyal employees. By 1915, they tripled the number of cars built at Ford. By 1924, Ford workers built two million new cars a year.

Henry Ford was a farmer, woodcutter, machinist, businessman, and the founder of the Ford Motor Company. Although many consider Ford a genius, he never learned to read above the fourth-grade level.

QUESTIONS FOR THE FIVE-DOLLAR-A-DAY JOB

1. What was the daily salary in 1914?

    _____

    _____

2. In what year did Ford decide to more than double the daily wages of assembly-line workers?

    _____

    _____

3. Why did hundreds of men flood Detroit for a chance to work for the Ford Company?

    _____

    _____

4. How many cars did Ford workers build in 1924?

    _____

    _____

5. What happened after people heard that Henry Ford was hiring men at a salary of five dollars a day?

    _____

    _____

6. What was the average daily salary before Ford more than doubled wages?

    _____

    _____

7. What one word best describes Henry Ford?

    _____

    _____

8. Why did the men hired by Ford become loyal employees?

    _____

    _____

9. Using the information in the first paragraph of the story, what might the average salary be in 2070?

_____

_____

10. Why do you think Henry Ford raised salaries so high?

_____

_____

11. Write a title for the story. Use as few words as possible.

_____

_____

12. Would men working at the Ford Company in 1915 work differently from the way they would at another car company? How would their work be the same? How would it be different?

_____

_____

13. In your own words, tell what happened when Henry Ford offered jobs paying five dollars a day.

_____

_____

14. Henry Ford's reading skills were low, yet he was able to build a major company. Would he be able to create a business today without strong reading skills? Why do you think so?

_____

_____

15. The story said, "Henry Ford believed in the hard work of the common people." Is this statement a fact or someone's opinion? How can you prove your answer?

_____

_____

16.

_____

_____

Name _____   Date _____

THE BIRTH OF McDONALD'S

ABOUT THE STORY

The story tells about the McDonald brothers who owned a clean, efficient drive-in restaurant. The brothers agreed to allow Ray Kroc to sell franchises. Within five years, Kroc set up 228 restaurants. In 1961, the brothers sold all their interests in McDonald's to Ray Kroc for 2.5 million dollars.

PREVIEW WORDS

McDonald's	Ray Kroc	efficient
eatery	profitable	franchise
trademarks	recipes	fad

PRIOR TO THE LESSON

Arrange for a field trip to a local McDonald's. Obtain the proper parent permission.

BOOKS TO READ

Better Mousetraps: Product Improvements That Led to Success, Nathan Aaseng (Lerner Publications, 1990).

The Fortunate Fortunes, Nathan Aaseng (Lerner Publications, 1989).

The Rejects, Nathan Aaseng (Lerner Publications, 1989).

The Unsung Heroes, Nathan Aaseng (Lerner Publications, 1989).

The Problem Solvers, Nathan Aaseng (Lerner Publications, 1989).

How to Turn Lemons Into Money: A Child's Guide to Economics, Louise Armstrong (Harcourt Brace Jovanovich, 1976).

Standing Up for America: A Biography of Lee Iacocca, Patricia Haddock (Dillon Press, 1987).

Henry Ford, Jacqueline L. Harris (Franklin Watts, 1984).

Grinding It Out: The Making of McDonald's, Ray Kroc (Henry Regnery, 1977).

McDonald's: Behind the Arches, John F. Love (Bantam Books, 1986).

Spaceburger: A Kevin Spoon and Mason Mintz Story, Daniel Pinkwater (Maxwell Macmillan, 1993).

Animal Cafe: Story and Pictures, John Stadler (Aladdin Books, 1986). A Reading Rainbow Book.

The Burg-O-Rama Man, Stephen Tchudi (Delacorte Press, 1983).

Dave's Way: A New Approach to Old-Fashioned Success, R. David Thomas (Putnam's, 1991).

Mr. Blue Jeans: A Story About Levi Strauss, Maryann N. Weidt (Carolrhoda Books, 1990).

Tomart's Price Guide to McDonald's Happy Meal Collectibles, Meredith Williams (Tomart Publications, 1992).

INTRODUCTORY ACTIVITIES

DAY ONE

Objective: The students will meet a speaker representing a McDonald's restaurant. The speaker will introduce them to the McDonald's system, and explain what a franchise is.
Curriculum subject: Social Studies

Invite a manager of a McDonald's restaurant or another McDonald's representative to class. The speaker should preview what the students will see and learn when they visit McDonald's. Tell him or her to prepare to answer questions about the McDonald's system and franchises.

Before the speaker arrives, help the students write who, what, when, where, and why questions. Write the questions on chart paper. Some example questions are:

◆ Who is the head of the McDonald's Corporation?

◆ What is a franchise?

◆ When did the first McDonald's open for business?

◆ Where are the McDonald's franchises located?

◆ Why is McDonald's so popular?

End the class with a question-and-answer period.

DAY TWO

Objective: The students will visit a local McDonald's.
Curriculum subject: Social Studies

Before going to the McDonald's, review what was learned on Day One. The students should look closely at how the McDonald's works. As they go to the restaurant, tell them to look for positive aspects of the restaurant, and for negative aspects. Did you wait a long time to be served? Were the tables clean? Did the McDonald's have play equipment for the children? Was the equipment kept in good condition?

After the trip, the students will write a letter to the manager of the McDonald's. They will thank the manager for his or her hospitality, as well as point out positive, and—if applicable—negative aspects of the restaurant.

Tell the students to visit the McDonald's a few months after this lesson. Has the manager made changes based on the students' observations?

DAY THREE

Story Lesson
Follow the *Presenting the Story Lesson* instructions in the Introduction. Each story lesson follows the same procedure; however, say the following in step 4:

"The title of the story we're reading today is *The Birth of McDonald's*. What do you think the story is about? What do you already know about McDonald's?"

EXTENSION ACTIVITIES

1. Read the chapter "The Fast-Food Pioneers: McDonald's" from the book *The Unsung Heroes.*

◆ Although the McDonald brothers saw the restaurant concept they created make millions of dollars, they never regretted selling the restaurant chain. Why do you think they felt this way?

2. Ask a representative of a local Ronald McDonald House to visit the class. What is the purpose of the house? How is the McDonald's Corporation involved? What does the Ronald McDonald House need?

◆ The students will work to find or make the supplies needed at the Ronald McDonald House. They can make latch hook rugs, toys, or quilts. The students might call local businesses and relatives to ask for donations of supplies they can't make themselves.

◆ The Ronald McDonald House might need volunteers to do work around the house. Does the yard need cleaning? Does the house need painting? What can the students do to help out?

THE BIRTH OF McDONALD'S

In 1954, Ray Kroc stopped at the only drive-in restaurant owned by the McDonald brothers. This clean and efficient eatery sold milk shakes, french fries, and fifteen-cent hamburgers. The first McDonald's was a busy and profitable business.

"I'd like to set up a franchise chain," Kroc told the brothers. "People will buy the right to use the McDonald's name and your system for making hamburgers. I'll pay you a percentage of what the restaurants earn, and I can use the McDonald's name and system." The McDonald brothers agreed, and Kroc set up 228 restaurants in five years. The new franchise business brought in 40 million dollars annually.

In 1961, the McDonald's brothers worried that their hamburgers were a passing fad. They sold their interests, recipes, trademarks, and 300 franchises to Kroc for more than 2.5 million dollars.

QUESTIONS FOR THE BIRTH OF McDONALD'S

1. Who stopped at a drive-in restaurant owned by the McDonald brothers in 1954?

   _____

   _____

2. What did the first McDonald's sell?

   _____

   _____

3. How many restaurants did Kroc set up in five years?

   _____

   _____

4. What did the McDonald's brothers sell to Kroc for 2.5 million dollars?

   _____

   _____

5. After five years, how much money did the new franchise business bring in annually?

   _____

   _____

6. How many McDonald's restaurants were there before Kroc set up the franchise chain?

   _____

   _____

7. What one word best describes Ray Kroc?

   _____

   _____

8. Why was the original McDonald's restaurant so popular?

   _____

   _____

9. Will the McDonald's restaurant chain continue to make large profits? Why do you think so?

_____

_____

10. Why do you think the McDonald brothers sold all their rights to McDonald's?

_____

_____

11. Write a title for the story. Use as few words as possible.

_____

_____

12. How are today's McDonald's like the original restaurant? How are they different?

_____

_____

13. In your own words, tell how the McDonald's franchise system began.

_____

_____

14. How did meeting Ray Kroc affect the McDonald brothers' lives?

_____

_____

15. The story said, "The new franchise business brought in 40 million dollars annually." Is this a fact or an opinion? How can you prove your answer?

_____

_____

16.

_____

_____

Name _____ Date _____

LEONARDO'S SECRET NOTEBOOK

ABOUT THE STORY

The story tells about a secret notebook kept by Leonardo da Vinci. In his notebook he drew pictures of his ideas, including a helicopter, bicycle, and parachute. Leonardo da Vinci wrote his notes in a secret code. To read them, you must look at them in a mirror.

PREVIEW WORDS

Leonardo da Vinci	secret code	machines
invented	blimp	helicopter
bicycle	lighter-than-air craft	

THROUGHOUT THE WEEK—During the lessons, the students will learn about people who kept diaries and notebooks. Some of these people are well known. Others simply witnessed or experienced history as it unfolded in their lives.

Throughout the week, read the book *Polar: The Titanic Bear* by Daisy Corning Stone Spedden (Boston, Massachusetts: Little, Brown, 1994). This is a true story about a family who sailed on the Titanic—told in a diary from the perspective of a young boy's toy bear.

BOOKS TO READ

A Gathering of Days: A New England Girl's Journal, 1830–32, Joan Blos (Scribner's, 1979). A Newbery Award book.

Pedro's Journal: A Voyage With Christopher Columbus, Pam Conrad (Caroline House, 1991).

Anne Frank: A Diary of a Young Girl, Anne Frank (Pocket Books, 1958).

Leonardo da Vinci, Richard McLanathan (H.N. Abrams, 1989).

Voices from the Civil War, edited by Milton Meltzer (Thomas Crowell, 1989).

The Fables of Leonardo da Vinci, Bruno Nardini (Hubbard Press, 1973).

Meet Edgar Degas: National Gallery of Canada, compiled by Anne Newlands (Harper & Row, 1988).

Leonardo da Vinci: The Artist, Inventor, Scientist in Three-Dimensional Movable Pictures, Alice and Martin Provensen (Viking Children's Books, 1984).

Leonardo da Vinci: Artist, Inventor and Scientist of the Renaissance, Francesca Romei (Peter Bedrick Books, 1994).

I, Columbus: My Journal, 1492–93, edited by Peter and Connie Roop (Walker, 1990).

A Weekend with Leonardo da Vinci, Rosabianca Skira-Venturi (Rizzoli, 1993).

Polar: The Titanic Bear, Daisy Corning Stone Spedden (Little, Brown, 1994).

A Book of Your Own: Keeping a Diary or Journal, Carla Stevens (Clarion Books, 1993).

Da Vinci, Mike Venezia (Childrens Press, 1989).

How to Make Your Own Book, Harvey Weiss (Thomas Crowell, 1974).

My Diary—My World, Elizabeth Yates (Westminster Press, 1981).

VIDEOS

Leonardo da Vinci: The Visionary Intellect (New York: Academic and Entertainment Video, 1992). Length 30 minutes.

CDS, RECORDS, AND CASSETTES

The Fables of Leonardo da Vinci, Bruno Nardini (Caedmon Records, Inc., 1974).

INTRODUCTORY ACTIVITIES

DAY ONE

Objective: The students will listen to a story about Leonardo da Vinci. They will look for pictures and notes from his notebook.

Curriculum subject: Language Arts or Art

Teacher: This week we'll learn about notebooks and diaries kept by famous people. We'll also look at notebooks kept by people who witnessed historic events, or whose lives teach us about the time in which they lived. Later, we'll make our own notebooks and diaries, and begin to write about our lives.

The first notebook we'll learn about was written by a man named Leonardo da Vinci. Before we can understand the importance of his notebook, however, we must know who Leonardo da Vinci was. Do you know who Leonardo da Vinci was? Do you know why his notebook is so interesting?

First, let's listen to a story about Leonardo da Vinci. The author, Rosabianca Skira-Venturi, wrote the book in a very special way. She doesn't just tell us about Leonardo da Vinci's life; she pretends she is Leonardo da Vinci. As I read the story, imagine you're listening to Leonardo da Vinci telling you about his life.

Also, look for pictures of pages from Leonardo da Vinci's notebook. Tomorrow we'll learn why his notebook is so special.

Read the book *A Weekend with Leonardo da Vinci* to the class. After the story, ask the students why Leonardo da Vinci is an important character in history. Why would someone want to read his notebook?

DAY TWO

Story Lesson

Follow the *Presenting the Story Lesson* instructions in the Introduction. Each story lesson follows the same procedure; however, say the following in step 4:

"The title of the story we're reading today is *Leonardo's Secret Notebook*. What do you think the story is about?" If the students mention Leonardo da Vinci, ask, "What do you already know about Leonardo da Vinci?"

EXTENSION ACTIVITIES

1. The students will listen to excerpts from historical diaries.

◆ Read from *I, Columbus: My Journal, 1492–93.* Read from the entries of Sunday, 9 September, 1492, to Tuesday, 25 September, 1492, on pages 22–26. Ask the students if hearing the story as told by Columbus makes the history seem more real to them. Why do they feel this way?

◆ Read from *Voices From the Civil War: A Documentary History of the Great American Conflict,* pages 183–187. This narrative is from the diary of Gideon Welles, Secretary of the Navy in Lincoln's cabinet. In his diary, Welles describes the death of President Lincoln. Ask the students if hearing a description of the death of President Lincoln made them feel the event in a way they had not felt it before. How did it make them feel? Why did it have such an impact on them?

2. The students will make diaries or notebooks. *How to Make Your Own Book* by Harvey Weiss is a good source of book designs. This book includes many types of book styles, bindings, covers, and so forth. The students can choose the style they want to use.

3. The students will begin making entries in their diaries. The goal of this activity is to take note of current events that may someday become important events in history. Explain to the students that their insights and perspectives on today's news will someday make history more real to their children. Their children will understand what it was like to grow up in this important time in history.

◆ Tell the students to watch the nightly news and bring a newspaper to class. Break the students into groups. The students read the headline news together and discuss what they learned.

◆ Next, the students will make an entry into their diaries or notebooks. They will tell about the facts of the events as well as how they feel about the event. How does this event affect their personal lives and the lives of their family and friends?

◆ Continue this exercise throughout the year. On the last day of school, the students will read from their diaries and talk about the year's events.

LEONARDO'S SECRET NOTEBOOK

Leonardo da Vinci lived from 1452 to 1519, long before the days of cars and planes. Most people think of Leonardo as an artist, but he also kept a secret notebook.

Leonardo drew pictures of his ideas in his notebook. The pictures look very much like the machines we use today. People invented these machines many years after Leonardo died.

Leonardo wrote his ideas in a 3,500 page notebook. He kept his notebook a secret. Leonardo even wrote his notes in a secret code. To read them, you must look at them in a mirror.

Here is a list of some of Leonardo's ideas, and the dates people invented them.

Leonardo's Ideas (1452–1519)	Year Invented
lighter-than-air craft (blimp)	1755
bicycle	1868
machine gun	1885
helicopter	1930s

QUESTIONS FOR LEONARDO'S SECRET NOTEBOOK

1. In what years did Leonardo da Vinci live?

   _____

   _____

2. How many pages were in Leonardo's notebook?

   _____

   _____

3. What must you do to read Leonardo's secret code?

   _____

   _____

4. What did Leonardo draw in his notebook?

   _____

   _____

5. Which was made first: Leonardo's notebook or the helicopter?

   _____

   _____

6. What do you have to do before you can read Leonardo's secret notes?

   _____

   _____

7. What one word best describes Leonardo da Vinci?

   _____

   _____

8. How did Leonardo feel about people reading his notebook? Why do you think so?

   _____

   _____

9. Will Leonardo's notebook continue to interest people in the future? Why do you think so?

_____

_____

10. Why do you think Leonardo kept a notebook?

_____

_____

11. Write a title for the story. Use as few words as possible.

_____

_____

12. If you kept a notebook, how would it be like Leonardo da Vinci's? How would it be different?

_____

_____

13. Describe Leonardo da Vinci's notebook in your own words.

_____

_____

14. Imagine if Leonardo da Vinci did not just write about a helicopter, but made one in 1500. Would this have changed human history? Why do you think so?

_____

_____

15. The story said, "Leonardo da Vinci lived long before the days of cars and planes." Is this a fact or someone's opinion? How can you prove your answer?

_____

_____

16.

_____

_____

Name _____   Date _____

ANTIPATER'S TRAVEL GUIDE

ABOUT THE STORY

In 200 B.C., a man named Antipater made a travel guide. His guide named wonderful places ancient tourists might want to see. He called these tourist spots "The Seven Wonders of the World."

PREVIEW WORDS

Antipater

tourists

destroyed

travel agent

sightseers

guide

Mediterranean Sea

ancient world

Egyptian

PRIOR TO THE LESSON

Contact local travel agents. Ask them if they have old travel guides or posters that they could donate to your class. Decorate the classroom with the posters and guides.

BOOKS TO READ

Take a Trip to New Zealand, Geoff Burns (Franklin Watts, 1983).

African Journey, John Chiasson (Bradbury Press, 1987).

Remember Me to Harold Square, Paula Danziger (Delacorte Press, 1987).

Take a Trip to Holland, Chris Fairclough (Franklin Watts, 1982).

Take a Trip to Ireland, Ian James (Franklin Watts, 1983).

Take a Trip to Cuba, Keith Lye (Franklin Watts, 1987).

Take a Trip to Greece, Keith Lye (Franklin Watts, 1982).

Take a Trip to Hong Kong, Keith Lye (Franklin Watts, 1983).

Take a Trip to India, Keith Lye (Franklin Watts, 1982).

Take a Trip to Jamaica, Keith Lye (Franklin Watts, 1988).

Take a Trip to Mexico, Keith Lye (Franklin Watts, 1982).

Take a Trip to Nepal, Keith Lye (Franklin Watts, 1988).

Take a Trip to Russia, Keith Lye (Franklin Watts, 1982).

Take a Trip to Scotland, Keith Lye (Franklin Watts, 1984).

Take a Trip to Peru, Keith Lye (Franklin Watts, 1987).

Take a Trip to Nicaragua, Keith Lye (Franklin Watts, 1988).

Take a Trip to Syria, Keith Lye (Franklin Watts, 1988).

Take a Trip to Turkey, Keith Lye (Franklin Watts, 1988).

Take a Trip to Venezuela, Keith Lye (Franklin Watts, 1988).

Take a Trip to West Indies, Keith Lye (Franklin Watts, 1983).

Take a Trip to Yugoslavia, Keith Lye (Franklin Watts, 1987).

Going Places: The Young Traveler's Guide and Activity Book, Harriet Webster (Scribner's, 1991).

INTRODUCTORY ACTIVITIES

DAY ONE

Objective: The students will make a list of seven places in the United States that everyone
should visit.

Curriculum subject: Social Studies

Teacher: This week we'll learn about interesting places to visit. We'll make travel posters and
travel guides. Today, we'll make a list of seven places in the United States tourists
should visit.

First, get into groups of four to five students. Talk about interesting places in the
United States. Make a list of seven places in the United States that tourists should
visit. Next to each name write three reasons why a tourist should go to this place.

Give the students time to work on their lists. Call on each group to name the places on
their list. Finally, the class as a whole will choose seven of the best tourist spots in the United
States. Write the list on chart paper. Label the chart "The Seven Wonders of the United States."

DAY TWO

Story Lesson

Follow the *Presenting the Story Lesson* instructions in the Introduction. Each story lesson follows the same procedure; however, say the following in step 4:

"The title of the story we're reading today is *Antipater's Travel Guide*. What do you
think the story is about? What do you already know about travel guides?"

EXTENSION ACTIVITIES

1. As a group, the students will make a list entitled "The Seven Wonders of (name of their city
or town)." The list can include buildings, monuments, and parks.

2. Break the students into seven groups. Assign each group one of the seven wonders from
the previous activity.

◆ The students will make a small travel guide telling about their "wonder." They can include
post cards, personal photographs, and so forth. Their guide should encourage tourists to
visit their "wonder."

◆ A good source for instructions to make various styles of books is *How to Make Your Own
Book* by Harvey Weiss (New York: Thomas Y. Crowell Company, 1974).

3. Staying in the group from the previous activity, the students will make a travel poster for
their "wonder." Encourage the students to make an eye-catching, creative poster.

◆ Display the posters on a bulletin board entitled "The Seven Wonders of (name of their town
or city)."

4. Read activities found in *Going Places: The Young Traveler's Guide and Activity Book* to
the class. For example, read the section called "Six Ways to Keep Busy While Standing in
Line" on pages 4–5.

◆ Ask the students if they have special games or tricks they use while they are on trips to help them remember the sights, learn more about what they see, or keep from getting bored. What games do you play on long car rides? Do your parents let you take something special on the trip? What can you do to help you remember all the sights you saw on your trip?

◆ Make a list of the students' ideas. After class, type out their ideas and suggestions on a master copy. Make copies to share with the students and parents.

ANTIPATER'S TRAVEL GUIDE

If you wanted to see places you'd never seen before you'd call a travel agent. A travel agent might show you travel guides. These books show pictures of places you might want to visit.

People of the ancient world also liked to travel. Ships sailed the Mediterranean Sea carrying eager tourists.

About 200 B.C., or over 2,000 years ago, a man named Antipater made a travel guide. Antipater knew that tourists wanted to know about the best places to visit. Like sightseers today, they wanted their trips to take them to the choice tourist spots in the world.

Antipater's guide was a list of seven amazing sights. The list included what we still call "The Seven Wonders of the World." These seven wonders were the finest buildings and works of art in Antipater's ancient world.

You can visit only one of these wonders today, the Egyptian Pyramids. Earthquakes, fire, and time destroyed the rest.

QUESTIONS FOR ANTIPATER'S TRAVEL GUIDE

1. Whom would you call if you wanted to see places you'd never seen before?

   _____

   _____

2. When did Antipater make his travel guide?

   _____

   _____

3. How many wonders did Antipater list in his travel guide?

   _____

   _____

4. Which one of these wonders can you visit today?

   _____

   _____

5. What might a travel agent show you before you went on a trip to see things you'd never seen before?

   _____

   _____

6. How many wonders of the ancient world remain after earthquakes, fire, and time destroyed the rest?

   _____

   _____

7. Did Antipater enjoy traveling? Why do you think so?

   _____

   _____

8. Did the people of the ancient world take vacations? Why do you think so?

   _____

   _____

9. Imagine looking at a travel guide in the year 2050. What seven wonders of the world (or universe) might the author list?

_____

_____

10. Why did Antipater write his travel guide?

_____

_____

11. Write a title for the story. Use as few words as possible.

_____

_____

12. How is the transportation used by tourists of the ancient world like the transportation used by modern tourists? How is it different?

_____

_____

13. In your own words, tell about the travel guide written by Antipater.

_____

_____

14. Do you think Antipater's travel guide changed the way ancient tourists planned their sightseeing trips? Why do you think so?

_____

_____

15. The story said, "Antipater knew that tourists wanted to know about the best places to visit." Is this a fact or Antipater's opinion? How can you prove your answer?

_____

_____

16.

_____

_____

Name _____   Date _____

THE SEVEN WONDERS OF
THE ANCIENT WORLD

ABOUT THE STORY

Antipater wrote about the Seven Wonders of the World in ancient times. This story names the wonders, and gives a short description of each.

PREVIEW WORDS

Antipater	Babylon	terraced
Zeus	columns	ivory
ebony	Colossus	Apollo
tomb	Halicarnassus	Pharos
lighthouse	pyramids	Egypt
Artemis	temple	

BOOKS TO READ

Ancient Worlds: Egypt, Peggy Ruth Cole and Ann Dearsley-Vernon (The Chrysler Museum).

Ancient Worlds: Greece and Rome, Peggy Ruth Cole and Ann Dearsley-Vernon (The Chrysler Museum, 1989).

Journey Through Ancient Civilizations, Roger Coote (Smithmark Publishers, 1992).

Ancient Rome, Cultural Atlas for Young People, Mike Corbishley (Facts on File, 1989).

Ancient Cities, Judith Crosher (Rourke Enterprises, 1985).

Ancient Egypt, A. Rosalie and Antony E. David (Warwick Press, 1984).

Ancient Rome, Sophia Harvarti Fenton (Holt, Rinehart and Winston, 1971).

Olympics, Dennis B. Fradin (Childrens Press, 1983).

Ancient Egypt, Cultural Atlas for Young People, Geraldine Harris (Facts on File, 1989).

Exploring the Past: Ancient Egypt, George Hart (Harcourt Brace Jovanovich, 1989).

Ancient Greece, John Ellis Jones (Warwick Press, 1983).

The Seven Wonders of the World, Kenneth McLeish (Cambridge University Press, 1985).

Sumer and Babylon, H.E.L. Mellersh (Thomas Crowell, 1964).

An Egyptian Pyramid, Jacqueline Morley, Mark Bergin, John James (Peter Bedrick Books 1991).

Ancient Greece, Cultural Atlas for Young People, Anton Powell (Facts on File, 1989).

Ancient Greece, Susan Purdy and Cass R. Sandak (Franklin Watts, 1982).

Drawing History: Ancient Egypt, Elaine Raphael (Franklin Watts, 1989).

Ancient Egypt, Charles Alexander Robinson, Jr. (Franklin Watts, 1984).

Ancient Greece, Charles Alexander Robinson, Jr. (Franklin Watts, 1984).

Ancient Rome, Charles Alexander Robinson, Jr. (Franklin Watts, 1984).

See Inside: An Egyptian Town, series editor R.J. Unstead (Warwick Press, 1986).

VIDEOS

The Seven Wonders of the Ancient World (Chicago, IL: Questar Video, 1990.) Length: 60 minutes

---

INTRODUCTORY ACTIVITIES

DAY ONE

Objective: The students will learn about the design of ancient buildings.

Curriculum subject: History or Social Studies

Teacher: This week we'll learn about the Seven Wonders of the Ancient World. Before we can truly understand the beauty of these wonders, we must have a picture in our minds of the type of art and buildings the ancient people created.

First, break into groups. Look through the books about ancient cities and worlds. Look at the designs of the buildings. How are Egyptian, Greek, and Roman buildings alike? How are they different? After looking at the pictures, can you tell which buildings are Egyptian? Can you recognize Greek buildings? What are Roman buildings like?

Discuss these questions in your group. Take notes on what you learned. After you finish your notes, continue to read the books about these ancient civilizations until everyone is finished. Then we'll discuss your answers.

Allow the students to explore the styles of construction. At the end of the lesson, discuss what the students learned with the entire class. Later in the week, the students will build a model of their favorite structure.

DAY TWO

Story Lesson

Follow the *Presenting the Story Lesson* instructions in the Introduction. Each story lesson follows the same procedure; however, say the following in step 4:

"The title of the story we're reading today is *The Seven Wonders of the Ancient World*. What do you think the story is about? What do you already know about the Seven Wonders of the Ancient World?"

EXTENSION ACTIVITIES

1. The students will make models of a building from Egypt, Greece, or Rome.

◆ The students return to the groups they were in on Day One. They will choose an ancient building, such as a nobleman's villa or the Pharos. They will design and make a model of this building. Try to encourage the students not to repeat a building made by another group.

◆ The students can use boxes, paper rolls for pillars, and so on, to make their models. Encourage the students to use their imaginations.

◆ Using masking tape and glue, the students make the skeleton of their model.

◆ Cover the skeleton with papier mâché. Let the model dry.

Papier Mâché

1. Soak sheets of newspaper overnight.
2. Mix 2 tablespoons of flour with 2 to 3 tablespoons of cold water.
3. Mix together until the paste is smooth.
4. Just before using the paste, the teacher pours in a little boiling water.
5. Stir until the paste is thick and shiny.

◆ Paint the model with gesso. Let the model dry.

◆ Glue the model to a piece of cardboard at least 6 inches wider than the model.

◆ The students paint the model and add landscape to the base. Tell the students to use the bright colors they see in the books about Egyptian, Roman, and Greek buildings. Did these ancient people decorate their walls with murals?

◆ The students can add toy figures or tiny clay pots.

◆ Some students enjoy making removable roofs and adding an interior. Allowing them to use their creativity is better than giving them a pattern to follow.

2. The students will make Greek tunics.

Materials

◆ a large white T-shirt (prewashed)
◆ pencils
◆ rulers
◆ fabric paint

Procedure

◆ Slide the T-shirt over a piece of cardboard. The cardboard should be large enough for the bottom of the T-shirt to fit snugly around it. Do not allow the T-shirt to stretch.

◆ Working on one side of the T-shirt, measure up 2 inches from the bottom of the hem and mark a small line with a pencil. Make several of these marks across the bottom of the T-shirt.

◆ Using the pencil marks as guides, connect the marks with a ruler.

◆ Measure up 1 inch from the straight line. Draw the following pattern on the T-shirt

Design:

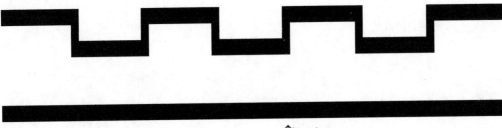

↑first line

◆ Using fabric paint, paint over the pencil lines.

◆ Let the paint dry.

◆ Turn over the shirt, and repeat the design on the back.

◆ Tie a decorative cord around the waist as a belt. Keep the cord very short as a safety precaution. Have the students remove the belts when they leave the room.

3. The students will hold Olympic games.

◆ Ask the physical education teacher to prepare races and other activities for a mini-Olympics.

◆ The students can compete with members of their class, or each class in a grade level can represent a country or team.

◆ The students wear their Greek tunics over pants for the games. Again, remove the cord belt before the games to avoid injury.

4. *Ancient Worlds: Greece and Rome* and *Ancient Worlds: Egypt* are activity books used in the social studies curriculum for the sixth grade in Virginia. The books contain lessons and activities on these ancient civilizations.

THE SEVEN WONDERS OF THE ANCIENT WORLD

Antipater wrote about the Seven Wonders of the Ancient World. Can you name them all?

The Hanging Gardens of Babylon—These terraced walls filled with beautiful plants rose up out of the hot, dry desert.

Statue of Zeus—The artist made the huge statue from stone, ivory, ebony, precious stones, and gold.

The Colossus—This ancient Statue of Liberty was a tribute to the god Apollo.

The Tomb at Halicarnassus—The great tomb was over 600 feet tall, with over 127 columns supporting the roof.

Pharos—A large fire burned on the top of this 600-foot lighthouse. A giant mirror reflected the light out to sea.

The Great Pyramid—With a bottom measuring 755 square feet, the Great Pyramid rises 481 feet off the desert floor.

The Temple of Artemis—The beautiful temple stood over 60 feet tall. 127 large columns held up the ceiling.

What happened to the Seven Wonders? Discover the answers as you learn more about the Seven Wonders of the Ancient World.

QUESTIONS FOR
THE SEVEN WONDERS OF THE ANCIENT WORLD

1. Name the Seven Wonders of the Ancient World.

   _____

   _____

2. What did the artist use to make the statue of Zeus?

   _____

   _____

3. What burned at the top of the Pharos?

   _____

   _____

4. How tall is the Great Pyramid?

   _____

   _____

5. What did the mirror at the top of the Pharos do after the fire was lit?

   _____

   _____

6. Which wonder of the ancient world did the author describe first?

   _____

   _____

7. Look up the word Colossus in the dictionary. Why do you think the statue of Apollo was called the Colossus?

   _____

   _____

8. How did the artist who built the statue of Zeus feel about the god? Why do you think so?

   _____

   _____

9. Will people continue to build expensive monuments like the statue of Zeus?

_____

_____

10. Why might a person build a garden in the middle of the desert?

_____

_____

11. Write a title for the story. Use as few words as possible.

_____

_____

12. How was the Colossus like the statue of Zeus? How was it different?

_____

_____

13. In your own words, tell about the Seven Wonders of the Ancient World.

_____

_____

14. Imagine walking for many days in the hot, dry desert. Suddenly, you see the hanging gardens of Babylon rising out of the desert. Beautiful green plants drape over the high walls. How would the sight of the gardens make you feel? Why do you think so?

_____

_____

15. The story said, "With a bottom measuring 755 square feet, the Great Pyramid rises 481 feet off the desert floor." Is this a fact or an opinion? How can you prove your answer?

_____

_____

16.

_____

_____

Name _____   Date _____

GEORGE WASHINGTON CARVER

ABOUT THE STORY

George Washington Carver began his life as a slave-born child. When he grew up, he earned advanced college degrees in agriculture. Carver invented new ways to recycle waste crops and improve farm production. Although he was offered jobs by both Thomas Edison and Henry Ford, Carver chose to work as an educator and researcher.

PREVIEW WORDS

George Washington Carver	kidnappers	slave-born
agriculture	educator	researcher
Thomas Edison	Henry Ford	waste crops
crop rotation		

PRIOR TO THE LESSON

Locate a colleague teaching a high school agricultural class. Coordinate lessons in which high school agricultural students visit your class. The high school students should prepare a lesson about starting a garden, and a discussion on why they enjoy working with food plants.

THROUGHOUT THE WEEK—Read *The Secret Garden* by Frances Hodgson Burnett (New York: Bantam Books, 1987) to the class. At the end of the story, ask the students why the secret garden was so important to the children. Would the students enjoy growing a garden? Why?

BOOKS TO READ

Growing a Garden: Indoors or Out, Katherine N. Cutler, (Lothrop, Lee & Shepard, 1973).

A Weed Is a Flower: The Life of George Washington Carver, Aliki (Prentice Hall, 1965).

George Washington Carver, Plant Doctor, Mirna Benitez (Raintree Pub., 1989).

Green Thumbs: A Kid's Activity Guide to Indoor and Outdoor Gardening, Laurie Carlson (Chicago Review Press, 1995).

Food Plants, Jennifer Cochrane (Steck-Vaughn Library, 1991).

Blue Potatoes, Orange Tomatoes: How to Grow a Rainbow Garden, Rosalind Creasy (Sierra Club Books for Children, 1994).

Dr. George Washington Carver, Scientist, Shirley Graham Du Bois (Washington Square Press, 1967, 1968).

Dooryard Garden, Ada and Frank Graham (Four Winds Press, 1974).

Greening the City Streets, Barbara A. Huff (Clarion Books, 1990).

From Seed to Jack-O'-Lantern, Hannah Lyons Johnson (Lothrop, Lee & Shepard, 1973).

Potatoes, Sylvia A. Johnson (Lerner Publications, 1984).

First Look at Growing Food, Claire Llewellyn (Gareth Stevens Children's Books, 1991).

A Pocketful of Goobers: A Story About George Washington Carver, Barbara Mitchell (Carolrhoda Books, 1986).

Growing Things, Ting and Neil Morris (Franklin Watts, 1994).

George Washington Carver, Peter Nabokov (Thomas Crowell, 1975).

In My Garden: A Child's Gardening Book, Helen and Kelly Oechsli (Macmillan, 1985).

The Power of Caring: Featuring the Story of George Washington Carver, Maurine Phillips and Phyllis Colonna (Eagle Systems International, 1984).

Grow It for Fun, Denny Robson and Vanessa Bailey (Gloucester Press, 1991).

Get Growing!: Exciting Indoor Plant Projects for Kids, Lois Walker (John Wiley & Sons, 1991).

The Victory Garden Kid's Book, Marjorie Waters (Houghton Mifflin, 1988).

INTRODUCTORY ACTIVITIES

DAY ONE

Objective: The students will listen to high school agricultural students tell why they want to work with plants. The high school students will explain how to plant a vegetable garden.
Curriculum subject: Science

Prepare for a visit from high school agricultural students. Help your students make a who, what, when, where, and why question list before class. Write the questions on a chart paper. For example:

◆ Who is an important figure in crop production in the United States?

◆ What do you need to make a vegetable garden?

◆ When is the best time of the year to plant your vegetables?

◆ Where is the best location for a vegetable garden?

◆ Why did you become involved in agriculture?

Give the high school students some freedom in creating their lesson. End the lesson with a question-and-answer session.

DAY TWO

Story Lesson
Follow the *Presenting the Story Lesson* instructions in the Introduction. Each story lesson follows the same procedure; however, say the following in step 4:
"The title of the story we're reading today is *George Washington Carver.* What do you think the story is about?" If the students mention growing crops or gardening, ask, "What do you already know about vegetable gardens?"

EXTENSION ACTIVITIES

1. The students will grow a vegetable garden. The design and plant selection will vary from school to school. If your school uses a year-round format, the students can start a garden to be cared for by other students. Teachers in the traditional Fall-to-Spring schedule might consider container gardens which the students can take home.

◆ There are several children's books on gardening that can help you put together a class garden. They include:

Get Growing!: Exciting Indoor Plant Projects for Kids

Greening the City Streets: The Story of Community Gardens

Growing a Garden: Indoors or Out

Green Thumbs: A Kid's Activity Guide to Indoor and Outdoor Gardening

2. The students will make decorative plant labels.

Materials

◆ 4" × 6" index cards

◆ tongue depressors

◆ seed envelopes

◆ black markers

◆ clear shelf paper

◆ glue

Procedure

◆ After planting the seeds, cut the front of the seed envelope from the back. Do not damage either side.

◆ Glue the front of an envelope to the front of an index card.

◆ Glue the back of the envelope to the back of the index card.

◆ Write the date the seeds were planted on the index card under the front envelope.

◆ Cover the index card with clear shelf paper. Make sure the shelf paper folds over the edges of the cards.

◆ Glue one tongue depressor to the back of the index card. Avoid covering the writing on the envelope.

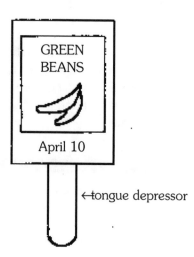

◆ Sink the tongue depressor into the dirt next to the seeds to identify the plants.

3. As the students grow their garden, they will make a notebook. They will keep a daily record of the plants' progress. They will list the plants they chose, and how they planted them. The notebook will tell which plants were successful, and which seeds did not sprout.

◆ Based on these notes, the students will make a class notebook about their garden. Include photographs of the plants as they grow.

◆ Finally, make a list in the class notebook of the top ten plants that produced the best vegetables. Next year's students can use this notebook as a guide, and add their findings to the notebook.

GEORGE WASHINGTON CARVER

In 1863, kidnappers took a slave-born baby. The owner of the child's mother paid for the baby's return with a horse worth $300. This was the beginning of the life of a brilliant American, George Washington Carver.

Although Carver's family had little money, he knew the key to his future was an education. Carver worked as a farmhand while he was in high school. This delayed his graduation until he was in his twenties.

In college, Carver earned advanced degrees in agriculture. Thomas Edison and Henry Ford saw Carver's talents, and asked him to work for them. Instead, Carver chose to work as an educator and researcher.

During the early 1900s, Carver traveled the South teaching farmers how to rotate their crops. This helped the farmers earn more money. Crop rotation also increased the food supply for all Americans.

Carver invented new ways to recycle waste crops. Farmers could now make dyes, soap, plastics, paper, and breakfast food from what they once threw away.

QUESTIONS FOR GEORGE WASHINGTON CARVER

1. What did George Washington Carver do to earn money while he went to high school?

   _____

   _____

2. How old was Carver when he graduated from high school?

   _____

   _____

3. In what subject did Carver earn advanced degrees?

   _____

   _____

4. What did Carver teach the farmers to make from waste crops?

   _____

   _____

5. What degree did Carver earn before he went to college?

   _____

   _____

6. What did Carver choose to work as after Thomas Edison and Henry Ford offered him jobs?

   _____

   _____

7. What one word best describes George Washington Carver?

   _____

   _____

8. How did Carver improve the lives of all Americans, not just farmers?

   _____

   _____

9. Will scientists continue to look for ways to make farms more productive? Why do you think so?

    _____

    _____

10. Edison and Ford offered Carver jobs that probably paid more money than that of an educator and researcher. Why do you think Carver chose to be an educator and researcher?

    _____

    _____

11. Write a title for the story. Use as few words as possible.

    _____

    _____

12. Reread the story The Five-Dollar-a-Day Job. How are George Washington Carver and Henry Ford alike? How are they different?

    _____

    _____

13. In your own words, tell what Carver taught the farmers of the South that helped them earn more money.

    _____

    _____

14. How did Carver's work in agriculture change the way American farmers worked?

    _____

    _____

15. The story said, "Carver invented new ways to recycle waste crops." Is this statement a fact or an opinion? How can you prove your answer?

    _____

    _____

16.

    _____

    _____

Name _____   Date _____

THE SMITHSONIAN INSTITUTION

ABOUT THE STORY

The Smithsonian opened its doors to America in 1855. James Smithson, an Englishman, left the Smithsonian to America as a gift after his death. He hoped to increase learning in the United States of America.

PREVIEW WORDS

Smithsonian	national	dinosaur
Washington, D.C.	James Smithson	England
museum	United States of America	

PRIOR TO THE LESSON

Make the necessary arrangements for a field trip to a museum. You can use any museum from art to science for this activity.

THROUGHOUT THE WEEK—Read to the class a nonfiction book that tells about the Smithsonian Institution. For example:

Stein, R. Conrad, *The Story of the Smithsonian Institution.* Chicago, IL: Childrens Press, 1979.

BOOKS TO READ

The Smithsonian Collection of Automobiles and Motorcycles, Smith Hempstone Oliver and Donald H. Berkebile (Smithsonian Institution Press, 1968).

The Smithsonian Book of Flight for Young People, Walter J. Boyne (Atheneum, 1988).

A Young Painter: The Life and Paintings of Wang Yani, Chen-Sun Cheng (Scholastic, 1991).

Sharks in Question: The Smithsonian Answer Book, Victor Gruschka Springer and Joy P. Gold (Smithsonian Institution Press, 1989).

The Smithsonian Institution: A Picture Story of Its Buildings, Exhibits, and Activities, Gene Gurney (Crown, 1964).

Seeds of Change: A Quincentennial Commemoration, Herman J. Viola and Carolyn Margolis (Smithsonian Institution Press, 1991).

Food and the Kitchen: Step-by-Step Science Activity Projects from the Smithsonian Institution, Smithsonian Institution (Gareth Stevens, 1993).

Games, Puzzles, and Toys: Step-by-Step Science Activity Projects From the Smithsonian Institution, Smithsonian Institution (Gareth Stevens, 1993).

Washington, D.C.: A Smithsonian Book of the Nation's Capital, Smithsonian Institution (Smithsonian Press, 1992).

The Story of the Smithsonian Institution, R. Conrad Stein, (Childrens Press, 1979).

More Science Activities From the Smithsonian Institution, Megan Stine (GMG Publishing, 1988).

Still More Science Activities From the Smithsonian Institution, Megan Stine (GMG Publishing, 1989).

VIDEOS

The Way We Wear: Smithsonian Institution, David Grubin (Washington, DC: WETA, 1988). Length: 58 minutes.

▬▬▬▬▬▬▬▬▬▬▬▬

INTRODUCTORY ACTIVITIES

DAY ONE

Objective: The students will learn the meaning of the word *museum*. They will visit a museum.
Curriculum subject: Language Arts

Today, students will visit a museum. Before leaving, discuss the meaning of the word *museum*.

Teacher: Long ago, the Greeks told stories about gods and goddesses who ruled over the people. The king of the gods was Zeus. Zeus had nine beautiful daughters called Muses. They were:

Clio, the Muse of history;

Euterpe, the Muse of lyric poetry;

Thalia, the Muse of comedy;

Melpomene, the Muse of tragedy;

Terpsichore, the Muse of music and dancing;

Erato, the Muse of love poems;

Calliope, the Muse of epic poems;

Urania, the Muse of astronomy;

Polyhymnia, the Muse of sacred hymns and harmony.

According to legend, Muses visit people in spirit form, and inspire them in the arts and learning.

We use the word *muse* in many ways. If you say a poet is museless, he or she has no inspiration. One word you know that comes from the word muse is museum. The word museum means "a place for the Muses." Is "a place for the Muses" a good way to describe a museum? Why do you think so?

Today, we'll visit a museum. As you look at the exhibits, think about the Muses. According to Greek mythology, the Muses not only inspired the person who made the exhibit, but they also send their spirit to inspire those who look at beautiful works of human achievement.

After the students return from the museum, ask how they felt when they saw the exhibits. In their own words, why do they think *museum,* or "a place for the Muses," describes the place they visited.

DAY TWO

Story Lesson

Follow the *Presenting the Story Lesson* instructions in the Introduction. Each story lesson follows the same procedure; however, say the following in step 4:

"The title of the story we're reading today is *The Smithsonian Institution*. What do you think the story is about? What do you already know about the Smithsonian?"

EXTENSION ACTIVITIES

1. The students will make a mural map of the Smithsonian Institution.

Teacher: James Smithson donated money for the Smithsonian Institution "for the increase and diffusion of knowledge." This means that Smithson wanted Americans to use the Smithsonian as a source of learning and information.

Many people call the Smithsonian "America's attic." America stores all the special items that remind the people of America's past at the Smithsonian.

It takes more than one building to house all the resources and museums that make up the Smithsonian Institution. Many of the Smithsonian's buildings stand in front of the Capitol Building in Washington, D.C. This area is called "the Mall."

Today, we'll make a map of Washington's Mall. We'll draw and label the streets and buildings that make up this historical area of our nation's capital.

◆ Give the students maps of Washington's Mall. (Refer to *The Smithsonian Institution* by Gene Gurney, page 2, or *The Story of the Smithsonian Institution* by R. Conrad Stein, pages 28–29. Discuss the names of the buildings and their locations on the Mall.

◆ Cut out a piece of bulletin board paper large enough to cover a bulletin board.

◆ The students will work together to draw a large map of Washington's Mall. They will label the buildings and streets.

2. The students will write about the buildings in the Smithsonian along Washington's Mall.

◆ Break the students into groups. Assign each group one Smithsonian building in the Mall.

◆ The students will write a research paper about the museum in their building. They will tell about the contents of the museum and why the items in the museum is important to America.

◆ The students will contact agencies in their building. Photographs and other materials are available to students and teachers.

  ◆ The National Museum of Natural History

  ◆ The Freer Gallery of Art

  ◆ The Smithsonian Institution Castle

  ◆ National Museum of American Art

  ◆ National Museum of American History

  ◆ Renwick Gallery

  ◆ Friends of the National Zoo

  ◆ National Portrait Gallery

  ◆ National Museum of African Art

  ◆ Arthur M. Sacker Gallery

  ◆ Anacostia Museum

◆ Arts and Industries
◆ The Hirshhorn Museum and Sculpture Garden
◆ The National Air and Space Museum
◆ Smithsonian Institution

Elementary and Secondary Education
900 Jefferson Dr. S.W.
Washington, DC 20560
Phone number: (202) 357-3049
Information: (202) 357-2425
Fax: (202) 842-6935

THE SMITHSONIAN INSTITUTION

Imagine a place where America keeps its memories—a place everyone can visit. In this place you can find everything from paintings to space capsules. To make it the perfect collection it would even have dinosaur bones.

You can find such a place in Washington, D.C. It's called the Smithsonian Institution.

James Smithson, from England, left the Smithsonian to America as a gift after his death. He hoped to increase learning in the United States of America.

The first Smithsonian Building, called "the Castle," took eight years to build. In 1855, the Smithsonian Institution opened its doors to America.

The Smithsonian prints magazines and makes educational television shows. The Institution has a library and plant displays. There is a National Art Museum and a Space Science Center. When you visit the Smithsonian Institution, you'll find the many treasures of America.

QUESTIONS FOR THE SMITHSONIAN INSTITUTION

1. Where is the Smithsonian Institution?

   _____

   _____

2. Who gave the Smithsonian Institution to America?

   _____

   _____

3. What country was James Smithson from?

   _____

   _____

4. Name two places you can visit at the Smithsonian Institution.

   _____

   _____

5. When was James Smithson's gift given to America, before or after his death?

   _____

   _____

6. Were other buildings added to the Smithsonian after the opening of "the Castle"?

   _____

   _____

7. What one word best describes James Smithson?

   _____

   _____

8. Why is the Smithsonian Institution important to the United States of America?

   _____

   _____

9. Will America add new displays and museums to the Smithsonian in the future? Why do you think so?

_____

_____

10. Why was the Smithsonian built in Washington, D.C.?

_____

_____

11. Write a title for the story. Use as few words as possible.

_____

_____

12. How are a zoo and an art museum alike? How are they different?

_____

_____

13. In your own words, tell about the exhibits found at the Smithsonian Institution.

_____

_____

14. How did James Smithson's gift affect the American people?

_____

_____

15. The story said, "To make it the perfect collection it would even have dinosaur bones." Is this statement a fact or an opinion? How can you prove your answer?

_____

_____

16.

_____

_____

Name _____   Date _____

FRANKLIN DELANO ROOSEVELT'S SECRET

ABOUT THE STORY

Franklin Delano Roosevelt walked to the podium on his inauguration with his son proudly by his side. Few in the cheering crowd realized the effort Roosevelt made to walk on one of the most important days of his life. At age 39, polio paralyzed Roosevelt's legs and lower stomach. Ten-pound braces supported his legs. He practiced his walk for months before the inauguration.

PREVIEW WORDS

Franklin Delano Roosevelt	paralyzing
Great Depression	polio
World War II	inauguration
virus	

THROUGHOUT THE WEEK—Read one of the following stories to the class. Each story deals with the polio virus.

Crofford, Emily, *Healing Warrior: A Story about Sister Elizabeth Kenny.* Minneapolis, Carolrhoda Books, 1989. Outstanding Science Trade Book for Children, NSTA-CBC Joint Committee and a Notable Children's Trade Book in the Field of Social Studies, NCSS-CBC Joint Committee.

Johnston, Julie, *Hero of Lesser Causes.* Boston: Little, Brown, 1992. The Governor General's Award for Children's Literature, Canada.

BOOKS TO READ

Healing Warrior: A Story About Sister Elizabeth Kenny, Emily Crofford (Carolrhoda Books, 1989).

Franklin Delano Roosevelt, Russell Freedman (Clarion Books, 1990).

Eleanor Roosevelt: A Life of Happiness and Tears, William Jay Jacobs (Coward-McCann, 1983).

The Value of Caring: The Story of Eleanor Roosevelt, Ann Donegan Johnson (Value Communications, 1977).

Hero of Lesser Causes, Julie Johnston (Little, Brown, 1992).

Franklin D. Roosevelt, Alice K. Osinski (Childrens Press, 1987).

Eleanor Roosevelt, Sharon Whitney (Franklin Watts, 1982).

INTRODUCTORY ACTIVITIES

DAY ONE

Objective: The students will discuss the meaning of the label "role model." They will list attributes that make up a good role model.

Curriculum subject: Social Studies

Teacher: During the week we'll look at what it means to be a "good role model." We'll look for people, both in the past and the present, whom you consider to be good role models.

First, what is a good role model? What do we mean when we say, "This man or this woman is a good role model?"

Let's make a list of characteristics you think a person must have in order to be called a role model. Can you name something you would look for in a role model?

Write the students' list on chart paper. Ask the students to give the list a title.

DAY TWO

Story Lesson

Follow the *Presenting the Story Lesson* instructions in the Introduction. Each story lesson follows the same procedure; however, say the following in step 4:

"The title of the story we're reading today is *Franklin Delano Roosevelt's Secret.* What do you think the story is about? What do you already know about Franklin Roosevelt?"

EXTENSION ACTIVITIES

1. The students will look for someone they consider a good role model.

◆ Ask the students if they think Franklin Roosevelt is a good role model. Why do they think so? Does he meet the requirements for a good role model the students listed on Day One?

◆ The students will begin a search for their own personal role model. The role model must meet most of the requirements the students listed on Day One.

◆ Take the students to the library or make reference books available. Ask the librarian to show the students reference books that list important people, both past and present. For example, there are reference books dedicated solely to biographies. Some of these reference books focus on society as a whole, while others list only people of a given ethnic group. These reference books generally give very short descriptions of the lives and accomplishments of each person.

◆ The students will look for a person they think is a good role model. This role model should have personal meaning to the student.

◆ Each student will write a short biography of the role model chosen. He or she will tell why this person is a good role model, and why the student admires the role model's accomplishments.

2. The students will write to their role models. The local library can help the students find addresses.

◆ If the person they chose no longer lives, they can contact an institution dedicated to the individual. For example, if a student chooses John F. Kennedy as a role model, the student can write to the John F. Kennedy Presidential Library.

◆ The Smithsonian is a wonderful resource for students and teachers. Many departments offer information about famous Americans. You can find lists of these departments in *Congres-*

sional Quarterly's Washington Information Directory (Congressional Quarterly, Inc.). Your local library should have a copy of this book in the reference section.

◆ It may take several weeks for the students to receive responses to their requests. Looking for information and photographs of role models is a wonderful exercise in using reference books and other library materials, however.

3. The students will make a bulletin board called "Our Role Models." They will display their reports, correspondences, photographs, and other material collected during their search.

With thanks & good wishes
Franklin Roosevelt

FRANKLIN DELANO ROOSEVELT'S SECRET

America was deep in the Great Depression. There were no jobs. Many homeless and hungry people searched for jobs to support their families. The president needed to be a strong leader. Also, America would soon be fighting in World War II.

In 1932, America elected Franklin Delano Roosevelt president. At his inauguration he walked straight-backed, his son proudly beside him. The cheering crowds didn't know that their new president had a secret.

When Roosevelt was 39 years old, he caught a disease called polio. The polio virus attacked Roosevelt's spinal cord, paralyzing his legs and lower stomach. Ten-pound braces supported his limp legs.

How did Roosevelt hide his secret? For months he practiced his inauguration walk. He held his son's arm tightly and pushed himself forward with a cane.

Americans elected Roosevelt president four times—more than any other president. His strong leadership guided America out of the Depression, and to victory in World War II.

QUESTIONS FOR
FRANKLIN DELANO ROOSEVELT'S SECRET

1. In what year did Americans elect Franklin Delano Roosevelt president?

   _____

   _____

2. How old was Roosevelt when he caught polio?

   _____

   _____

3. Which parts of Roosevelt's body did the polio virus paralyze?

   _____

   _____

4. How many times did Americans elect Roosevelt president?

   _____

   _____

5. What happened to Roosevelt's legs and lower stomach after he caught the polio virus?

   _____

   _____

6. Did Roosevelt catch polio before or after he became president?

   _____

   _____

7. What one word best describes Franklin Delano Roosevelt?

   _____

   _____

8. Did Roosevelt's disability prevent him from being an effective president? Why do you think so?

   _____

   _____

9. Would you vote for a presidential candidate if he or she were in a wheelchair? Why do you think so?

_____

_____

10. Why did Roosevelt want people to believe he could walk?

_____

_____

11. Write a title for the story. Use as few words as possible.

_____

_____

12. Think about America's current president. How are the President and Franklin Delano Roosevelt alike? How are they different?

_____

_____

13. In your own words, describe how Roosevelt walked at his inauguration.

_____

_____

14. How did Roosevelt's paralysis affect his presidency? Why do you think so?

_____

_____

15. The story said, "His (Roosevelt's) strong leadership guided America out of the Depression, and to victory in World War II." Is this a fact or an opinion? Why do you think so?

_____

_____

16.

_____

_____

Name _____   Date _____

THE MARCH OF DIMES

ABOUT THE STORY

The story tells about the history of the March of Dimes. Franklin Roosevelt enjoyed swimming in the soothing waters of Warm Springs, Georgia. He wanted to share the experience with others who could not afford the trip to the springs. Roosevelt donated his own money to needy polio victims. This act of charity inspired the March of Dimes.

PREVIEW WORDS

polio virus

Warm Springs, Georgia

donated

President Roosevelt

research

crutches

vaccine

PRIOR TO THE LESSON

Contact a person who uses a wheelchair. Local volunteer organizations, veterans organizations, or physical therapists can direct you to someone who might be willing to visit your class. Meet with the individual, and explain that the students are learning about people who use wheelchairs. Is it possible to give a demonstration of the tools a wheelchair user needs to use during his or her daily tasks? Discuss what the person will talk about so that you will be prepared to introduce the lesson.

THROUGHOUT THE WEEK—Continue reading *Healing Warrior: A Story about Sister Elizabeth Kenny* by Emily Crofford (Minneapolis, Carolrhoda Books, 1989) or *Hero of Lesser Causes* by Julie Johnston (Boston: Little, Brown, 1992), which you began during *Franklin Delano Roosevelt's Secret*.

BOOKS TO READ

Eddie's Blue Winged Dragon, Carole S. Adler (Putnam's, 1988).

The Physically Disabled, Connie Baron (Crestwood House, 1988).

The Berenstain Bears and the Wheelchair Commando, Stan and Jan Berenstain (Random House, 1993).

On Our Own Terms: Children Living With Physical Handicaps, Thomas Bergman (Gareth Stevens Children's Books, 1989).

Picking Up the Pieces, Patricia Calvert (Scribner's, 1993).

Helping Hands: How Monkeys Assist People Who Are Disabled, Suzanne Haldane (Dutton Children's Books, 1991).

Different and Alike, Nancy P. McConnell (Current, 1982).

Ted Kennedy, Jr.: He Faced His Challenge, Patricia Stone Martin (Rourke Enterprises, 1987).

The Monument, Gary Paulsen (Delacorte Press, 1991).

Our Teacher's in a Wheelchair, Mary Ellen Powers (A. Whitman, 1986).

Hometown Heroes: Successful Deaf Youth in America, Diane Robinette (Kendall Green Publications, Gallaudet University, 1990).

Move Over, Wheelchairs Coming Through!: Seven Young People in Wheelchairs Talk about Their Lives, Ron Roy (Clarion Books, 1985).

Stephen Hawking: Unlocking the Universe, Sheridan Simon (Dillon Press, 1991).

A Service Dog Goes to School: The Story of a Dog Trained to Help the Disabled, Elizabeth Simpson Smith (Morrow Junior Books, 1988).

Colt, Nancy Springer (Dial Books for Young Readers, 1991).

Jim Abbott: Against All Odds, Ellen Emerson White (Scholastic, 1990).

INTRODUCTORY ACTIVITIES

DAY ONE

Objective: The students will listen to a true story about disabled people who use wheelchairs.
Curriculum subject: Social Studies

Throughout the week, the students will learn about people who use wheelchairs. Tomorrow, a wheelchair user will visit the class. By listening to a true story about people who use wheelchairs, the students are better prepared to ask educated questions.

There are several books on the market that tell about the lives of wheelchair users. Two of these books are:

Roy, Ron, *Move Over, Wheelchairs Coming Through!: Seven Young People in Wheelchairs Talk About Their Lives*

Powers, Mary Ellen, *Our Teacher's in a Wheelchair*

Before reading the story, ask the students what they know about people who use wheelchairs. How do they feel when they see someone in a wheelchair? What do they think the wheelchair user's life is like? Write the list on the board.

After the story, discuss what the students learned. Review the list they wrote before hearing the story. Have any of their ideas and feelings changed? Why?

DAY TWO

Objective: The students will meet a person who is confined to a wheelchair. They will learn about the daily life of a person with disabilities.
Curriculum subject: Social Studies

Today the students meet a person who uses a wheelchair. Before the lesson, review what they learned yesterday. Next, help the students make a who, what, when, where and why list. Write the list on chart paper. For example,

1. Who are the people who helped you learn to work with a wheelchair?

2. What should I do when I see a person in a wheelchair at the store?

3. When did you start to use a wheelchair?

4. Where do you go to have fun with your friends?

5. Why do you use a wheelchair?

After the lesson, conduct a question-and-answer session. Later, the students will write thank-you notes to their visitor. They should tell what they learned about people in wheelchairs that they did not know before.

DAY THREE

Story Lesson

Follow the *Presenting the Story Lesson* instructions in the Introduction. Each story lesson follows the same procedure; however, say the following in step 4:

"The title of the story we're reading today is *The March of Dimes*. What do you think the story is about? What do you already know about the March of Dimes?"

EXTENSION ACTIVITIES

1. Contact a teacher in the school district who works with physically disabled children. Work together to match a physically disabled child with one of your students. Begin a pen pal program between the classes. The students can write letters, or communicate by computer modem.

2. Make arrangements for your students to meet their physically disabled pen pals. The setting depends on your situation; however, you might consider a picnic or pizza party.

◆ Work with the teacher of the physically disabled students to design games the children can play together. Focus on games that require interaction between the students.

◆ Encourage the students to continue writing to their pen pals after the school year is over.

THE MARCH OF DIMES

Along with thousands of Americans, President Roosevelt was paralyzed by the polio virus. He knew what it was like to carry the weight of heavy leg braces. Crutches rubbed his arms raw. The only time Roosevelt found relief was in the waters at Warm Springs, Georgia. He could take off his braces and swim free.

Roosevelt wanted to share this wonderful feeling with other polio victims, so he donated his own money to help them visit the springs. Still, there wasn't enough money to keep the springs open to everyone who wanted to go. How could they raise more money?

If everyone in America sent in one dime, there would be enough money. America would begin the March of Dimes. Suddenly, Americans sent 150,000 dimes a day to the White House. The money not only paid for Warm Springs, but also research. In 1955, exactly ten years after Roosevelt's death, doctors introduced a vaccine to prevent polio.

If you look closely at a dime, you will see a picture of a president. Can you guess which president it is?

QUESTIONS FOR THE MARCH OF DIMES

1. Who was the president paralyzed by the polio virus?

   _____

   _____

2. Where did Roosevelt find relief from the braces and crutches?

   _____

   _____

3. What did the money raised by the March of Dimes pay for?

   _____

   _____

4. In what year did doctors introduce a vaccine to prevent polio?

   _____

   _____

5. Who donated money for polio victims to visit Warm Springs before the March of Dimes?

   _____

   _____

6. How many dimes did Americans send each day to the White House after the March of Dimes began?

   _____

   _____

7. President Roosevelt gave his own money to help polio victims visit Warm Springs, Georgia. What one word describes President Roosevelt's actions?

   _____

   _____

8. Did Americans want to help polio victims? Why do you think so?

   _____

   _____

9. Could a campaign like the March of Dimes help doctors find a vaccine for the AIDS virus? Why do you think so?

_____

_____

10. Name two reasons why someone might send money to the March of Dimes.

_____

_____

11. Write a title for the story? Use as few words as possible.

_____

_____

12. How is President Roosevelt's donation to Warm Springs like the donations other Americans gave to the March of Dimes? How is it different?

_____

_____

13. In your own words, tell why President Roosevelt enjoyed going to Warm Springs, Georgia.

_____

_____

14. How did learning about President Roosevelt's donation to Warm Springs make you feel about giving to charities? Why do you feel this way?

_____

_____

15. The story said, "In 1955, exactly ten years after Roosevelt's death, doctors introduced a vaccine to prevent polio." Is this a fact or an opinion? How can you prove your answer?

_____

_____

16.

_____

_____

Name _____   Date _____

THE SECRETS OF THE ROSETTA STONE

ABOUT THE STORY

For many years, archaeologists wondered about the meaning of the strange markings called hieroglyphics, or sacred carvings. In 1799, soldiers led by Napoleon dug ditches along the coast of Egypt near the city called Rosetta. They uncovered a carved rock known as the Rosetta stone. Twenty-five years later, a man named Champollion deciphered the hieroglyphics of the Rosetta stone.

PREVIEW WORDS

Rosetta stone	Egyptian	hieroglyphics
scholars	ancient	Greek
language	Champollion	

THROUGHOUT THE WEEK—Read the book *The Reluctant God* by Pamela F. Service (New York: Atheneum, 1988) to the class. The story, which takes place in Egypt, revolves around a young girl and her father, an archaeologist. Continue to read the story into the next story lesson, *Reading Hieroglyphics.*

BOOKS TO READ

Egypt to the End of the Old Kingdom, Cyril Aldred (McGraw-Hill Book Company, 1965).

Mysteries From the Past: Stories of Scientific Detection from Nature and Science Magazine, edited by Thomas G. Aylesworth (Natural History Press, 1971).

Egyptian Language: Easy Lessons in Egyptian Hieroglyphics, Sir Ernest Alfred Wallis Budge (Dover Publications, 1983).

History As Evidence Ancient Egypt, A. Rosalie and Antony E. David (Warwick Press, 1984).

Ancient Egypt: A Book to Begin On, Sophia Harvati Fenton (Holt, Rinehart and Winston, 1971).

Science and the Secret of Man's Past, Franklin Folsom (Harvey House, 1966).

Archaeology As a Hobby, Virgina J. Fortiner (C.S. Hammond, 1962).

Science—Hobby Book of Archaeology, Virginia J. Fortiner (Lerner Publications, 1968).

How the World's First Cities Began, Arthur S. Gregor (Dutton, 1967).

Signs, Letters, Words: Archaeology Discovers Writing, W. John Hackwell (Scribner's, 1987).

Ancient Egypt, Susan Gold Purdy (Franklin Watts, 1982).

The Illustrated Atlas of Archaeology, Sue Rollin (Warwick Press, 1982).

Egyptian Hieroglyphs for Everyone: An Introduction to the Writing of Ancient Egypt, Joseph Scott and Scott Lenore (HarperCollins Children's Books, 1990).

Behind the Sealed Door: The Discovery of the Tomb and Treasures of Tutankhamen, Irene Swinburne (Sniffen Court Books, 1977).

INTRODUCTORY ACTIVITIES

DAY ONE

Objective: The students will visit an archaeological museum.

Curriculum subject: Science

Teacher: Archaeology is defined in the dictionary as "the study of past human life and activities, as shown by the relics, monuments, etc., of ancient peoples." What does this mean? Imagine you are a scientist digging in the desert looking for pieces of Native American pottery. You were looking for the pottery to learn more about ancient Native American life and activities. You would call yourself an archaeologist.

If you put the pottery pieces in a museum for other people to learn about ancient Native American life, the museum would be called an archaeological museum.

Today we'll visit an archaeological museum. You'll need to take a plain piece of white paper, a piece of notebook paper, and a pencil. You'll also need a notebook or book to use as a writing table.

As we walk through the museum, look for an item that tells about the lives and activities of ancient people. You might find a piece of pottery, arrow heads, statuary, or tools. Draw a picture of the relic. Write the name of the relic over your picture. On the notebook paper, jot down notes about the relic. Who used the relic? What is the relic? When was the relic made? Where was it used? What does the relic tell you about the people who made or used it? Why is the relic important to our understanding of ancient people?

DAY TWO

Objective: The students will add details to the drawing they made on Day One. They will make another drawing of ancient people using the relic. They will write a short paper about the relic.

Curriculum subject: Science

Discuss the relics the students drew yesterday. What did they learn about the people who used the relics?

The students will add details to their drawings. Each student will draw another picture of ancient people using the relic.

Next, the students write a short, one-page paper about the relics. The paper will answer the questions posed on Day One.

Finally, mount the two drawings and the paper on a colored poster board. Display the posters around the room.

DAY THREE

Story Lesson

Follow the *Presenting the Story Lesson* instructions in the Introduction. Each story lesson follows the same procedure; however, say the following in step 4:

"The title of the story we're reading today is *The Secrets of the Rosetta Stone*. What do you think the story is about?" If the students mention archaeology, ask, "What do you already know about archaeology?"

EXTENSION ACTIVITIES

1. In this activity, the students go on a mock archaeological dig.

◆ Line five copy paper boxes with large trash bags.

◆ Fill half of each box with sand.

◆ Hide three artifacts in the sand (for example, a spoon, a rock statue). Do not use pottery or other breakables that might cut the students if they break.

◆ Divide the class into five groups. Give each group one box.

◆ Using small shovels and brushes, the students will look for the artifacts. They must measure the depth at which they found the artifacts, and draw a picture showing how the artifacts were laid out in the box.

◆ Archaeologists make special notes about the exact location of the artifacts they find. Why is this important information? Imagine an archaeologist quickly digging up an artifact. If the archaeologist did not take special notes about the location of the relic on the site, how would this affect our understanding of how ancient people used the artifacts?

2. Invite a professional or amateur archaeologist to class.

◆ Ask the archaeologist to describe the digs he or she was on. Did they take special notes about the site? How did they dig out the relics without breaking them? How did your visitor get involved in archaeological digs?

◆ End the lesson with a question-and-answer session.

◆ After the visitor leaves, have the students write thank-you notes. They should name specific points of the lesson they enjoyed the most.

THE SECRETS OF THE ROSETTA STONE

Imagine a room with walls covered in beautiful paintings. You also find line drawings of people, animals, circles, and triangles.

The drawings are the lost writing of the Egyptians called hieroglyphics, or "sacred carvings." No one understood these strange writings. Scholars could only dream of the stories told on ancient Egyptian walls.

In 1799, soldiers dug ditches along the coast of Egypt near the city called Rosetta. They uncovered a carved rock we now call the Rosetta stone.

On the Rosetta stone they found a story. The person who told the story wrote it three times in three different languages: Egyptian hieroglyphics, common Egyptian, and Greek. People could read the Greek language, but no one could match the Greek words to the pictures of the hieroglyphics.

It was not until twenty-five years later that a man named Champollion explained the hieroglyphics. Champollion's work unlocked the secrets of the lost Egyptian writing.

QUESTIONS FOR THE SECRETS OF THE ROSETTA STONE

1. What is the name of the Egyptian writing that means "sacred carvings"?

   _____

   _____

2. When was the Rosetta stone found?

   _____

   _____

3. What was carved on the Rosetta stone?

   _____

   _____

4. Who explained the meaning of the hieroglyphics?

   _____

   _____

5. Which happened first, the discovery of the Rosetta stone or Champollion's reading of the hieroglyphics?

   _____

   _____

6. What did the soldiers find after they began to dig ditches along the coast of Egypt?

   _____

   _____

7. Is the Rosetta stone an archaeological relic? Why do you think so?

   _____

   _____

8. The story said, "On the Rosetta stone they found a story. The person who told the story wrote it three times in three different languages: Egyptian hieroglyphics, common Egyptian, and Greek. People could read the Greek language, but no one could match the Greek words to the pictures of the hieroglyphics."
   What does this tell you about the difficulty of decoding the hieroglyphics?

   _____

   _____

9. Now that we understand Egyptian hieroglyphics, do you think people will use hieroglyphics in their everyday writing? Why do you think so?

_____

_____

10. Why do you think Champollion worked so hard to read the Rosetta stone?

_____

_____

11. Write a title for the story. Use as few words as possible.

_____

_____

12. How are hieroglyphics like today's English writing? How are they different?

_____

_____

13. In your own words, tell how the Rosetta stone was found, and what writings are on the stone.

_____

_____

14. What effect did the translation of hieroglyphics have on the study of ancient Egyptian people?

_____

_____

15. The story said, "In 1799, soldiers dug ditches along the coast of Egypt near the city called Rosetta. They uncovered a carved rock we now call the Rosetta Stone." Is this statement a fact or an opinion? How can you prove your answer?

_____

_____

16.

_____

_____

Name _____   Date _____

READING HIEROGLYPHICS

ABOUT THE STORY

Hieroglyphics use three major types of symbol systems: sound-signs, sense-signs, and word-signs. The students learn the meaning of these terms, and how they are used in Egyptian hieroglyphics.

PREVIEW WORDS

hieroglyphics	sound-signs	sense-signs
word-signs	consonants	vowels
masculine		

THROUGHOUT THE WEEK—Continue reading *The Reluctant God* by Pamela F. Service (New York: Antheneum, 1988) to the class. Discuss the references to hieroglyphics presented in the story.

BOOKS TO READ

Egyptian Language: Easy Lessons in Egyptian Hieroglyphics, Sir Ernest Alfred Wallis Budge (Dover Publications, 1983).

The Story of Writing: From Cave Art to Computers, William and Rhoda Cahn (Harvey House, 1963).

Ancient Egyptian Calligraphy, Henry George Fischer (H. N. Abrams, 1994).

Indian Signals and Sign Language, George Fronval (Bonanza Books, 1985).

Signs, Letters, Words: Archaeology Discovers Writing, W. John Hackwell (Scribner's, 1987).

Indian Picture Writing, Robert Hofsinde (William Morrow Junior Books, 1959).

Hieroglyphs: The Writing of Ancient Egypt, Norma J. Katan and Barbara Mintz (Atheneum, 1981).

Dictionary of Symbols, Carl G. Liungman (ABC-CLIO, 1991).

Language and Writing, Miriam Moss (Bookwright Press, 1988).

Writing and Numbers, Nonverbal Communications, Nigel Nelson (Thomson Learning, 1994).

Egyptian Hieroglyphs for Everyone: An Introduction to the Writing of Ancient Egypt, Joseph Scott and Scott Lenore (HarperCollins Children's Books, 1990).

WHT's YR NM?, Margaret C. Taylor (Harcourt, Brace & World, 1970).

Prehistoric Rock Art, Marinella Terzi (Children's Press, 1992).

Hieroglyph It, Sue and Stephen Weatherill (Barron's Educational Series, 1995).

INTRODUCTORY ACTIVITIES

DAY ONE

Objective: The students will decode a message in a secret writing.
Curriculum subject: Language Arts or History

      Make copies of the secret code and key only; don't copy the answer key. Transfer the pages to overhead projector film or chart paper.

Teacher: Imagine you're an archaeologist, digging for ancient treasures among the pyramids of Egypt. You gently remove each artifact from the ground. Carefully, you dust away the dirt from thousands of dusty, desert years. As you brush away the layers of sand, you begin to see the indentations of strange markings. The lines form beautiful eagles, cats, and geometric shapes. What do the strange symbols mean? What secrets of the past would these lost writings of Egypt tell us?

            Last week we learned about the Rosetta stone, which is the key to reading hieroglyphics, or sacred writings. This week we'll learn how to read the symbols. First, we'll break a secret code of our own. Look at this secret message.

SECRET MESSAGE

Teahcer: Can you read this message? What if I give you a clue. Look at the key. The key is like the Rosetta Stone. It tells you what some of the symbols mean. Using this key, can you solve the mystery?

♦ « » ✓ ‼ ✳ ‼   » ✓ ¿ ⌐ ♣ ✳.

® ¥ ¿ » ‼   ¿   ✳ « ¤ ☺ ‼ ♦   » ✓ ‼   ♂ ‡ ✳ » ‼ ¥ ‡.

♣ ¿ ☺ ‼   » ✓ ‼   ♀ ♥ ♀ ‼ ¥   » «   » ✓ ‼   » ‼ ♥ ★ ✓ ‼ ¥.

♣ ‼ »   ♥   ✳ ⌐ ¥ ♀ ¥ ¿ ✳ ‼.

KEY

» ✓ ‼   ✳ ‼ ★ ¥ ‼ »   ♂ ‼ ✳ ✳ ♥ ♣ ‼

T H E   S E C R E T   M E S S A G E

Teacher: Break into groups. Work together to solve the secret message.

Answer key (for the teacher's eyes only):

A	B	C	D	E	F	G	H	I	J	K	L	M	N	O	P	Q	R	S	T
♥	△	★	♦	‼	♪	♣	✓	¿	♠	‡	¤	♂	⌐	«	♀	⌐	¥	✳	»

U	V	W	X	Y	Z
⌐	☺	®	□	‡	♪

Answer:
Do these things.
Write *I solved the mystery.*
Give the paper to the teacher.
Get a surprise.

As the students bring their papers to you, give them a reward. The reward might be a sticker or a stamp on their paper.

DAY TWO

Story Lesson
Follow the *Presenting the Story Lesson* instructions in the Introduction. Each story lesson follows the same procedure; however, say the following in step 4:
"The title of the story we're reading today is *Reading Hieroglyphics.* What do you think the story is about? What do you already know about hieroglyphics?"

EXTENSION ACTIVITIES

1. The students will make a clay cartouche necklace.

◆ When you see a cartouche (⬭), around hieroglyphics this means that the symbols are part of a name. Cleopatra's name looks like this:

The students will make clay cartouches of their names, using this design.

◆ Lay a 1-inch wide piece of clay on wax paper. The clay must be long enough to spell out the student's name. Lay the clay horizontally in front of the student.

◆ Gently roll a round pencil or marker over the clay to make the surface flat.

◆ Using a sharp pencil, poke a hole in the far left side of the clay. The hole must be large enough to thread a string through.

◆ Using a sharp pencil, etch any hieroglyphic symbol you like in the far left side of the clay. Next, write your name in the clay, from left to right.

◆ Encircle your name with a cartouche.

◆ Let the clay dry.

◆ String a decorative cord or string through the hole. The string must be large enough to go over the student's head.

◆ Now the students can wear the cartouche necklaces.

Example:

2. Like the ancient Egyptians, we leave messages. You can find these messages in plaques that mark important places. These plaques might mark a historical site, a scenic view, or a grave.

◆ The students will collect rubbings of plaques they find in their community.

◆ Take the class to a plaque at your school. Discuss why the plaque is at the school. Does it mark an important event, or name important people?

◆ Lay a large piece of light-colored paper over the plaque. Rub the side of a crayon or charcoal pencil over the paper. The raised words of the plaque will begin to appear on the paper.

◆ Give each student a large piece of paper. They will look in their community for a plaque that marks an important place. They might want to make a rubbing of a plaque that is of personal importance to them.

◆ When the students bring their rubbings to class, discuss what the plaque is telling the people who read it. What do you think people thousands of years from now will think of the plaque?

3. The students will make frames for the rubbings.

◆ Cut a piece of white poster board 2 inches larger than the rubbing.

◆ Put glue from a glue stick on the back edge of the rubbing. Do not put glue all over the back of the rubbing.

◆ Glue the rubbing to the center of the white poster board.

◆ Choose a colored poster board. Cut four pieces of the poster board 2 inches wide. Measure and cut the four pieces to fit as a frame around the rubbing.

◆ Glue the colored poster board pieces around the outside edge of the rubbing as a frame.

◆ Display the rubbings around the room.

> **Note:** Students can collect rubbings from plaques they find on their vacations. Framing the rubbings gives the students a collection of beautiful artwork that also reminds them of the places they have seen.

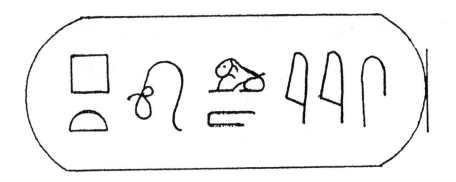

P   t   o   l   e   m   y

K   l   e   o   p   a   t   r   a

READING HIEROGLYPHICS

Hieroglyphics use three major types of symbol systems: sound-signs, sense-signs, and word-signs.

Sound-signs: In modern languages, such as English, every letter or group of letters represents a sound. Some letters stand for consonants, while others stand for vowels. This is how sound-signs work. Hieroglyphic sound-signs represent only consonants, however. A drawing of a human face stands for the sound hr.

Sense-signs: Sense-signs are pictures that give the general idea or "sense" of a word. For example, the symbol of the sun stands for ideas related to the sun. It can mean day, light, time, or eternity.

A picture of a man gives a word the "sense" or idea of something male. Any masculine name or title includes a picture of a man.

Word-signs: Word signs mean exactly what the picture shows you. A picture of a boat means "boat."

Hieroglyphic Pictures

human face

sun

man

boat

QUESTIONS FOR READING HIEROGLYPHICS

1. What are the three major types of symbol systems used in hieroglyphics?

   _____

   _____

2. What sound-sign represents the sound hr?

   _____

   _____

3. What can the sense-sign of the sun mean?

   _____

   _____

4. What are word-signs?

   _____

   _____

5. Which type of hieroglyphic symbol system does the story describe first?

   _____

   _____

6. Which type of hieroglyphic symbol system does the story describe last?

   _____

   _____

7. What one word would describe the people who created the writing system we call hieroglyphics?

   _____

   _____

8. Would it be easy to learn to write and read hieroglyphics? Why do you think so?

   _____

   _____

9. Over hundreds of years, letters have changed to fit new languages. For example, there once was a letter that was a picture of an ox head. Over time the ox head turned into the simple drawing ∀. Today the ox head looks like A.
Do you think the alphabet we use today will change in the next thousand years? Why do you think so?

_____

_____

10. Why do you think Egyptians invented their writing system?

_____

_____

11. Write a title for the story. Use as few words as possible.

_____

_____

12. The hieroglyphic letter O was a simple drawing of an eye. How is a drawing of an eye like the letter O? How is it different?

_____

_____

13. Explain what sense-signs are in your own words.

_____

_____

14. How do you think the invention of writing changed the daily lives of Egyptians?

_____

_____

15. The story said, "Hieroglyphics use three major types of symbol systems: sound-signs, sense-signs and word-signs." Is this statement a fact or an opinion? How can you prove your answer?

_____

_____

16. _____

_____

Name _____   Date _____

THE GREAT EXPLOSION OF 1908

ABOUT THE STORY

On June 30, 1908, an explosion rocked Siberia. People living 250 miles away heard the blast. Shock waves knocked over horses 150 miles from the explosion. Although there are many explanations for the explosion, many scientists believe a large meteor struck Earth.

PREVIEW WORDS

Siberia	Siberian	explosion
atomic bomb	black hole	antimatter

THROUGHOUT THE WEEK—Read the book *The Year of the Comet* by Roberta Wiegand (Scarsdale, NY: Bradbury Press, 1984) to the class. The Junior Literary Guild named *The Year of the Comet* an outstanding children's book. As you read the story, ask the students why the people in the story were afraid of the comet. What did they think would happen when Halley's Comet passed Earth?

BOOKS TO READ

Did Comets Kill the Dinosaurs?, Isaac Asimov (Gareth Stevens, 1987).

Comets and Meteors, Isaac Asimov (Gareth Stevens Children's Books, 1989).

Comets and Meteors: Visitors from Space, Jeanne Bendick (Millbrook Press, 1991).

Halley's Comet, Dennis B. Fradin (Childrens Press, 1985).

Edmond Halley: The Man and His Comet, Barbara Hooper Heckart (Childrens Press, 1984).

The Comet and You, Edwin C. Krupp (Macmillan, 1985).

Voyagers From Space: Meteors and Meteorites, Patricia Lauber (Crowell, 1989).

Sky Dragons and Flaming Swords: The Story of Eclipses, Comets, and Other Strange Happenings in the Skies, Marietta D. Moskin (Walker, 1985).

Peterson First Guide to the Solar System, Jay M. Pasachoff (Houghton Mifflin, 1990).

Exploring Your Solar System, Elizabeth Rathbun (National Geographic Society, 1989).

VIDEOS

Newton's Apple: Dinosaurs, Bullet-Proof Glass, Whales, Sharks, Comets, Warts, Heartburn (PBS Home Video, 1990, PBS 216). Length: 60 minutes.

INTRODUCTORY ACTIVITIES

DAY ONE

Objective: The students will listen to a story about a meteor hitting Earth as told by a witness to the event.

Curriculum subject: Language Arts or Science

Teacher: Throughout the week, we'll learn about comets and meteors. Most meteors break and burn up in Earth's atmosphere; however, some meteorites don't completely burn up, and they hit the ground.

One famous meteorite crater is in the Arizona desert. Arizona's Meteor Crater is about 50,000 years old. The meteorite fell to Earth at a speed of seven miles a second. You can visit the crater, which is 4,150 feet wide and 600 feet deep.

Today we'll read a story by Patricia Polacco called *Meteor!*. Patricia Polacco begins the story with this dedication, "To my family—who actually lived this remarkable event."

Read the story *Meteor!* by Patricia Polacco (New York: Dodd, Mead, 1987) to the class. After the story, ask the students if this is a true story. Why do they think so? How do the people in the story react to the meteorite? Why were they excited about the story? Why did the family use the meteorite for their grandmother's headstone?

DAY TWO

Story Lesson

Follow the *Presenting the Story Lesson* instructions in the Introduction. Each story lesson follows the same procedure; however, say the following in step 4:

"The title of the story we're reading today is *The Great Explosion of 1908*. What do you think the story is about?" If the students mention meteors or meteorites, ask, "What do you already know about meteors or meteorites?"

EXTENSION ACTIVITIES

1. Read the book *The Log of Christopher Columbus* by Christopher Columbus, selections by Steve Lowe (New York: Philomel Books, 1992), to the class. Pay particular attention to the entry for Saturday, September 15, 1492. A meteorite fell into the ocean about twelve miles from the ship. How did Columbus's crew react to the meteorite? What did Columbus tell his men to make them feel better? How do you think Columbus felt about the meteorite?

◆ Another account of the meteorite is in the book *I, Columbus: My Journal, 1492–93* edited by Peter and Connie Roop (New York: Walker and Company, 1990).

◆ The students will write a narrative about the meteorite falling in the sea. They will imagine they are members of Columbus's crew. Speaking in the crewman's voice, what did he think about the meteorite? Was he frightened? Had he seen meteorites fall into the sea before? How did he feel after he heard that Columbus had seen meteorites fall into the ocean on many occasions? Why did this information affect the way the man felt?

2. Read Chapter 6 of *Voyagers from Space: Meteors and Meteorites* to the class. The chapter gives a detailed description of the 1908 Syberian explosion.

◆ Point out the Syberian region on a map. Note how close the region is to the Arctic.

◆ The students will break into groups. The groups will discuss what they think caused the explosion, and write a brief paper about their conclusions. They must give specific reasons for their conclusions.

◆ Other books that discuss the explosion of 1908 are:

Asimov, Isaac, *Comets and Meteors,* p. 25.

Moskin, Marietta D., *Sky Dragons and Flaming Swords,* pp. 62, 70.

3. The students will look for meteor showers that occur close to the time of the lesson. If possible, hold a Meteor Shower Party at school the night of the shower. Share the following "Meteor Messages" with your students.

◆ Meteor showers are made up of fragments of disintegrated comets. As Earth moves around in its orbit, it passes through the paths of the broken comets. Therefore, the meteor showers are set, annual events.

◆ One meteor shower, the Perseid Shower, is also known as St. Lawrence's Tears. The shower occurs each year during St. Lawrence's Feast, July 24 to August 18.

◆ Meteor showers are seen in the constellations for which they are named. To see the meteor shower Orionids, look toward the constellation Orion.

◆ Meteor Showers:

Quadrantanids	January 1–5
Lyrids	April 19–24
Aquarids—Eta	May 1–4
Aquarids—Delta	July 15–August 15
Perseids	July 24–August 18
Orionids	October 16–26
Taurids	October 20
Leonids	November 16
Geminids	December 7–15
Ursids	December 17–24

THE GREAT EXPLOSION OF 1908

On June 30, 1908, an explosion rocked Siberia. The blast was so big that it burned and knocked down trees more than 20 miles away. People living 250 miles away heard the explosion. A "pillar of fire" reached up from the ground. Many others said they saw a blue streak in the sky just seconds before hearing the explosion.

Shock waves rolled across the earth, knocking over horses 150 miles away. Earthquake machines picked up the waves in Washington, D.C. It was not until thirty-seven years later that scientists invented the atomic bomb. Even with the power to destroy large cities, the blast from an atomic bomb could not equal the strange Siberian explosion.

What caused this blast? Many scientists believe a large meteorite hit Earth. Some people think a tiny black hole or a small bit of antimatter fell into Earth's gravity. A stranger theory tells of an alien spaceship crashing in the Siberian forest, causing its engine to explode.

QUESTIONS FOR THE GREAT EXPLOSION OF 1908

1. Where did the explosion of 1908 occur?

   _____

   _____

2. How far away was the explosion of 1908 heard?

   _____

   _____

3. What did people see reaching up from the ground?

   _____

   _____

4. Where did earthquake machines pick up the waves of the explosion?

   _____

   _____

5. What did people see in the sky before the explosion?

   _____

   _____

6. Name two things that happened after the explosion.

   _____

   _____

7. Are people interested in learning the cause of the explosion of 1908? Why do you think so?

   _____

   _____

8. How did the people near the explosion feel when they experienced it?

   _____

   _____

9. Do you think a similar explosion could happen again? Why do you think so?

_____

_____

10. Why do people find this story interesting?

_____

_____

11. Write a title for the story. Use as few words as possible.

_____

_____

12. How was the explosion of 1908 like an earthquake? How was it different from an earthquake?

_____

_____

13. Imagine witnessing the explosion of 1908. Reread the story, putting yourself in the place of a person who was there. Summarize what you would see, hear, and feel as you experienced the explosion of 1908.

_____

_____

14. How do you think the explosion of 1908 affected the people living near the explosion?

_____

_____

15. The story said, "Some people think a tiny black hole or a small bit of antimatter fell into Earth's gravity." Is this a fact or someone's opinion? How can you prove your answer?

_____

_____

16.

_____

_____

Name _____   Date _____

THE GOOD MASTER KUNG

ABOUT THE STORY

The story tells about the life of a man named K'ung Chung-ni, or Confucius. Confucius hoped to unify his people by reminding them about their regal past. He taught his followers to practice honesty, self-control, and the Golden Rule. Over 2,500 years later, we still quote the proverbs of Master Kung.

PREVIEW WORDS

K'ung Chung-ni   prosperous   Confucius

regal   Tao   proverbs

Confucianism

THROUGHOUT THE WEEK—Read the book *Tongues of Jade* by Lawrence Yep (New York: HarperCollins, 1991) to the class. *Tongues of Jade* is a collection of stories from China.

BOOKS TO READ

China Past—China Future, Alden R. Carter (Franklin Watts, 1994).

Chinese Brush Painting Techniques: A Beginner's Guide to Painting Birds and Flowers, Stephen Cassettari (Angus & Robertson Publishers, 1987).

Confucianism (World Religions Series), Francis X. Clooney (Facts on File, 1992).

The Sleeper, David Day (Ideal Children's Books, 1990).

A Magic Tapestry: A Chinese Folktale, Demi (Holt, 1994).

A Taste of China, Roz Denny (Thomson Learning, 1994).

Leaving Point, Betty Vander Els (Farrar, Straus & Giroux, 1987).

Lóng Is a Dragon: Chinese Writing for Children, Peggy Goldstein (China Books and Periodicals, 1991).

Why Snails Have Shells: Minority and Han Folktales From China, Carolyn Han (University of Hawaii Press, 1993).

Count Your Way Through China, James Haskins (Carolrhoda Books, 1987).

A Family in China, Peter Otto Jacobsen and Preben Sejer Kristensen (Bookwright Press, 1986).

The Value of Honesty: The Story of Confucius, Spencer Johnson (Value Communications, 1979).

China: The Culture, Bobbie Kalman (Crabtree Publishing, 1989).

China: The Land, Bobbie Kalman (Crabtree Publishing, 1989).

China: The People, Bobbie Kalman (Crabtree Publishing, 1989).

The Chinese, Pamela Odijk (Silver Burdett Press, 1991).

Marco Polo: His Notebook, Susan L. Roth (Doubleday, 1990).

Women in Society, China, Pamela Tan (M. Cavendish, 1993).

Tongues of Jade, Lawrence Yep (HarperCollins, 1991).

The Wisdom of Confucius, edited by Lin Yutang (Modern Library, 1938).

VIDEOS

Chinese New Year (Bala Cynwyd, PA: Schlessinger Video Productions, 1994). Length: 30 minutes.

Yeh-Shen: A Cinderella Story From China (Beverly Hills, CA: Fox Video, 1992). Length: 25 minutes.

INTRODUCTORY ACTIVITIES

DAY ONE

Objective: The students will read proverbs of Confucius and write a story about how they can use what they learned in their lives.

Curriculum subject: Language Arts or History

Teacher: Throughout the week we'll learn about a man named Master Kung, or Confucius. Confucius lived in China over 2,500 years ago. He was a teacher in the truest sense of the word. He not only taught the importance of reading and learning, but also how good literature and learning can make you a better, more true, person.

Confucius is best known for his proverbs. Proverbs are wise sayings. Many people study the proverbs of Confucius to help them learn to become true, or better, people. Today we'll read some of the proverbs of Confucius. I'll give each of you a proverb. Read the proverb silently, then write a story about how you can use the proverb in your everyday life. Be as specific as possible.

The girls must change their proverbs if they use the words *he, his,* or *man.* Change the words to *she, her,* or *woman.*

Don't share your proverb with anyone yet. Tomorrow we'll read the proverbs and the stories.

Copy the two pages of proverbs. Cut out the proverbs along the solid lines, and give one proverb to each student. If there are more than twenty-two students in your class, you can find more proverbs in *The Wisdom of Confucius,* edited by Lin Yutang. Remember to rewrite the proverbs to a sixth-grade level. Choose only proverbs that are appropriate to your students' age and maturity.

DAY TWO

Objective: The students will review what they learned on Day One. They will share their proverbs and stories with the class.

Curriculum subject: Language Arts

Review what the students learned yesterday about Confucius. The students will share their proverbs and stories with the class. After each story, discuss how the proverb will help them to live better lives. Is the proverb as true today as it was 2,500 years ago? Why do you think so? Why do you think people all over the world enjoy learning the proverbs of Confucius? After reading all the proverbs, what do you think Confucius was trying to teach people?

There are trees that grow up, and never flower. There are other trees that flower, but do not bear fruit.

When you see a good man, try to copy his example. When you see a bad man, look for his faults in yourself.

A good person blames himself, while a common person blames others.

Listen much, look much, watch closely, and you will rarely have cause to regret.

A person who makes a mistake and does not correct it is making another mistake.

I probably will not meet a saint today, but I will be happy if I meet a good person.

A good person is shamed when his words are better than his deeds.

If a ruler does what is right, he can influence his people without giving orders. If a ruler does not do right, his people will not follow his orders.

A person who reviews what he has already learned, and gains a better understanding, is worthy to be a teacher.

Learning that requires a person to remember things in order to answer another person's questions does not make a teacher.

Students of long ago studied for their own self-improvement. Students of today study to please others.

A president who rules a country with honor is like the North Star, which remains in place while the other stars revolve around it.

Remember these four things: read good literature, follow good personal conduct, be your true self, and be honest with those around you.

A person who brags without shame cannot live up to his bragging.

Do not deny the truth, even when it is spoken by someone you do not like.

Learning prevents you from becoming narrow-minded.

Do not worry if people do not recognize your ability, worry about not having it.

All people fail in areas in which they are weak. Therefore, true people know this, and do not criticize or shame others for failing.

Remember, being a true person depends only on yourself. What does anyone else have to do with it?

If a person looks inside himself, and feels he has done right, what does he have to fear or worry about?

What a superior man seeks is in himself. What a small man seeks is in others.

To study without thinking about what you learn is a waste of time. Thought, unassisted by learning, is dangerous.

DAY THREE

Story Lesson

Follow the *Presenting the Story Lesson* instructions in the Introduction. Each story lesson follows the same procedure; however, say the following in step 4:

"The title of the story we're reading today is *The Good Master Kung.* What do you think the story is about? What do you already know about Confucius?"

▬▬▬▬▬▬▬

EXTENSION ACTIVITIES

1. Read the story *The Value of Honesty: The Story of Confucius* to the class.

Teacher: What was Confucius trying to teach his students? Was Confucius a good teacher? Why do you think so?

◆ End the session by reading the Historic Facts on page 63 of *The Story of Confucius.*

Teacher: What was the most interesting fact about Confucius? Why do you think so?

2. The students will make a wall hanging of the Confucius proverb assigned to them on Day One. Remind the girls to change the masculine words to feminine words.

Materials

◆ bulletin board paper in light colors

◆ white glue

◆ two wooden dowels per student, cut to the width of the wall hanging

◆ one ruler per student

◆ black markers

◆ decorative cord

Procedure

◆ Cut bulletin board paper in 36-inch lengths. Cut one length for every two students (one page).

◆ Cut each page in half lengthwise.

◆ Give one page to each student.

◆ Draw a line 2 inches from the top. Draw another line 2 inches from the bottom.

◆ Between the two lines, use a ruler to mark lines like the lines on writing paper. Draw the lines 2 inches apart.

◆ On a piece of scratch paper, the students write out their proverb so that it fits onto sixteen lines. Short proverbs can have one word per line. Lay out the proverb in a "poem-like" fashion. (See the example in this activity.)

◆ Write the proverb onto the bulletin board paper lightly in pencil in your best handwriting. *Do not write above the top line, or below the bottom line!* Remember to make the letters large. Look at your proverb. Does it look nice on the page?

- ◆ When you are pleased with the look of the proverb, write over it in black marker.
- ◆ Run a thin bead of white glue just above the top 2-inch line. Fold the top of the paper over to the 2-inch pencil line.
- ◆ Run a thin bead of white glue just under the lowest 2-inch line. Fold the bottom of the paper up to the 2-inch pencil line.
- ◆ Let dry. This makes top and bottom sleeves for the dowels.
- ◆ Slide one dowel into the top sleeve, and one dowel into the bottom sleeve.
- ◆ Tie a decorative cord onto each end of the top dowel.
- ◆ Hang the proverb on the wall.

Example:

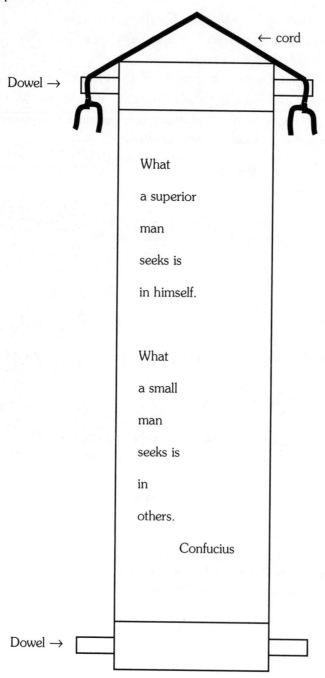

THE GOOD MASTER KUNG

From 551 to 479 B.C., a man named K'ung Chung-ni began his quest to create a peaceful and prosperous China. His people called him Master Kung. Others called him Confucius.

The Master hoped to unify his people by reminding them about their regal past. He believed that the study of history and myth could bring the people out of their suffering.

According to Confucius, deep within everyone's heart is a Way to Heaven or Tao. Confucius taught his followers that they must practice honesty, self-control, and the Golden Rule: "Never do to others that which you would not like done to you." He said, "When all people cherish one another, the world will experience the Great Family. All mankind will seem like One Man only."

Today we continue to quote the proverbs of Confucius. Many people practice a religion called Confucianism. "No matter what religion the Chinese practice, in their hearts they are followers of the Good Master Kung."

QUESTIONS FOR THE GOOD MASTER KUNG

1. When did K'ung Chung-ni begin his quest to create a peaceful and prosperous China?

   _____

   _____

2. According to Confucius, what is deep within everyone's heart?

   _____

   _____

3. What did Confucius teach his followers to practice?

   _____

   _____

4. What did Confucius's people call him?

   _____

   _____

5. What did Confucius believe his people must do before they can bring themselves out of their suffering?

   _____

   _____

6. According to Confucius, what will happen to the world after all people cherish one another?

   _____

   _____

7. What one word best describes Master Kung (Confucius)?

   _____

   _____

8. After reading the story, how do you think Master Kung felt about people?

   _____

   _____

9. Do you think Master Kung's vision of the Great Family will ever come true? Why do you think so?

_____

_____

10. According to historians, Master Kung never intended his ideas and proverbs to become a religion. The story tells us, however, that many people practice a religion called Confucianism. Why do you think the followers of Master Kung worship his beliefs as a religion?

_____

_____

11. Write a title for the story. Use as few words as possible.

_____

_____

12. Compare how your classmates treat one another now, and how they would act if they experienced the Great Family. How would your classmates stay the same? How would they change?

_____

_____

13. In your own words, explain what people must do to experience the Great Family according to Master Kung.

_____

_____

14. Imagine that everyone in your school practiced honesty, self-control, and the Golden Rule: "Never do to others that which you would not like done to you." How might your school change?

_____

_____

15. The Master said, "When all people cherish one another, the world will experience the Great Family. All mankind will seem like One Man only." Is this a fact or Master Kung's opinion? Why do you think so?

_____

_____

16.

_____

_____

Name _____ Date _____

BIBLIOGRAPHY

Aaseng, Nathan, *The Unsung Heroes: Unheralded People Who Invented Famous Products,* pp. 67–75. Minneapolis: Lerner Publications Company, 1989.

Angelucci, Enzo, and Attilio Curcari, *Ships,* p. 152. New York: Greenwich House, 1983.

Benitez, Mirna, *George Washington Carver, Plant Doctor.* Milwaukee: Raintree Publishers, 1989.

Brinton, Crane, John B. Christopher, Robert Lee Wolff, *A History of Civilization.* Englewood Cliffs, NY: Prentice Hall, 1967.

"Carver, George Washington," *People Who Made America,* 3, 197. Skokie, IL: United States History Society, 1973.

Cooper, Ilene, "Geisel, Theodor Seuss," *The Americana Annual* (1992), 404-405. Canada: Grolier Inc., 1992.

David, A. Rosalie, and Antony E. David, *History As Evidence: Ancient Egypt.* New York: Warwick Press, 1984.

Freedman, Russell, *Franklin Delano Roosevelt.* New York: Clarion Books, 1990.

Ilin, M., "From Pictures to Letters," *Our Wonderful World: An Encyclopedic Anthology for the Entire Family* (1962), 1, 166–173.

Johnson, Spencer, *The Value of Honesty: The Story of Confucius.* La Jolla, CA: Value Communications, Inc., 1979.

Lauber, Patricia, *Voyagers from Space: Meteors and Meteorites,* pp. 50–55. New York: Thomas Y. Crowell, 1989.

Marshall, Richard, ed., *Great Events of the 20th Century,* pp. 60–63. Pleasantville, NY: The Reader's Digest Association, Inc., 1977.

Moskin, Marietta D., *Sky Dragons and Flaming Swords: The Story of Eclipses, Comets, and Other Strange Happenings in the Skies,* pp. 62–70. New York: Walker and Company, 1985.

Oehser, Paul H., "The Smithsonian Institution," *Encyclopedia Americana* (1964), 25, 131–135.

Potter, Charles Francis, *The Faiths Men Live By.* Englewood Cliffs, NJ: Prentice Hall, 1954.

Robb, David M., "Leonardo da Vinci," *Encyclopedia Americana* (1964), 17, 289–289b.

"Roosevelt, Franklin D.," *People Who Made America,* 15, 1162–1163. Skokie, IL: United States History Society, Inc., 1973.

"The Seven Wonders of the Ancient World," *Our Wonderful World: An Encyclopedic Anthology for the Entire Family* (1962), 18, 20–21.

Scott, Joseph, and Scott Lenore, *Egyptian Hieroglyphs for Everyone: An Introduction to the Writing of Ancient Egypt.* New York: HarperCollins Children's Books, 1990.

Stein, R. Conrad, *The Story of the Smithsonian Institution.* Chicago: Childrens Press, 1979.

Reader's Digest Editorial Staff, *Strange Stories, Amazing Facts of America's Past,* p. 107. Pleasantville, NY: Reader's Digest General Books, 1989.

Swanson, June, *David Bushnell and His Turtle: The Story of America's First Submarine.* New York: Atheneum, 1991.

"Wages: Not What They Used to Be," *The Americana Annual* (1993), 50. Canada: Grolier Inc., 1993.

Yutang, Lin, ed., *The Wisdom of Confucius.* New York: The Modern Library, 1938.